ENVIRONMENTAL
INTERACTION

Psychological Approaches
to our Physical Surroundings

by

David Canter, Peter Stringer

with

Ian Griffiths, Peter Boyce, David Walters and Cheryl Kenny

INTERNATIONAL UNIVERSITIES PRESS, INC.

New York

First published 1975, Surrey University Press,
    450 Edgware Road, London W2 1EG, England
First American edition, International Universities Press, Inc.,
    1976
Library of Congress Catalogue Card Number: 75-37077
ISBN: 0-8236-1685-1

Contents

The Contributors

PETER STRINGER read Classics at Christ Church, Oxford, followed by Psychology and Philosophy. He taught and did research for eight years at the School of Environmental Studies, University College, London. At present he is teaching Social Psychology and the MSc course in Environmental Psychology at the University of Surrey.

IAN GRIFFITHS is Senior Consultant in Environmental Psychology in Atkins Research and Development's Environmental Consultancy. He has in the past carried out research into subjective response to road traffic noise, investigated human factors in the thermal environment, performed experiments in the lighting field and studied open plan environments in schools and offices.

PETER BOYCE has been a Research Officer at the Electricity Council Research Centre at Capenhurst since 1966, where his work has been concentrated on lighting, although some fringe areas have touched thermal comfort and satisfaction with environmental conditions in modern office buildings.

DAVID WALTERS has studied music at the Royal College of Music and Architecture at Liverpool University. He specialized in architectural acoustics and lectured on this subject at Birmingham School of Architecture. He is now a Senior Lecturer in the Department of Architectural, Planning and Urban Studies at the University of Aston in Birmingham.

CHERYL KENNY is currently engaged in the MSc course in Environmental Psychology at the University of Surrey.

iv

Preface

The design of a shopping centre, university campus, or any other large building complex may be approached in one of two ways. Either by giving the project to a single design team and allowing this team to design and manage the work—this has the advantages of comprehensiveness, but the dangers of monotony. Or, by setting up an overall plan and giving individual parts to different designers—here the management of the project may not be as smooth, but the greater variety and the opportunity to choose for each part a designer who excels in that particular form must make this means preferable.

The planning and writing of *Environmental Interaction* presents an analogous situation to the second alternative. At the risk of sacrificing overall coherence, I invited the participation of contributors, each of whom was an expert in his own field.

Not only this, but the way in which people interact with their surroundings is a wide ranging field of study drawing upon numerous subject areas and many different approaches; hence it lends itself to multi-author treatment.

This does not mean that the book is without coherence. Indeed, this has been provided in two ways. Firstly, a direct and obvious structure has been used—the simple leading on to the complex. As with all that is obvious, closer examination reveals intricacies. The first chapter, therefore, elaborates the ideas behind the sequence of topics. Although, intuitively at least, the sequence from heat, light and sound by way of space and buildings to urban and natural environments, has an undeniable appeal. In providing this first, introductory chapter and a concluding chapter which pinpoints the potential relevance to practical problems, I have sought to make the book a coherent entity.

The second way in which coherence has been provided is in the recurrence of themes throughout the book; whether stated explicitly or merely implied in the text, it is amusing and instructive to look at these and follow them through the different chapters. One of the most dominant is that people bring to their surroundings as much as they take from them. Attitudes, expectations, existing habits and skills, perceptual sensitivites, all influence the implications which our physical environment has for us. It is from this theme that we have taken our title, *Environmental Interaction*. It is the concern with people's *interaction* with their surroundings which links the wide range of subjects in this book.

Another significant theme is also embedded in our title. Although our approaches to environmental interaction are un-ashamedly psychological, we do not insist on their being part only of *psychology*. In other words, although our level of analysis is the individual, taken in relation to the groups of which he is a member, we do not draw the boundaries of our interest around the discipline of existing academic psychology.

Unfortunately the title of our area has been labelled in North America, *Environmental Psychology*, implying a development within mainstream psychology. It is in the nature of our interactions with our surroundings that many perspectives are of value. As a consequence in the present book, material from as far afield as physiology and physics to sociology and geography will be found. Furthermore, the contributors include a physicist and an architect as well as psychologists who have worked closely with planners and engineers.

Other themes also link the different parts of the book. One is the recurrent questioning of how research activities and results may be integrated to the environmental decision-making process. The answers to this questioning are not straightforward (some of the approaches are discussed in the final chapter) and they often lead to a re-examination of the whole design process. One extreme of this questioning leads to involvement in public participation exercises as discussed in chapter eight. The other extreme leads to the development of computer models and regression equations which may produce design recommendations. Between these two extremes there are many possibilities, a large number of which have not yet been explored.

A further theme running through the book is the importance of identifying the particular context before the process of environmental interaction can be understood. In other words, just as it is difficult to generalize across broad aspects of the environment, so care must be taken in dealing within aspects. Examples of the necessity of identifying the particular context abound in this book. Thermal comfort at any temperature relates to the individual and the activities in which he is engaged. Overall satisfaction with a building relates to a person's particular role and objectives within that building. The reactions which people will have to a city or a national park will be influenced by where they are within it and why. This is something different from the psychologist's fight with the great variations existing between people. It is a more focused emphasis on the reasons people have for being in a particular place, their context and its meaning.

The meanings or implications then of the physical setting may be taken as a final thread which ties the various approaches in this book together. We are not concerned solely with the impact, or effect, of the environment but with the interpretations people make of it and themselves within it. In turn we wish to know how these interpretations interact with behaviour and moderate environmental responses.

The ambiguities of our title, *Environmental Interaction*, may be seen as encompassing the essential ambiguities of the physical environment and our relationships with it. In a technical sense, our physical surroundings may be thought of as being composed of variables which confound the links between various aspects of behaviour. Our environment interacts with our emotional responses and with determined courses of action, but the various aspects of the environment interact with one another. Response to temperature is modified by response to noise. The third and most recurrent reference is to the interactions people have with their surroundings. They manipulate as much as they are manipulated. In this book we are concerned with processes underlying environmental interaction. This book is thus predicated upon the assumption of the ultimate importance, if not the conscious significance, of the full range of the physical environment.

I see the book being used in a number of ways. For some it will be a matter of reading only certain chapters while for others it will provide a means of obtaining an overall view of the current man-environment studies. It is this use of the book which I personally find the most instructive. It follows from the fact that although the authors do believe that the material covered in this book conceptually belongs under one umbrella, it is clear to me from reading the chapters that the research was never carried out as part of one general concern. Yet while editing and contributing to this book it became apparent that there are many points at which the different studies would complement one another.

Let me emphasize this potential use of the book. It is to stimulate others to look for gaps in the study of environmental interactions. Having found them I hope they will then question whether they exist because of the vagaries of the developments of various research activities or because of conceptual holes in the umbrella. This questioning should lead to fruitful new areas of investigation. We have tried to present the broad outlines of research as we see them, in the hope of facilitating informed appraisal and healthy growth.

David Canter
University of Surrey

Acknowledgements

The authors wish to acknowledge kind permission from the following people and organizations:

Mr J.B. Collins for permission to reproduce Figure 4.3 from *The Ergonomics of Lighting*.

The Illuminating Engineering Society (London) for permission to reproduce Figure 4.1 from *Light and Lighting 1955*. Figure 4.4 from *Light and Lighting 1972* and Figure 4.6 from *Lighting Research and Technology 1969*.

Professor R.G. Hopkinson for permission to reproduce Figure 4.3 from *The Ergonomics of Lighting*.

Jim Doveton for permission to use photographs from his collection.

Chapter One

An Introduction to Environmental Psychology

David Canter

Fable has it that the fish will be the last to discover water. This discovery will be made too late, as the fish lies dying, having jumped out of the stream onto the dry earth. At times it would appear that man has made the same mistake with his physical environment. Only discovering its essential, all embracing properties, when it is too late to act upon that knowledge.

We may develop our comparison by referring to a modern fabulist, Sigmund Freud. For in much the same way as an earlier generation saw a stimulating mixture of excitement and evil in sexual behaviour, so today a confusion arises from trying to take advantage of and, at the same time, to maintain the pristine quality of, our newly discovered surroundings. This confusion often leads us to curse ourselves for our distorted environmental behaviours.

Given this excited state of man/environment relations it is surprising, but not uncommon, to find academic psychologists who insist that the physical environment has little relevance for behaviour. Some insist that the amount of variation in human response produced by the physical environment is minimal compared with that produced by the social, institutional or cultural environment. One of the starting points for this book is

1

the quantity of evidence that is accumulating which suggests that this is not the case. But even if it were the case that the physical environment played only a small part in the total matrix of influences on behaviour, it would still be necessary to examine those influences. This is necessary because of the colossal cost of producing and maintaining our physical surroundings. We must identify even the smallest impact to ensure that resources are effectively utilized.

A very large proportion of the resources of any society is spent upon the creation, development and maintenance of the environment in which it lives. These resources are spent in order to achieve certain social goals—goals which can best be achieved by providing an appropriate environment for human activities. Until we can develop a scientific understanding of our interactions with the physical environment many of the resources spent on physical surroundings will be wasted. They will be wasted because it is only by the development of a *scientific* understanding of people's interactions with their surroundings that we may move steadily towards a better environment; instead of the ill-directed meandering which constitutes progress based upon 'experience' and 'rules of thumb'.

Indeed, the construction industry is a major industry in any advanced culture and in most developing cultures. It was possibly one of the earliest specialist crafts to develop as mankind became 'civilized'. Yet from the earliest writings on the product of this industry its psychological function was apparent. For as Vitruvius points out (Morgan, 1960) whether a building is being produced for defensive, religious or utilitarian purposes it "must be built with due reference to durability, convenience and beauty".

'Durability' may well be the general concern of the civil engineer but no psychologist seriously interested in human activities can turn away from the potential relevance to him of 'convenience' and 'beauty'. It is true, of course, that taking the broad spectrum of behaviour the search for the relevance of the physical environment is often masked by psychological and social processes but if there is *no* relevance, the conceptualizations and economic mechanisms of our society, which place such emphasis on our physical surroundings, must be gravely at fault. Of course, the implications of the environment we build for ourselves and the

2

natural environment we use, frequently appear to be of economic or functional importance but psychologically, trivial. Buildings keep the rain out and keep us warm; cities provide the milieu for trade and commerce and the fields may be used to feed cattle and grow grapes. It only takes a little exploration of the scale and complexity of our use of our environment to see that these psychological trivialities are quickly overgrown by plants of a sturdier stock. Why do buildings have windows? What are the advantages of gardens? By what process can we learn to cope with the complex, and complexly changing, stimuli which make up our surroundings? As this book unfolds many, many other questions will emerge and, possibly, a few answers.

If one central impetus for examining the environment is the amount spent upon it, it might be expected that this impetus would pick up momentum in times of scarce resources. Historically, this would appear to have been the case.

Historical development

Probably, the first major attempts to assess the impact of the physical environment upon behaviour, outside of the laboratory, were the Hawthorne investigations of the late 1920s (Roethlisberger and Dickson, 1939). In a time of impending economic crisis, every attempt to use the environment and other aspects of working conditions, in such a way as to maximize productivity, was considered. Thus manipulation of lighting levels was tried together with a variety of other modifications of working conditions. Given the context and a variety of other aspects of these studies (discussed for instance by Landsberger, 1961), it is not surprising with hindsight, that the investigators found the social milieu of considerably more significance than the physical milieu in influencing behaviour. Partly because of this finding, and partly because of the other developing trends in applied psychology, the concern with the psychological effects of the physical environment was dropped by psychologists and passed into the hands of environmental engineers, architects and planners.

These design professions kept the concern warm until the end

3

of the Second World War when, once again, some social scientists turned their attention to problems in environmental design. The major interest now saw the light of day in Britain. As a result of the war there were scarce resources but a vast amount of building was necessary. Yet this rebuilding was being attempted in a new ideological environment, with the commitment to the building of a new society, and the move towards a welfare state. The main research approach was to instigate social surveys. The results of these eventually became part of government legislation. Some of the surveys, such as that by Chapman on Sunlight Penetration (Chapman and Thomas, 1944) have given rise to design codes and legislation throughout the world.

The concern, in those days, with the importance of creating an appropriate physical environment was expressed succinctly by Churchill when opening the debate on the rebuilding of the bomb-blasted House of Commons. "We shape our buildings and afterwards our buildings shape us"(Hansard, 1943). He went on to demonstrate his concern that the building's *inefficiencies* should be maintained as integral to Parliamentary government, saying that "buildings which give to every Member, not only a seat to sit in but often a desk to write at, with a lid to bang, has proved fatal" (Hansard, 1943). Thus, the rebuilding was not seen as brought about by simple functional necessity but as the need to maintain a form which complemented the social and psychological processes of an institution. Indeed, Churchill said that an important characteristic of the House of Commons was that "it should not be big enough to contain all its Members at once without over-crowding"(Hansard, 1943).

Once the major task of rebuilding was under way and post-war affluence began to emerge, the examination of the physical environment slowed in pace to a trickle of government sponsored studies.

Some 20 years later in the late 1960s the effect of awareness of the importance of the appropriate use of limited resources re-emerged once again; but this time it was the environment itself which was conceived of as a limited resource, one which is ever more rapidly being spent. The need to examine this resource, what we can do with it and what it does to us, has thus surfaced again on a scale before unknown.

Origins in psychology

The above historical sketch has drawn on only those studies which were directly linked to decision making. Indeed, they were usually commissioned by decision makers. There have always been, however, academics carrying out research into the relationship between psychological processes and the physical environment. In fact, the problems which exercised the skills of the founders of experimental psychology (for example, Fechner and Wundt) were the relationships between subjective experience and physical stimulus. In developing their science the early psychological experimenters borrowed from the methods and formulations of the natural sciences. In essence, this was the minutely controlled laboratory experiment. As a consequence, from their earliest studies psychologists literally abstracted stimuli for their natural environment and carried them (one is tempted to say, screaming) into their laboratories.

Much of the traditions which developed in those pioneering days have proved valuable and their impact today may be discerned in the early chapters of this book, but much also, as we shall see, has led to bad habits.

These early psychologists gave birth to an experimental psychology which had as its central core, perception. Thus, the experimental study of perceptual phenomena became a distinguishing characteristic of scientific psychology. Many developments have taken place within it so that there is now a fat and heavy body of literature in this area. As Helen Ross (1974) so impishly puts it:

"We know a great deal about the perception of a one-eyed man with his head in a clamp watching glowing lights in a dark room but surprisingly little about his perceptual ability in a real-life situation".

Thus it would appear that the sins of the founding fathers have been visited upon their academic children. Not that there have been no attempts to break away. The Gestalt School of Psychologists had as one of its specific goals an attack upon Wundtian Psychology, but with hindsight we can see that the battle was confused because they used each other's weapons. For all their pleas that stimuli had structural properties which were lost if parts of them were dissected for analysis, they still concerned them-

5

selves with stimuli, albeit line drawings of optical illusions, taken into their laboratories for assessment by subjects.

The influence of the Gestalt School

Nonetheless, the Gestalt School of Psychologists had the effect of making us aware of the importance of the relationships between stimuli for the sense we make of them. With that they brought attention to the importance of context, both the context within which the stimuli occur and the context provided by the particular interests or goals of the observer. These two types of context have produced complementary streams in perceptual psychology.

The first was given particular impetus by Brunswick (1956) and later in a somewhat different way by Gibson (1966). They both saw the need to explore and emphasize in their writings, the nature and prevalence of available cues for perception in people's daily environment. Brunswick (1956) painstakingly recorded his subject's judgements of the size of a representative sample of objects which were in her vision during the day. He carried out this study as part of his insistence that the stimuli we use in our experiments should be as carefully sampled as should our subjects. He thus pointed the way to the examination of the total stimulus field and thus to the environment. Gibson (1966) went a stage further by arguing that it is the frequently occurring properties of the daily visual field, such as texture gradients, which structure our perception.

The second growing stream of perceptual psychology has been to look further into the cognitive structures which make perception possible; so much so that one of the most significant, relatively recent books, dealing with topics formerly considered under the heading of perception is entitled 'Cognitive Psychology' (Niesser, 1971). Yet Niesser traces his origins to Bartlett (1932) a psychologist who had much sympathy with the Gestalt approach. For Niesser, as for Bartlett, perception of simple or complex objects is only possible because we have an array of cognitive structures which allow us to process, and indeed distort, the information we receive from our environment.

Given these two developments it is becoming possible for perceptual psychologists to begin to examine the real environ-

6

ment. Unfortunately, this growing maturity has brought with it the bad old habits. None of the above studies has moved much beyond a consideration of single variables at a single point in time under controlled conditions. Thus, it is far easier for the psychologist to think about perception in a space capsule, which has many similarities to their laboratories or the judgement of the distance to circular discs under water at Wied-iz-Zurrieg, collected by the same Helen Ross quoted earlier.

As a consequence, the present book is not about the psychology of perception. Few, if any, of the psychologists referred to above will be referred to again. Even the following four chapters on heat, sound, light and space, will draw little on perceptual psychology as practised by academic psychologists, although the research discussed therein is often as vigorously controlled and usually as laboratory based as any in the laboratories of Wundt and Niesser. We find ourselves, therefore, in a position in which the development of perceptual psychology gives us a broad framework and a confidence to examine the physical environment psychologically, but gives us little specifically to draw upon. The reasons for this lie in the differences, now becoming clear to us, between the perception of the environment and the perception of objects. Differences to which we now turn our attention.

Stimuli and the environment

To say that the environment is a collection of stimuli is to miss the point. The perception of the environment derives as much from the structure of the stimuli in it as from the properties of the stimuli themselves.

The most crucial property is that our experience of our environment is notably temporal and sequential. As you read this page, what is behind you has a relevance to your present actions and perception although you may not at the present moment sense it. The environment carries us around with it wherever we go. We can never shake free of it. An object which can be lifted or nailed to the wall may possibly be perceived and reacted to instantaneously and then forgotten. Of course, this is unlikely to happen if we see it as a significant part of our environment.

7

(Hence the need, when studying *object* perception, to take the objects into a special environment, which is defined as non-existent, the laboratory.)

The fact that the environment is all around us means, of course, that we can only 'perceive' it by building up a conceptual system from our sequential experience. Whereas with objects debate is possible about the role of cognitive structures in relation to distortion, say, at the sense organs, with environment perception such debate seems frivolous. For example, the way in which I perceive the depth present in a drawing of a room, given the structure of the eye, is open to much psychological and physiological discussion, especially, if we forget that I have experienced rooms. However, my perception of the depth of the room in which I am may more usefully be linked to the facts of my entering it, taking two paces, and sitting at the window. In this case my perception and my knowledge are difficult to disentangle. The fact that my conceptual system containing the knowledge that a six-foot mattress fits exactly from wall to wall, under the wide shelf I use as a desk, provides a knowledge of the room which will have a great influence upon the perceptual judgements.

The confusion of perception and cognition which appears inevitable in the environmental context has many other implications for the types of psychological research which are relevant, both to our understandings of our interactions with the environment, and to the possibilities for providing environmental designers with useful information. That the environment is all around us, that we are always participants in the environment, also implies that our presence in the environment is purposive. We are always present in a particular place because of a set of roles which we are performing within that environment. This further indicates that any consideration of a person's interactions with his environment leads to consideration of the activities in which that person is involved and his role within those activities. It also follows, that when studying individuals within any particular environmental setting that the types of interactions they have with other individuals must also be taken into account. Thus, the individual within the environment, is usually a member of a group. The isolated subject in a laboratory making judgements of a perceptual stimulus thus draws upon a very different paradigm from the individual within a building making perceptual judgements.

Behaviour/environment interaction

The ways in which the environment and behaviour interact has been considered in a number of publications. However, they generally may be reduced to three key processes (Canter, 1969). Clearly, one of these is the environment providing perceptual stimuli; but these stimuli are always present together with their implications, and their links to the conceptual structures which facilitate our interactions with the environment. Beyond providing perceptual stimuli the built environment may also be thought of as a filter. A building, for example, allows in the light and fresh air which we require but keeps out the nasty noises and the rain. This filter process has given rise to many of the outgrowths of environmental engineering. The requirements which people have for heat, light and sound are the basis for engineering design and thus the environmental psychologist is often involved in research which will provide the requisite information.

A third process of interaction is the degree to which the environment encourages or inhibits interactions between individuals. This may be the sort of spatial relationship which we will consider in later chapters or it may be the roles which it allows us to perform. The example of the various role possibilities within the natural landscape is an interesting example of this. Given that we are always in the environment to carry out certain activities, and we usually carry out these activities with other individuals, the recurrent impact of our surroundings on social processes is not to be under-emphasized. This is one of the reasons why so much of what is considered under environmental psychology seems to have its roots more deeply in social psychology than in experimental perceptual psychology.

There is one further, very important, aspect of the environment which removes it from consideration as a set of stimuli. This is the fact that we actively modify, build and influence our physical surroundings. As has been discussed earlier the resources involved in this process are considerable. It is not only the financial resources which are considerable, nor even the resources in terms of human energy. It is also the psychological resources which we call upon, the skills, the insights and the imagination which we bring to bear upon our physical milieu which are such a considerable portion of social activities. It is thus not surprising that action on the physical environment is a major political issue. The processes or organization and social interaction which give rise to modifications of our surroundings must be kept in mind when considering the types of interactions we have with those surroundings.

It should now be apparent why this book is not just a glorified text on perceptual psychology, or why there are many aspects of the material covered by it which would be hard to place within any specific area of theoretical or experimental psychology; why it is that we must consider this as a book on *environmental* psychology. We interact with the environment over time and over space. These interactions are related to social and personal goals. Our interaction with the environment is always part of our interaction with others.

Origins in sociology

If we go back to the last century the early empirical research on the London poor revealed links between the incidence of illness and crime and areas of the city. Further, much of the early research was guided by a deterministic view which even the most mechanistic psychologists eschewed. The notion could be summarized as the belief that slums caused delinquency. In some instances this view was taken so far as to suggest that the physical climate almost completely determined the cultural patterns (Whitbeck, 1918; Huntington and Cushing, 1921).

Empirical research developed beyond the early naive determinist notions. By the late 1920s people such as McKenzie (1933) plotted the spatial occurrence of many forms of social behaviour such as delinquency and vice as well as psychological aspects such as mental illness, (see for example, Faris and Dunham, 1939). This eventually merged into the ecological psychological studies so common today (for example Barker, 1968).

The recurrent concern of all these studies was to demonstrate that there were parallels between the patterns of *behaviour* which could be discerned and the patterns present in the *physical* environment in cities. It was the evolution of sociology that gave rise to an understanding that the researcher was dealing with a complex, developing, interactive system in which slums and delinquency were related and presumably supported one another because they both had their origin in similar social processes.

Nonetheless, there emerged from this early work the realization that there were links between aspects of the physical environment and behaviour. This realization did, in part, give rise to the post-war surveys to which we have already referred. Perhaps of more importance was their influence on planning concepts. Such notions as a 'catchment area' and 'planning zones' developed in relation to the consideration of the links between proximity and behaviour. Recently, of course, planners and geographers have taken many of these notions much further. As we shall see in later chapters (especially Five and Eight) there have now been many studies of the interactions between social and behavioural patterns and the form of housing layouts, communities and cities.

The approach of this book

Where does all this leave us? Having seen all these ifs and buts, the variegated, not to say piebald, origins of the study of man's interactions with his environment, how can we structure the diverse material into a cogent text for the student? Clearly, it is still too early in the development of our field to expect, or even to look for, a definitive and final structure. A structure which will allow a steady, unbroken, unfolding of the concepts, methods, theories and applications which shall make up our field.

In structuring this text all we can do is to start with the more simple issues and move towards those which are more complex. By simplicity, we mean something quite specific. We imply that man's interactions with *certain* aspects of his environment may, at this stage, be predicted with a degree of confidence and with some understanding of the processes involved. Because we can predict and understand, the interactions may be explained in relatively

11

simple terms. Thus, an underlying notion of the move from simplicity to complexity is that there exists a range of different interactions between the individual and his surroundings. We are not positing one overall structure which explains all interactions.

An obvious example of this approach may be taken by comparing one of the earlier discussions, say, that on the thermal environment with the discussion in the later chapters such as that dealing with the natural environment. In the thermal environment chapter specific correlations and formulae can be put forward which will predict a person's comfort ratings from knowledge of the thermal conditions. No such simple formulae can be derived for the natural landscape. We can explain many aspects of human thermal reactions by an understanding of the physiological basis of thermal mechanisms within people. However, the full richness of the processes, discussed above, which distinguish the environment from 'stimuli' are brought to bear when we consider the natural landscape.

It is important to emphasize the evolving model of interaction with our physical surroundings which underlies the development through this book because it is easy to fall into the 'atomistic trap'. It is easy to believe that if you can understand heat, sound and light that these can be built up into an ever increasing understanding of the complexities of our interactions with our environment. By now it should be clear that we will never be able to understand our interactions with the 'wilderness', for example, on the basis of our understanding of our reactions to heat, light and sound. Any particular environmental variable, or aspect of the environment, which we select to consider is part of a complex system of other environmental variables and of human reactions. However, it is necessary to study environmental variables separately. This necessity arises for pedagogic reasons. We must divide the field in order to study it. It also arises for related decision making reasons. The architect or planner must decide how much money is to be spent on a heating system or on a road system. He must consider each environmental problem and make decisions about it. The designer (or design team) must also divide their design problem into manageable units in order to solve them.

The sequence of this book

As we move from the earlier chapters, considering aspects of heat, light and sound, to the later chapters, dealing with the urban environment, it will be apparent that the problems with which we are concerned will become increasingly multivariate. As a consequence, the central chapter, (Chapter Six), which acts as a bridge from the first half to the second, will be concerned in part with identifying the key dimensions underlying the many aspects of our reactions to buildings. In part it will deal with the ways in which we can structure the relationships between those different dimensions.

As we move beyond the scale of buildings, we are more and more concerned with the implications of the social and psychological processes for people's interactions with their physical surroundings.

In this book then, we are not pretending that there is some unified viewpoint which will enable us to explain the whole complex array of interactions which people have with their physical environment. Each researcher or writer on the subject will, quite rightly, have his own opinion. Indeed, in a review of bibliographies of what was referred to as the 'sociophysical technology' literature (Archea, 1970) it was found that:

> "there is only a ten per cent overlap between the specific references listed in the different bibliographies and only a twenty-five per cent correspondence between the authors cited".

We have felt it to be important that each chapter should have an author's name associated with it. Together with the name comes a distinct viewpoint on the topic of concern. The great strength of this is that it has enabled us to explore environmental issues in a number of different ways. Although we believe that none of these ways are incompatible with any of the others, anyone who skims through this book may be surprised at the range of approaches it encompasses. However, as has been argued the physical environment surrounds and supports all human activities. It is therefore to be expected that the study of the human environment should be as complex and multi-faceted as is the range of studies of human behaviour.

Having emphasized the diverse coverage of this book, it is

important to state clearly the theme which links it together. This theme can be summarized as the basic structure of all of the studies which are considered in this book. This structure consists of two parts, psychological and physical. It contains on the one hand, variables which are drawn from the physical environment; light levels, distances between people, types of landscape, etc. On the other hand, it contains psychological reactions, responses or interactions with those physical variables. We can go a step further and emphasize that the physical variables are drawn from those which exist in the natural and manmade environment, normally available to people and the psychological variables are meaningfully available in normal everyday existence.

Difficulties of environmental research

In carrying out research into the physical environment a number of methodological difficulties arise. These are brought about by the many practical and theoretical difficulties involved in the study of the physical environment. In later chapters we shall return again to many of these problems but for the present we may summarize them.

Scale—When looked at from the viewpoint of conventional psychological research, the scale of the physical environment is enormous. Buildings, for example, typically contain many people, spread over many thousands of square feet. They also exist for many years. When we further take into consideration the natural environment these aspects of scale are increased by orders of magnitude. The vastness of the phenomena central to environmental psychology frequently implies that research methodology should be employed which is different in a number of respects from that common in experimental psychology. The aim will be to reduce the scale to manageable terms. This is achieved either by concentrating on a particular set of variables or by taking individual environmental settings for examination. A further method is to concentrate upon topics such as crowding but this is more of a descriptive device than a methodological one.

14

Variety—When attention is turned to the comparison of environmental settings, it is apparent that they exist in great variety and profusion. Not only is the number of actual forms of buildings, cities or landscapes, very great indeed but so is the number of goals of their users. The varieties of physical environment are as numerous, if not more so, than the variety of human activity. This variety is present whether we are concentrating on a particular building form, for example, or trying to examine a particular institutional setting.

Occurrence—The third difficulty which, to some degree, derives from a combination of variety and scale, is that the occurrence of identical environments is likely to be very rare. Similar people doing similar things with similar goals in any given location, housed in the same building form, may usually only be found if the level of similarity with which we concern ourselves is very broad. This orients the research worker towards studies which will provide generalities, rather than specific predictions.

Implementation—Although there are tendencies to distinguish between applied environmental psychology and other sorts there would seem to be some general consensus amongst researchers that if it is not geared to decision making the research is eventually frivolous. However, with regard to the physical environment there is one particular practical difficulty produced by this approach. This is the fact that many aspects of the environment require decisions to be made about them before they are actually in existence. The decision maker frequently requires to know the ways in which people will interact with the environments he proposes to create before he has created them.

Simulating the environment

There are, of course, many other difficulties which grow out of the involvement with environmental decision makers and these will be dealt with in the final chapter. However, for the present, we need to draw attention to the fact that is an integral part of environmental research to consider environments which exist only in some conceptual form. The way of resolving these difficulties is

15

to *represent* the environment of interest by some means. The potential variety of these 'simulations' is very large but they all have in common an attempt to veridically represent some aspects of the environment and to assess human response to them. Thus, for example, in the study of noise annoyance, sounds may be played to people as representations of noises they may hear outside of the laboratory. In the study of townscapes, people may be shown slides of buildings and asked to identify them. Here again, it is the slides as representations of *existing* environments that is the central concern.

In the design of environments generally, various forms of representations of the potential environment are common. Drawings, models, perspectives and plans are regarded as part of the apparatus of the design decision maker. However, although there are links it is important not to confuse a research strategy with a design tool. The former has to be made part of an integral scientific process, whereas the latter is often of most value to the designer himself, ellucidating his own ideas.

Having made this distinction, it is clear that there exists a validation problem in the use of environmental simulations. The simulation is not of interest in its own right. It is, therefore, necessary to validate it by comparison with some criterion.

Interestingly enough the problem of simulation does exist in psychology in general but there is rarely any attempt even to examine what the most appropriate criteria for validation of the simulation might be. For, unless psychologists really are interested in only dots, dashes, flashing lights and the other components of their laboratory stimuli, there is the very real question of what these stimuli represent and how might their representativeness be tested. Thus, in some ways this problem bears a relationship to Brunswick's (1956) on the representative design of psychological experiments. However, in the environmental field the problem goes further than ensuring that the experimental stimuli are truly representative of those which exist in the natural environment. This is the case because the stimuli which the environmental psychologist uses are transposed into some alternative mode, whether this be, for instance, the production of heat in a heat chamber or movement round an art gallery by the selection of slides.

Validating simulations

The problem of validating environmental simulations is an intricate one because there is usually no clear understanding of what is the 'real' environment being simulated. For, if a valid comparison is the actual environment in use, the question arises as to how long it should be in use, by whom, and viewed from what perspective. There are many occasions upon which people are more familiar with some representation of the environment than with experience of living within it, such that the representation may have a reality far greater than the environment itself. Big Ben, The White House or the Taj Mahal are all environments such that there is a sense in which it is meaningless to ask if judgements of the commonly available simulations bear any resemblance to judgements of the original object. This question, of course, begs a fundamental question about the nature of the environment and our interactions with it. As the examination of this problem recurs throughout this book we need not spend time on it now. All that we need to mention is that there are many forms of representations feasible for our surroundings and that there are many ways in which we may experience them. The validation exercise, as a consequence, consists of relating one form of environmental experience to another form, in a situation where both environmental experiences are drawn from a common source.

In recent years the centrality of the simulation/validation problem has emerged and as a consequence a number of investigators have explored it. Winkel and Bonsteel (1968) carried out studies of an art gallery, comparing the movements of people actually in the gallery with those who selected a route on the basis of slides which they were shown. Canter and Wools (1970) compared evaluations of room interiors using drawings, with those made on the basis of photocopies, Lau (1970) compared judgements of a full scale mock-up with judgements of a small model. There have also been a number of studies relating to outdoor environments. Acking and Kuller (1973) compared judgements made using a film based on a model, with films and drives around an actual area. Shafer and Richards (1974), and Howard *et al* (1972) also compared responses to slides referring to the actual environment. When dealing with actual landscapes Cunningham *et al,*

(1973) compared the simulations of streets using video recordings and other means. In all these cases close similarities are found between the judgements in the various media. The one exception is the study by Winkel and Bonsteel (1968) in which movement speeds were different in the real environment from the simulated one, although the routes selected were very similar. Indeed, on the basis of these studies we may predict that the results of the large scale expensive studies in progress by Appleyard *et al* (1974) will now produce little that is surprising.

Variety in research procedures

These studies and the conceptual clarification that they have generated helps us to move a stage further in the discussions that have developed in this chapter. On the one hand we have insisted that laboratory, experimental research is unlikely to omit much which is of significance in the environment. On the other hand, we have demonstrated the great difficulty of studying the physical environment *in situ*. The solution to this conflict lies in two directions. Firstly, as wide a variety of techniques as possible needs to be drawn upon. Secondly, the careful, cautious use of environmental simulations may prove to be very fruitful. The fact that some compromise is necessary is made particularly clear by reference to discussion in a recent introductory environmental psychology text (Ittelson *et al,* 1974). In that book the authors argue fulsomly for the need for field research in environmental psychology, yet in their central chapters refer again and again to laboratory experiments of a most artificial kind. Indeed, it is difficult to reconcile their advocacy of observational studies in real world situations with references to the Ame's distorted rooms demonstrations (Ittelson, 1952).

The argument that emerges from our consideration of these issues is that laboratory type simulations are worthwhile provided they are examined as simulations of the real environment. This implies both the establishment of the studies so that the environment is simulated as adequately as possible, as well as checks wherever possible that a valid simulation is being used. Furthermore, the results grow in value as the range of experiences, ways of representing and interacting with the environment is increased during the research programme. This approach is in accord with the argument expressed earlier, that a complex model of man's interactions with his environment is the only one likely to be generally valid. A model which assumes a whole range of interactions with the physical environment, with a variety of different processes underlying this interaction, also requires a variety of research procedures and strategies drawing upon a variety of environmental experiences. Within this there is plenty of room for the single variable experiment, carried out under conditions of laboratory control. However, the problems of simulation which we have discussed always need to be considered.

Our environmental locus

Environmental psychology has not yet developed to the full level of reflexivity advocated by George Kelly (1955) for psychological theories in general. We still cannot explain what it is in the physical environment which makes it possible for us to be environmental psychologists. However, we are at the level of sophistication where we should expect to be aware of the effects our physical surroundings may have on the approach we take to environmental psychology. In doing this, we at least point the direction for future PhD dissertations! We may also help the reader to put this book in some clearer perspective.

While it would be invalid to push this too far, or to over stress the role of the existing locale it is of value to point out that we take cities and urban development as less of a threat than many authors and conceive of both as more closely integrated with the rural scene. We further see an unbroken continuum from the minutiae within a building to the expanses of the wilderness. The distinct categories so often created by our American colleagues draw upon a different cultural viewpoint. We think it worthwile, also, to note that they draw upon a different environmental context.

Chapter Two

The Thermal Environment

I.D. Griffiths

We start our detailed examination of the psychological effect of the physical surroundings by turning our attention to the thermal environment. With the acoustic and luminous environment (dealt with in Chapters Three and Four respectively) it provides one of the major sub-environmental categories commonly considered, whether by researchers or practitioners. There is a simple logic in these sub-divisions in that each is associated with identifiable physiological mechanisms and psychological processes. Not until Chapter Six will we have the opportunity to look at the relationship between the responses to each of these aspects of our surroundings.

The reason for commencing our detailed accounts with the thermal environment, derives from the overall development of this book from those aspects of the environment which have a long history of study through the measurement of relatively few variables, to those aspects which have emerged more recently as of interest and have given use to studies dealing with their multi-variate complexity. This development from 'simple' to 'complex' also parallels a number of other developments, the move from laboratory oriented research to field studies and from research which is being applied to that which is still raising more questions than it answers, being two of the most obvious.

As will unfold as this chapter proceeds, the 'simplicity' of the

21

thermal environment relates, essentially, to our ability to predict comfort votes accurately from only a few physical variables. The picture is far less clear when we turn to the stressful effects of the thermal environment rather than rated comfort. It may well be that, in that context, issues dealt with in later chapters such as the effects of 'urban stress' (Chapter Eight) will someday coalesce with the issues dealt with in the present chapter to demonstrate that human reactions to the thermal environment are rather complex as well!

This chapter concerns itself only with the range of thermal conditions likely to be encountered inside inhabited spaces. These do not, in general, constitute physical hazards and points at which such hazards arise have not, therefore, been indicated. (Those interested in the effects of extreme heat and cold should consult Carlson and Hsieh, 1965 and Fox, 1965).

The present chapter contains three main sections. The first concerns the physics and physiology which are basic to an understanding of thermal sensations. Heat production and exchange, and the measurement techniques for the assessment of real environments are discussed briefly. This section then deals with the control responses of the body to heat and cold and finally summarizes the physiology of thermal sensation. The second section gives a description of present knowledge of subjective responses to the various physical parameters which describe thermal environments; air and mean radiant temperatures, air velocity and humidity, some other physical variables not dealt with in heat exchange equations, and relevant human variables. The final section deals with the relationship between human performance and temperature.

Responses to heat and cold

Human beings, like other warm-blooded animals, attempt to maintain constant internal thermal conditions. If ambient conditions are too warm for a person to lose the amount of heat his metabolic activity is producing, changes occur in the body which will maximize heat loss. At levels which allow loss and production to approximate to one another, dilation of peripheral blood vessels, which allows a greater amount of blood to pass its heat to the outer surface of the body, takes place. At higher temperatures thermal sweating is introduced (at an ambient temperature of about 33°C for a nude resting man), which increases to a very marked degree the heat loss by evaporation. There is also some evidence of another physiological response to raised ambient temperature, reduced heat production. This is achieved by a reduction in activity level. As well as these physiological changes there are, of course, a large number of behavioural adjustments to raised temperature. Wyon (1970) has shown that there are marked postural changes in high ambient temperatures. These consist largely of changes which maximize the body surface area presented to the environment, the most extreme being the 'spread-eagle' posture. People will also adjust their clothing, increase ventilation rates by various means, seek shade, and so on.

There are also responses which are specific to cold environments. There is generally an increase in metabolic rate. The directly physiological and involuntary methods of doing this include shivering, increased muscular tension and increased oxygen uptake by the body. There are hormonal changes, involving such functions as thyroid activity and adrenalin output. There are also heat conserving responses: peripheral blood vessels become constricted so as to reduce blood flow and consequently heat loss to the exterior surface of the body. Again, there are behavioural changes: posture is often modified to reduce exposed surface area (as in crouching), activity level may be raised voluntarily, and once more, there are clothing modifications.

The changes mentioned so far are for the most part short term, but there are some changes which occur in long term exposure. These are generally referred to as adaptation effects. Acclimatization to elevated temperatures consists largely of developing an increased ability to sweat (Leithead and Lind, 1964) and to vasodilate peripherally (Fox, 1965). As we shall see later, this leads to greater tolerance of extreme conditions rather than to a preference for higher temperatures. Cold adaptation consists largely of an increase in metabolic rate, with a consequent increase in food consumption. Adaptation to cold can be considered an academic problem, in that cold is easily dealt with by increases of clothing under normal circumstances. Social pressures, presumably, having many parallels to those of space use (dealt with in Chapter Five), prevent similarly easy modes of dealing with higher temperatures. Unfortunately, there is little research directly related to the exploration of these pressures.

Physics of thermal sensation

Metabolic activities produce heat. The basic problem for man, or any homeothermic animal, is to maintain a constant internal temperature. This is achieved by matching the amount of heat lost with the amount produced. If heat production exceeds heat loss, heat storage takes place in the body and conversely, if there is an excess of loss over production body temperature falls. Rate of heat production varies with activity: there is much greater heat production from an active person than from a sedentary one. Some representative values for heat production are given in Table 2.1. The values are expressed in Watts per square metre of body

Table 2.1 Representative values for heat production at various activities

Activity	Metabolic heat production per unit surface area W/m^2
Basal metabolism	45
Seated at rest	60
Standing at rest	65
Office work	75
Walking on level ground at 3.2 km/h	115
at 8.0 km/h	340
Heavy manual work	250
Digging	320

surface area, since it is at the body surface that heat transfer takes place. For a young adult the body surface area varies between perhaps 1.3 m^2 and 2.2 m^2 (Macmillan *et al*, 1965).

Heat is lost from or gained by the body in a number of ways, namely: radiation, convection, evaporation and conduction. Radiation takes place from the body to surrounding solid surfaces, convection to the surrounding air, and evaporation from the skin and lungs. Conduction losses are usually small. The proportion of heat lost by each of the three major processes is determined by environmental conditions. For example, as air velocity increases and air temperature falls, the proportion of heat lost convectively will increase.

To be of use, then, the physical values chosen to describe the thermal environment must relate to the avenues of heat loss. The physical variables employed to cover convective losses are air temperature and velocity; to cover radiant losses, the mean radiant temperature; and to cover evaporative losses, absolute or relative humidity (plus air temperature and air velocity).

A full description of the techniques for measuring these variables is given by Thomas Bedford (1964). It is to be noted that these four variables constitute a minimum for the description, in thermal terms, of an environment: it is unfortunately true, however, that it is seldom that they all appear in descriptions of psychological studies of thermal stress.

One further value essential for the description of the thermal exchange between a person and his environment is a description of the thermal insulation of the clothing ensemble worn. The unit of clothing insulation is whimsically called the *clo* (1 clo = 0.16 $m^2 \,°C/Watt$) or, less often, and quite definitely restricted to the UK, the *tog* (1 tog = 0.645 clo). Values for particular clothing ensembles are achieved by direct measurement of insulation values, using a heated manikin. Table 2.2 gives the insulation

Table 2.2 Insulation values of a variety of clothing ensembles in *clo*

Clothing	Insulation
Light sleeveless dress, cotton underwear	0.2
Light trousers, short sleeve shirt	0.5
Warm long sleeve dress, full length slip	0.7
Light trousers, vest, long sleeve shirt	0.7
Light trousers, vest, long sleeve shirt, jacket	0.9

values of a variety of outfits. Newburgh (1968) discusses the thermal characteristics of clothing in great detail. Fanger (1973) gives a purely physical account of how the variables of heat loss and heat production can be evaluated.

Physiology of thermal sensation

Early studies of the relation between subjective measures of comfort and physiological variables were concentrated on skin temperature. Houghten *et al* (1929) found that people described their sensations as pleasant at skin temperatures of 33.5°C. More recently, Fanger (1967) has shown that this is only the case for people at low rates of activity. At higher rates of activity he found that his subjects preferred to have lower skin temperatures and, for instance, at a rate of activity equivalent to heavy manual work (250 W/m²) they preferred to have a skin temperature about 3°C lower. These findings make it difficult to believe that the only stimulus for the thermal sensation is the temperature of the skin.

However, human beings are extremely sensitive to changes in the temperature of the skin and the search for particular sensory structures for the thermal sense has a long history. Von Frey (1904) proposed specialized nerve endings for the sensations of warmth and cold: Ruffini cylinders and Krause end bulbs respectively. More recently this has been discredited and it is now believed that free, unspecialized nerve endings are the relevant structures; they are unspecialized only in the sense that they are not distinguishable morphologically. Hardy (1960) suggests that some only respond to downward changes in skin temperature, while others respond only to upward. Kenshalo and Nafe (1962) argue that the free nerve endings are not in fact the receptors as such but act as mechanical transducers of direct thermal changes in the characteristics of the muscles of the blood vessels in the skin. According to this view, the wall of a blood vessel will dilate when its temperature rises and constrict when it falls, and these changes will have a direct mechanical effect on the free nerve endings embedded in the muscle.

As we have seen, skin sensation cannot be the whole story and in fact considerable attention has been paid to direct thermal sensitivity of the hypothalamus. It has been shown that direct heating of the anterior hypothalamus induces sweating (Andersson *et al*, 1964) and Benzinger (1959; 1960; 1961; 1963) has shown that in experimental conditions where skin temperature is low and cranial temperature is high sweating is induced. There is no sweating, on the other hand, where a high skin temperature is associated with a low cranial temperature. Benzinger (1963) also used his technique of putting skin and cranial temperature in opposition to one another in studies of the warmth sensation; he found that reports of warmth increased as the cranial temperature was raised, although skin temperature was maintained at a constant high value. Benzinger and his collaborators (1961) showed that physiological heat responses were more affected by skin sensation: reductions of skin temperature against a constant cranial temperature produced very large increases in body heat production. The scale of the heat production response is, however, modulated by the cranial temperature: increases in cranial temperature reduce the scale of the metabolic change, which does not occur at all, in fact, if the cranial temperature reaches that equivalent to thermal neutrality, that is, 'body temperature' ($37.5°C$). As far as the sensation of cold is concerned, Benzinger's (1963) experiments show that this is entirely a function of skin temperature and is unaffected by cranial temperature.

Benzinger's experiments are models of ingenuity and elegance, but perhaps because rather than in spite of this, seem artificial and unrelated to normal environmental conditions. However, the general principles do seem to apply for fairly extreme conditions where body temperature changes are involved. Where ambient conditions are close to thermal neutrality changes in heat loss are brought about by dilation and constriction of peripheral blood vessels.

It is interesting to compare this section with the description of the relevant physical variables. You will remember that there were four processes by which heat is lost. The physiological account, however, reads as if there were only one variable which leads to changes in the temperature of the skin or of the blood in peripheral blood vessels. When we come to discuss (in the next section) the sensations reported by people in a variety of thermal

27

conditions one of the questions we shall be asking is the degree to which the different physical variables have distinct subjective effects.

Thermal sensations

In turning our attention to the reported experience of variations in the thermal characteristics of the environment, i.e. subjective reports, we may proceed in one of two ways. We could begin with the major physical characteristics of the thermal environment and postulate a sensation to relate to each of these. We would thus look, in turn, for the subjective correlates of air temperature, radiant temperature, air movement and humidity. In addition, there might be subjective differentiation relating to the variability of these, either in space or in time. There might be also subjective factors related to specific interactions of the physical variables. Finally, and for practical purposes perhaps the most important of all, some or all of the subjective correlates would be evaluated and as a consequence we would need to introduce the concept of comfort. All of the above would be subject to interaction with activity level and degree of clothing insulation.

Another approach would involve the construction of a thesaurus of the words used by a population in their descriptions of the thermal aspects of the environment. This would be followed by an analysis of the variation in the use of the terms in the thesaurus, in order to extract the smallest number of factors which explain the variation in the terms used.

Whichever approach is followed it is clear that any set of subjective variables would need to be validated against physical variables by correlational studies. Unfortunately, research has tended to start at the correlational end with the result that, while there are many *ad hoc* studies relating temperatures and subjective variables, there have been few attempts to define the range of subjective responses or their factor structure. With few exceptions, studies have concentrated on the single thermal sensation of warmth, and not even the evaluative factor, which would appear to be most important practically, has received any concentrated attention.

In the absence of any coherent approach from the psychological end of the problem it seems most reasonable to proceed from the physical end.

A major cause of the lack of a coherent psychological attack on the problems raised here has been the belief that warmth is the only subjective variable and that studies of even this factor are unnecessary because the problem of warmth is a simple physical one. It is a commonly held view that the only problem in providing a thermal environment which meets the needs of its users is that of matching the rate of heat loss to the environment with the rate of heat production. This is indeed desirable, but far from being the whole picture. It is clear that, for instance, thermal balance can be attained in many ways, some of which, *a priori,* are unacceptable; for example, compensation for a large heat loss from a particular part of the body by use of a very large heat gain on another part of the body. In addition, it might well be that people prefer some methods of heat loss to others. Fanger (1967), has shown that people who are at a high level of activity prefer to have a lower skin temperature than people who are less active, even though they can achieve thermal balance in physical terms with normal skin temperatures. The final criterion for non-harmful environments must be a subjective one: physiological and physical considerations can provide information about situations in which human beings can come to physiological harm, but within the great range allowed by those considerations what is important is the relevant subjective assessment.

Before going on to consider particular investigations it is necessary to briefly distinguish between field surveys and laboratory experiments. This is particularly important because historically, subjective investigations have largely been of the survey variety, which has led paradoxically to a certain amount of artificiality and consequently to a degree of disagreement with laboratory studies.

Laboratory experiments consist basically of the exposure of a sample of people to the conditions provided in a climatic chamber, which provides control over most or all of the physical variables important in thermal exchange, and clothing and level of activity are generally under the control of the experimenter as well. In the case of the field study, none of these controls exists and in addition the range of variation of the physical variables that is

Figure 2.1 The control panel of the environmental chamber at the Electricity Council Research Centre. (Each small dial records the temperature of a portion of the chamber's inside surfaces. The two large central controls are for dry and wet bulb air temperatures)

Figure 2.2 The interior of the environmental chamber

possible in the chamber is absent. It is unlikely that temperatures of the workplaces in which these studies are carried out are allowed to stray from the comfort region, because of the humanity of the management or the complaints of the staff. Most buildings involved will be conventional and thus, for instance, the mean radiant temperature will tend to have very similar values to the air temperature. People in these places who are too warm or too cold will be able to make the behavioural changes necessary to compensate for the displacement from the optimum. In all, survey work will tend to concern very restricted ranges of physical conditions and the lack of experimental controls will tend to make the range of subjective variation smaller than is desirable for scientific evaluation of the results. Generally, field surveys will tend to underestimate effects and to have confounded physical variables.

In what follows the discussion will largely revolve around laboratory work, for the reasons given, and the information will be presented as it relates to the important physical variables. It is important to note that even laboratory experiments have re-stricted ranges of variation: most experiments relate to people with 0.5—0.8 clo clothing, to low air velocities and low levels of activity. Experimental results are generalizable to other situations only by use of the physical heat balance equations.

Air and mean radiant temperatures

Physical considerations would lead us to suppose that the mean radiant temperature and the air temperature would be of roughly similar importance in determining subjective warmth when air velocities are low. This is certainly the conclusion of Mackey (1944) and Neilsen and Pedersen (1952). Their expectation would only apply at air velocities below 0.1 m/s. In this velocity region the natural convection currents which arise when the body is warmer than the surrounding air are the sole avenue of convective heat loss. At velocities outside this region the relative importance of air temperature should increase, convective heat loss increasing as the square root of the air velocity.

Experiments in which subjects reported the warmth of their

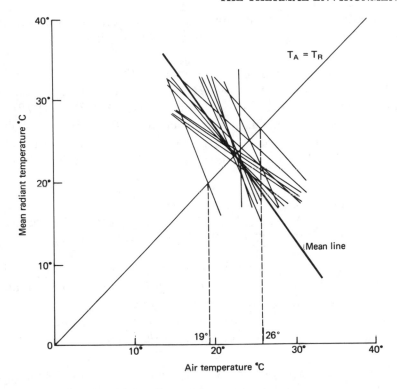

Figure 2.3 Lines of equal warmth for the combination of air and mean radiant temperature. (Each faint line is based on observations on one subject: the range of preferred temperatures is from 19°C to 26°C. The heavy line is the mean for all observations. (McIntyre and Griffiths, 1972))

Table 2.3 The Bedford Warmth Scale

Description	Numerical value
Much too cool	1
Too cool	2
Comfortably cool	3
Comfortable, neither cool nor warm	4
Comfortably warm	5
Too warm	6
Much too warm	7

33

environment by using the numerical values of the Bedford Warmth Scale (Table 2.3) do not give results which differ greatly from these expectations.

Typically, the magnitude of correlation between the subjective and the physical variables is acceptable, for example, the regression equation, reported by McIntyre and Griffiths (1972), is associated with a correlation coefficient of 0.84. It is probably most useful to produce an equation which averages the results of a number of independent studies (from Griffiths and McIntyre (1972)):

Bedford Scale Score = $0.20Ta + 0.16Tr - 4.19$

(Ta = air temperature; Tr = mean radiant temperature)

The Bedford Scale Score varies linearly with temperature and it can be seen that each scale interval approximates to $3°C$ in mean radiant and air temperature. Inserting an optimum mean scale score in the equation gives a preferred temperature of a little above $23°C$. This applies to sedentary people in light clothing (0.75 clo) at low air velocities (less than 0.1 m/s).

It has been generally believed that environments of high mean radiant temperature and lower air temperature are differentiated subjectively from those with a higher air temperature and low mean radiant temperature. Munro and Chrenko (1949) exposed 145 subjects to a hot wall situation, a cool wall situation and a neutral wall situation. The differences between mean radiant and air temperature were up to about $3°C$. A small but statistically significant correlation between reports of 'freshness' and the size of the difference was found and 73 per cent of the subjects found the warm walls preferable to the cool. However, it is not easy to accept these experimental results since very long periods elapsed between the subjects' experiencing the three different conditions: neutral walls were experienced in January and February, cold walls in March and April and warm walls in May and June.

McIntyre and Griffiths (1972) had subjects respond on a wide range of subjective rating scales (including scales for pleasantness and freshness) and found no differentiation between radiant and convective environments. Thus the total heat loss was noticed by subjects, but not the ways in which the loss occurred. Subjects

34

reported environmental conditions as fresh when both temperatures, or the combination of the two according to the warmth
equation above, were low.

Air velocity

Very little investigation of the subjective effects of differing air
velocities has taken place. If air temperature is lower than outer
surface temperature of the (perhaps clothed) body then the
convective heat loss will vary as the square root of the air velocity.
Thus, any increase in air velocity can in principle be compensated
for by an increase in air or mean radiant temperature. The air
velocity (if any) beyond which this compensation cannot be
achieved has not yet been established. Compensation by air velocity
for air temperatures above body temperature cannot be achieved
since in this case increasing air velocity will in fact increase warmth.

Draught is a special case of convective cooling, in that the word
is generally used in relation to localized, rather than general,
cooling. Andersen and Olesen (1968) have established that, for
clothed persons, there is no discomfort from a high unilateral air
velocity (c. 1 m/s) if the temperature is correctly regulated
according to one of the comfort equations. The sensitivity of
different areas of the body to draught has not received exhaustive
study. A DIN Standard (Anon, 1960) can be used to assess draughts
in practical situations, in the absence of experimental data. Finally,
since we have seen that people do not distinguish between radiant
and convective cooling and heating, it is to be expected that
radiant cold spots will give rise to reports of draughts.

Humidity

The amount of moisture in the atmosphere has been shown to
affect sensations of warmth. Nevins *et al* (1966), for example,
demonstrated very high correlations between subjective estimates
of warmth and temperature and humidity. He exposed 360
sedentary subjects wearing light clothing (0.52 clo), for three hours
to relative humidities between 15 per cent and 85 per cent at air
and mean radiant temperatures in the range 19°C to 28°C.

The regression equation derived from the experiment predicts a

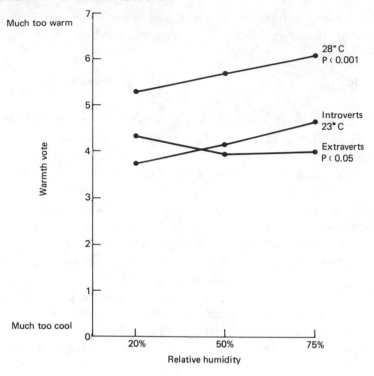

Figure 2.4 The effect of relative humidity on warmth at two air temperatures. (The significant main effect of humidity on subjective warmth at 28°C is shown. The weak interaction at the lower temperature indicates that humidity is probably unimportant at 23°C, as far as warmth is concerned. (Griffiths and McIntyre, 1973a))

difference in warmth vote of about half a scale interval (that is, approximately equivalent to 1.5°C) between 20 per cent and 75 per cent relative humidity at both comfortable and warmer temperatures.

Rasmussen (1971) investigated the direct perception of humidity, rather than its effect on warmth, after three hours' exposure for sedentary subjects in 0.6 clo clothing. His statistical analysis shows a significant difference in scores on a five-point scale from 'very dry' to 'very humid' between humidities of 30 per cent and 80 per cent at 28°C but not at the other lower temperatures he used, the lowest being 21°C.

A slightly different result is reported by Griffiths and McIntyre

(1973). They found that humidity differences for 20 per cent, 50 per cent and 75 per cent were perceived as such at *both* high (28°C) and low (23°C) equal air and mean radiant temperatures, when inactive subjects in indoor clothing had been exposed to them for six hours. At the normally comfortable temperature of 23°C subjects preferred 50 per cent relative humidity, reporting high and low humidities as more oppressive and less comfortable. The difference in mean warmth assessment from 20 per cent to 75 per cent was significant and amounted to 0.8 of a warmth scale interval, that is the equivalent of 2.5°C. As might be expected, a higher temperature (28°C) led to a preference for the lowest humidity.

Clearly, different levels of humidity are distinguishable at comfortable air temperatures, and a moderate humidity level is preferred to higher or lower values. It seems reasonable to conclude, as far as the effect of humidity on warmth is concerned, that there is little effect in the region of comfortable air temperatures, but that, in warmer temperatures, a change in relative humidity from 20 to 75 per cent could be equivalent subjectively to raising the temperature by 1.5°C.

In the three sections above we have discussed the physical variables of immediate importance in determining the sensation of warmth. Now we come to those which probably do not effect that sensation but which, one might expect, would influence the perceived desirability of a set of environmental conditions. The parameters which have received scientific attention in this respect are those concerned with the uniformity of temperature; uniformity over space and uniformity over time.

Temperature variation over space

To take spatial uniformity first: both radiant and convective heating or cooling systems will more often lead to non-uniformity than to uniformity. Hot air rises and this phenomenon often leads to vertical gradients in air temperature. Radiant heat sources tend to be relatively small in relation to the surface area of the enclosure and non-heated surfaces are imperfect reflectors of thermal radiation. The consequence of this is also non-uniformity.

Little or no work has concerned convective non-uniformity but considerable attention has been paid to the radiant problem. Chrenko (1953) exposed 160 subjects to radiation from ceiling panels at a height of 2.6 m for 30 minutes. The physical parameter used to quantify the radiant asymmetry was elevation of mean radiant temperature at head level. He found this to correlate well with reports of discomfort: 20 per cent of subjects reported conditions to be unpleasant at an elevation in mean radiant temperature of 2.2°C and 60 per cent at 5.3°C. He concluded that 2.2°C was the discomfort threshold.

Although Chrenko's experiment is basic to European standards of acceptability adopted since, it has two major failings. The first is that there was no uniform condition in the experiment so that we may not assume that the 20 per cent discomfort rate at 2.2°C elevation is an increase over a base rate. Secondly, subjective warmth was not constant between conditions so that subjects experiencing higher ceiling temperatures were also generally warmer than people experiencing lower panel temperatures, and not simply subject to greater non-uniformity.

More doubt is cast on Chrenko's findings by subsequent work which has not suffered these deficiencies. It has tended to show greater tolerance of asymmetry. Schlegel and McNall (1968) exposed subjects to a wall up to 6.7°C hotter than the surroundings, without discomfort. McNall and Biddison (1970) exposed 234 subjects to considerably more extreme conditions, using both walls and ceilings as heat sources. With air and mean radiant temperatures at 25.6°C (thermal neutrality for their subjects) a hot ceiling at 54°C produced no discomfort. Griffiths and McIntyre (1974) exposed 24 subjects to four ceiling temperatures from 26.5°C (equivalent to mean radiant temperature) to 45°C. Air temperature, velocity, and humidity were the same in all conditions and, by controlling wall panel temperatures, it was possible also to maintain a constant mean radiant temperature.

As we shall discuss in greater detail in Chapter Six, it is often of value to identify the dimensional structure of the human response under study, in the present case statistical analysis of the questionnaire responses showed four basic underlying variables: evaluation (or comfort); warmth; humidity and a factor resembling freshness. Only warmth was affected by the experimental manipulation: greater asymmetry led to lower warmth. There was thus no discomfort produced specific to the asymmetry.

McIntyre (1973) concludes that a large ceiling (or possibly wall) should probably not have a surface temperature exceeding the mean radiant temperature by more than 10°C. Such results can probably be related generally to problems such as solar overheating and radiant asymmetry caused by high level lighting installations.

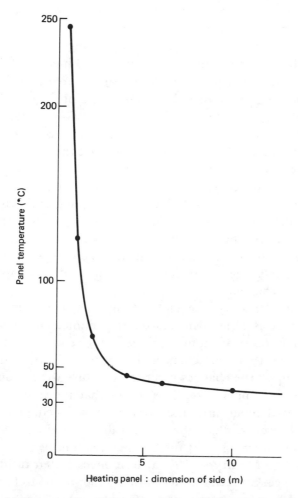

Figure 2.5 Limiting temperatures for ceiling heating panels of different sizes. (The line gives the maximum surface temperatures for square panels of different sizes. (Griffiths and McIntyre, 1974))

39

Temperature variation over time

Temperatures also vary over time in a regular and semi-regular fashion due to control functions of heating and ventilation apparatus or irregular fashion due to weather changes or movement of personnel between enclosures. We may distinguish three types of temperature variation which have been investigated: ramp, transient and cyclic changes. Unfortunately transient changes have not yet been studied scientifically and so we will deal only with ramp and cyclic changes in this section.

Wyon *et al* (1971) investigated ramp changes, that is changes which are linear over time, as a way of looking at the limits of acceptability for each phase in a cycle. The experimental method was to expose subjects, naked or in 0.6 clo clothing, to changes in air temperature at rates of 0.15 or 0.50°C/min, while either performing a mental task or resting. Subjects were asked to signal 'too hot' or 'too cold' when they noticed that the temperature was no longer comfortable and at that point the direction of change was reversed. Clothed subjects tolerated a median range between 'too hot' and 'too cold' of 9.2°C when working and 5.6°C when resting, at the higher rate of change. Naked people had slightly greater tolerances when resting and slightly smaller when working. At the lower rate of change, only naked subjects were tested and their tolerated ranges were lower than for naked people at the higher rate of change.

If we consider only the clothed subjects it appears that the tolerated range is large. The matter is complicated, however, by the fact that only air temperatures are given: the authors do however state that the changes in mean radiant temperature consequent upon the changes in air temperature were about 25 per cent of the air temperature. This means that the tolerated ranges in subjective temperature are somewhat reduced. The authors conclude, however, that the large values obtained cannot be accepted as realistic without further investigation.

Griffiths and McIntyre (1974a) have investigated rather slower rates of change. Sixteen clothed subjects (approximately 0.75 clo) experienced four levels of change in temperature: 0°, 0.5°, 1° and 1.5°/h over an exposure period of six hours. Changes were linear over time and the mean temperature was in each case 23°C.

Mean radiant temperatures and air temperature were always equal to one another and the changes were made in both upward and downward directions. Subjects reported their warmth sensations at hourly intervals and provided a more comprehensive assessment at the end of the whole exposure period.

Of some note was the fact that the hourly warmth votes of the subjects revealed even the smallest rate of change in temperature. The final assessment showed that larger rates of change were less pleasant and more uneven than the control and low rate of change conditions. The mean warmth votes at each hour were directly predictable from the normal warmth equations and neither change nor the direction of change produced any visible effect of the means or standard deviations of the warmth assessments.

We can conclude from this work that, as far as linear changes in temperature at these rates are concerned, the degree of dissatisfaction can be predicted from the instantaneous temperatures without difficulty. There seems to be no case for the existence of thermal boredom. If people were to dislike the lack of stimulation produced by invariant thermal conditions they would presumably prefer the lower rates of change to the control conditions.

Human variables

We have so far considered human responses to thermal stimulation only in terms of group responses. It is important to have some idea of the range of differences between individuals and the differing characteristics of specific sectors of the population.

Sex is often considered to be the source of differences in thermal preferences, but surprisingly disappears as an important variable when subjected to experimental investigation. McNall *et al* (1967) in an experiment involving clothed subjects (0.6 clo) at three different activity levels, found small and inconsistent differences between male and female subjects at the different activity levels. Fanger (1972) found no significant differences in preferred temperature between the sexes for Danish subjects, but did find a small but statistically significant difference between the sexes for American subjects (females preferred a temperature 0.3°C higher than males). He concludes that such a geographical/

sex interaction is inexplicable and not to be believed. It is clear that any difference, if real, is too small to be of practical significance. It is likely that the sex differences in thermal comfort often found in field studies are due to the differences in clothing between the sexes.

It is generally assumed that there are differences in preferred temperature between different age groups. The problem of hypothermia in the elderly may have led to the common belief that older people require higher temperatures for comfort. Physiological evidence seems at first sight to support this, since older people have lower basal metabolic rates and thus do not generate as much heat as younger people. However, Fanger (1972) has shown that evaporative heat loss falls with age, and subjective determinations of preferred temperatures show no differences between college age Danes and elderly (mean age 68 years) Danes.

Griffiths and McIntyre (1973b) investigated the relative importance for the warmth sensation of air temperature and mean radiant temperature in a group of elderly (>60 years) women. They found a significant difference in preferred temperature between this group and a previously investigated group of young men, but this was small and probably explicable in terms of clothing differences. These subjects did not differ from the previous group in terms of the effects of varied combinations of mean radiant temperature and air temperature upon them; there was no subjective differentiation between the two temperatures and the warmth equation derived for the young men was acceptably accurate.

In general, therefore, it seems reasonable to conclude that there are no important differences in preferred warmth or thermal sensitivity between young and old adults. However, in practical situations it should be borne in mind that activity levels and, consequently, body heat production, will be lower for the older group. This will necessitate the provision of temperatures suitable for that level of activity. At the other end of the age scale we find that children below the age of 11 or 12 years have higher metabolic rates than adults, and Humphreys (1973) has shown in school field studies that their preferred temperature would be considerably lower than that of their teachers, perhaps lying as low as 18°C.

The degree of acclimatization of subjects (in sociological guise, this can be referred to as geographic location) is often referred to as an important variable in determining preferred temperatures. Much of the work in this area is field work in tropical regions rather than the laboratory work to which we have restricted our attention, and seems superficially to indicate that preferred temperatures are higher for both Europeans and local inhabitants in such places as New Guinea (Ballantyne *et al*, 1967) and Singapore (Ellis, 1953). However, Fanger (1972) has inserted the values of the relevant physical variables in his comfort equation, which is based on experimental work with Americans and Europeans in temperate climates, and found that the preferred temperatures so predicted are remarkably similar to those obtained in the field studies. Ballantyne *et al* (1967) found an optimal temperature for 34 acclimatized Caucasian subjects in New Guinea to be 25.8°C. The subjects were tropically clothed and sedentary, the relative humidity was 80 per cent and the air still. For such conditions Fanger's equation produces an optimum of 25.8°C. Ellis's subjects were 152 Europeans and Asians, resident in Singapore and tropically clothed (estimated at 0.4 clo). The optimal temperature was 27°C at a relative humidity of 80 per cent and an air velocity of 0.4 m/s. The comfort equation produces 27.4°. Fanger (1973b) has also carried out studies, in the climatic chamber, of the preferred temperature of subjects just after their arrival in Copenhagen by aeroplane from hot climates. The preferred temperatures were very similar to those of residents. In general, we may conclude that geographic location may have some influence on what you will put up with and how you will dress, but does not produce any shift in preferred temperature.

In general, we have seen that the three major non-physical human variables of sex, age and geographical location do not have important effects upon preferred temperatures. The preferred temperature is, however, not the whole thermal story and only one of the experiments referred to concerned possible differential effects of the physical variables we discussed initially. Future research may find that, for instance, age affects sensitivity to atmospheric humidity. However, at the present state of knowledge it is reasonable to treat groups of people as homogeneous for the purpose of determining suitable thermal environments. That is not to say that there are not differences in thermal response between individuals, but simply to say that this variation is not explicable in terms of age, sex, or degree of acclimatization.

At a given temperature we find that the standard deviation of warmth vote is 0.8 of a Bedford Scale interval (Griffiths and McIntyre, 1974a) and does not vary significantly over the range we have so far investigated (this is in the near optimum region: 18.5°C to 27.5°C for sedentary subjects in indoor clothing and still air). Fanger (1972) has produced a chart which enables the prediction of the percentage of people dissatisfied with a particular degree of subjective warmth, from knowledge of the mean warmth vote of the group. A similar chart, Figure 2.6, constructed on the

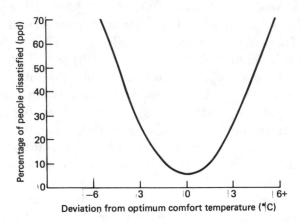

Figure 2.6 Percentage of people dissatisfied as a function of the deviation of the actual subjective temperature from the optimum subjective temperature

basis of the standard deviation given above, is shown here and allows this prediction from the deviation of the temperature from the optimum. Both define 'dissatisfied' as having a vote outside the three central intervals of a warmth scale. Comparison of the two would indicate a very high degree of agreement: Fanger's standard deviation must therefore be near the present estimate of 0.8.

Summary of human comfort responses

Since this section concerns matters of considerable practical

44

importance and has concentrated on describing experiments rather than the practical conclusions that follow on from them, it is reasonable to provide a summary and a guide to practical decisions. For a fuller treatment of how to arrive at a suitable temperature for a group of people at a given level of activity in given clothing, Fanger's (1972) account has much to recommend it. For those requiring a briefer version of the approach, McIntyre (1973) has provided a summary.

Assuming still air and sedentary subjects dressed in indoor clothing (*c*. 0.75 clo) then the air and mean radiant temperatures must be such as to provide a temperature of about 23°C when combined appropriately, that is, in the ratio 0.56 to 0.44. A more complex formulation is necessary if the air velocity exceeds 0.1 m/s (McIntyre, 1973).

There is no subjective differentiation between heating or cooling which is predominantly convective and that which is predominantly radiant. Humidity affects sensations of warmth in high air temperatures (above 26°): at 75 per cent relative humidity the sensation of warmth will be greater than that at 20 per cent to an extent equivalent to 1.5°C. Humidity is itself directly perceived and at moderate air temperatures (that is, when it has no warming effect) a moderate humidity of, say, 50 per cent will be preferred to 20 per cent or 75 per cent. Little is known of the effects of non-uniformity in air temperature but people seem to be quite tolerant of radiant non-uniformity and large surfaces such as ceilings and walls can probably be allowed to reach temperatures 10° higher than their surroundings. Changing temperatures appear to present no particular problems: they can be assessed as a series of separate instantaneous temperatures. Age, sex and degree of acclimatization do not affect preferred temperature; the magnitude of differences between individuals is known but its causes are not understood.

From a research point of view, we may note the deficiencies of the account that has been presented. The subjective variable has been, over and over again, warmth. Comfort, the dimension which immediately springs to mind in this context and which is frequently used, perhaps in error, to describe this field of work, seldom appears as a significant variable: points of discomfort are not often reached experimentally. This may be caused by the relative ease of having subjects operate as physical meters and the relative difficulty of measuring affective aspects of experience. If this is the case, then probably a more sophisticated approach to subjective assessment is needed.

In addition, the results presented do not give indications that any particular sort of environment is preferred: in the field of air velocity, for instance, there is no scientific indication that a discernible air velocity at a high air temperature is desirable. In general, our everyday experience would indicate that we do evaluate thermal environments and often have strong preferences and quite an extensive vocabulary of atmospheric and thermal terms. These aspects do not appear at all in the research literature at present and will not do so until the problem is attacked systematically from the human end rather than in an almost totally *ad hoc* manner on the basis of thermal physics.

Performance under thermal stress

Most studies of the effects of temperature upon the performance of intellectual and psychomotor tasks have concentrated on the comparison of comfortable temperatures with higher ones. Low temperatures have been neglected, possibly because they can be easily compensated for, by the use of heavier clothing, for example: similar compensation is difficult in the case of heat. No clear picture of the effects of temperature emerge: a large number of studies show that elevated temperatures produce decrements, some show no effects, and yet others show that adverse conditions produce improved performance.

Mackworth (1950) studied the effects of elevated temperatures on Europeans in Singapore. Military personnel were required to work at simulations of real-life tasks which were familiar to them; morse code reception, a visual vigilance task (the Clock test), a coding task, and a tracking task using a pursuitmeter, for periods of 2—3 hours (in 67 per cent humidity).

The first three tasks showed a progressive reduction in performance with increasing temperature (the minimum temperature was 29°C) with a maximum of 41°C. In the signal detection experiment, temperatures 5° above and below 29°C showed significantly deteriorated performance. The subjects were lightly dressed (that is below the waist only) and allowances for this and the high air velocity (0.5 m/s) suggest that an air temperature of 28°C would be optimally comfortable. Therefore, the results can be taken to indicate that temperatures within five degrees or so of the optimum can lead to measurable performance decrements. Pepler (1958) has replicated these results. Teichner and Wehrkamp (1954) showed that short duration (five 20 second periods) working on the pursuit rotor over five days, was significantly affected by air temperature and that 13° and 29° produced lower efficiency than 21°.

Poulton and Kerslake (1965) studied the effect of entry into a warm environment (in this case a simulation of a commercial aircraft cockpit) on performance of two tasks. The vigilance task involved scanning five dials for a moving needle (this happened pseudorandomly every 4—8 seconds) while listening for a repeated letter in a sequence of ten letters (an average of 5 responses/min). After practice at 21°C their performance was assessed at air temperatures of 45°C or 25°C (humidity 13mb, air velocity 2.5 m/s). The listening task was performed reliably less well on the first day in the cool condition, although by the end of the second day the cool condition was reliably better. Colquhoun and Goldman (1968) raised their subjects' body temperature by exercise and exposure at 39.5°C air temperature, 50mb absolute humidity and found on a signal detection task that both correct detections and false reports increased.

Studies showing no apparent effect are less often published. Dean and McGlothlen (1965) exposed ten pilots to 70 or 110 dB noise, together with air temperatures between 17° and 43°. The subjects performed simultaneously two slow monitoring tasks (17 events/minute) and a tracking task. There was no temperature effect on performance and no noise effect.

It is difficult to draw conclusions from evidence like this about the nature of thermal effects on psychomotor performance (if indeed there are any). Pepler (1963), on the basis of a far more extensive review than I have attempted here, concludes that small but measurable decremental effects are visible in temperatures 3—5° different from normal, in either direction. He states that tasks requiring greater physical or mental effort are most affected but that such effects can in many cases be offset by incentives or knowledge of results. He attempts to distinguish between the distracting effect of temperature, and other specific effects due to heat. He concludes that heat has different qualitative effects on performance at different temperatures, although there is a central attentional effect.

Provins (1966) reviews performance under thermal stress from the point of view of body temperature. Electrophysiological evidence shows a minimum amount of arousal (in the sense of activity of the reticular activating system) at thermal equilibrium or normal body temperature. Increasing or decreasing the body temperature produces arousal. Arousal interacts with the characteristics of the task in a complex way: differing tasks have different levels of arousal for optimum performance. In addition tasks may have characteristics which are themselves arousing. To evaluate the effect of a change in body temperature on performance it is therefore necessary not only to know the magnitude of any change in performance but also to know the activation level (or effort) involved, degree of difficulty of the task as well as the level of achievement. Temperature is stressful, he suggests, when the degree of arousal produced is higher than the optimum for the task.

Wyon (1970) extends Provins' ideas to the extent of relating them to moderate degrees of environmental heat rather than relating arousal only to body temperature (which is affected only by extreme environmental conditions). Holmberg and Wyon (1969) exposed children of nine and eleven years in 0.1 clo clothing to an air temperature of $20°$, $27°$ and $30°C$. Significant effects of temperature on performance were observed for a number of normal school activities, such as reading speed and comprehension. In general performance was worse at $27°$ than $20°$, and worse at $30°$ than $20°$, but performance at the highest temperature was better than at $27°$. In a number of other studies of schoolchildren (Ryd and Wyon, 1970) Wyon has shown differences in performances between $20°$ and $27°C$ air temperature. Johansson and Lofstedt (1969) have, however, shown the complex relationship for the performance of naked children at $30°$, $36°$ and $41°C$. These temperatures are equivalent to $20°$, $27°$, $30°C$ for children in 1 clo clothing. Wyon argues that these results show that arousal level is reduced by moderate levels of thermal stress (that is temperatures $c.27°$ compared with a comfortable $20°C$ and increased by higher levels (that is, $30°$). The Tsai-Partington test (Ammons, 1955) was administered to these subjects and has been shown (Eysenck and Willet, 1962) to be sensitive to arousal. The test was performed best at the intermediate temperature: this seems to argue for Wyon's explanation of his results.

Arousal theory (Duffy, 1962) is often criticized for its ability to explain all experimental outcomes. This implies that those who use it must make specific rebuttable hypotheses about outcomes. Griffiths and Boyce (1971) have done this for a version of Provins' theory which relates to environmental rather than to body temperature. They hypothesized that in the near comfort range simple tasks would be insensitive to temperature, or show increments with deviation from neutrality, since their optimal level of arousal would be high, but that complex tasks would be sensitive to temperature and show decrements with deviation from a comfortable temperature, since their optimal level of arousal would be low. The temperatures were in the range $16°-27°C$ (mean radiant temperature equal to air temperature, relative humidity 50 per cent, air velocity less than 0.13 m/s).

Two simple tasks were used: a pseudo-tracking task (subjects had to contact a series of randomly placed dots on a rotating disc, viewed one at a time through a narrow sector at a rate of 1 dot/s), and a task which required the classification by three criteria of groups of three digits (presented at approximately 22 groups/minute). A much more complex task consisted of the two tasks described above performed simultaneously. Both hypotheses were confirmed: performed singly the tasks were not affected by temperature, but performed together there was a significant temperature effect. The best performances were at $18°$ and $21°C$, with lower performances at $16°$ and $24°C$. Subjects would be expected to be maximally comfortable at $21°C$. However, there was a significant increment in performance at $27°$ as compared with $24°C$. This suggests that, as hypothesized, arousal is at a minimum at a comfortable temperature (say $21°$ for these subjects) and increases as temperature rises to $24°$ and then (inexplicably) decreases at $27°$. Thus, although the results disagree with Wyon's prediction, to the extent that they show a minimum arousal at the most comfortable temperature (he would predict minimum at 27°C) they do agree about the relative decrease in arousal at 27°C (for 0.8–1 clo) although in this case it is relative to a lower rather than to a higher temperature.

What can we conclude from this appraisal of theoretical approaches to the problem of performance decrements caused by thermal stress? A simple distraction theory will not provide an answer to the problem (not even as elaborated by Broadbent (1958)): it can explain neither the increments in performance under stress which are observed occasionally, nor the apparent non-linearity in decrement as temperature increases. An arousal theory is clearly necessary to explain the first of these and can be extended to cover the second. However, this is done only with some difficulty since one would expect arousal to increase linearly with level of thermal stimulation, which leaves the significance of 27°C to people in 0.8–1 clo clothing a mystery. Practically this mystery is of little significance because of Provins' (Provins, 1966) equation of degree of arousal with cost or effort: clearly, efficient performance caused by raised arousal rather than minimum stress can be maintained only while it is possible to continue to incur costs. In general, we must conclude that people work most efficiently at comfortable temperatures. It follows further since subjective studies are more sensitive to thermal effects than performance measurements, that it is probably wise to use the data on subjective optima to predict performance optima.

Conclusion

Human beings, by their basic metabolic activities, produce quantities of heat which they must dissipate to their environment. The dissipation takes place by radiation, convection, evaporation and, less importantly, by conduction. The physical values chosen to describe the environment must, as a minimum, cover the first three of these and thus we find that the necessary physical parameters are air temperature, mean radiant temperature, air velocity, and a measure of humidity. Clothing insulation is the final required physical value. The human body responds to thermal conditions in such a way as to maintain a constant internal temperature and to lose just the amount of heat produced. In heat, these mechanisms are vasodilation, sweating, decreased metabolism, and behavioural changes. In the cold, metabolic rate is increased, and vasoconstriction, shivering, and other increases in muscular tone take place. Again, there are behavioural changes. Thermal sensation is probably achieved by free nerve endings acting as mechanical transducers to the changed muscular states of the peripheral blood vessels. The hypothalamic region of the brain is also directly sensitive to the temperature of its blood supply. It is reasonably clear that warmth is the major subjective variable in thermal studies, but other, more specific, sensations probably exist as well. Laboratory studies are probably more dependable as research investigation than field surveys, because of the restricted facilities for control outside environmental chambers. Research has concentrated on investigation of subjective warmth as a function of the four major physical variables, but work has begun on other physical variables such as non-uniformity. A method of predicting warmth from mean radiant temperature and air temperature (which cannot be subjectively differentiated) is available. There has been little or no subjective study of air velocity but work on humidity has shown that the amount of moisture in the air is perceived as such, as distinct from any effect on subjective warmth. Human beings are very sensitive, but also very tolerant, to thermal non-uniformities. The major demographic characteristics, such as age and sex, have no effect on thermal sensation. Human beings work most efficiently at psychomotor tasks when at comfortable temperatures.

The general picture that has emerged is that the work of the psychologist in this field has only just begun. There is a clear knowledge of how to produce a given level of subjective warmth from the variables which are known to be physically important: warmth appears to be a robust sensation, not affected by such variables as the surface colours of rooms (Berry, 1961). However the whole area of the possible variety of other sensations has not yet received any concentrated attention, and the investigation of subjective responses to such variables as spatial and temporal variation has only just begun. Furthermore, we know little of the way in which thermal aspects of the environment combine to influence response with other aspects, such as the acoustic, luminous and spatial aspects with which we will be concerned in subsequent chapters. It has been established that the best psychomotor performance is achieved at comfortable air temperatures. The arousal approach suggests that, since it is total stimulation which is important, the various equations for combining physical variables to predict warmth will also predict performance decrement. This cannot however be deduced *a priori*.

Chapter Three

The Acoustic Environment

David Walters

Some physics and physiology

Whether we like it or not, we are all exposed for the whole of our lives, from before birth until death, to an acoustic environment of some sort. The delicate mechanisms of ear and brain are constantly responding to those minute fluctuations, like ripples on the surface of the ambient atmospheric pressure, which we interpret as sound. Only in highly artificial situations, such as might with considerable difficulty be contrived in an acoustical laboratory, can conditions be achieved in which these air pressure fluctuations are almost stilled.

The existence of a relatively straightforward set of physical variables, sound pressure waves, which have clearly associated with them identifiable psychological responses, whether it be the delight of a pop group's fans or the annoyance of their neighbours, places the study of the acoustic environment in a similar bracket to the study of the thermal environment, discussed in the previous chapter. It has added complexities, as we shall see, which grow partly from the increased importance of temporal factors, but more directly from the great range of common sound producing sources.

c

Study of the acoustic environment shares with the luminous environment, as we shall see in Chapter Four, a necessity to take into account the significance, or 'meaning', of the physical stimuli not at all prominent in the study of the thermal environment. Concert hall acoustics are a clear example of this, which we shall discuss, for it is difficult to study concert hall acoustics without exploring what meanings such terms as 'good acoustics' may have.

The human auditory system, ear and brain, is an extremely sensitive transducer and interpreter of sound pressure. Typically the normal atmospheric pressure is in the region of 100 000 newtons per square metre (N/m^2); a sound pressure of $1 N/m^2$ would be a very loud noise indeed, such as might exist in a factory machine shop. At the other end of the scale the ear can respond to sound pressures as small as about $0.00002 N/m^2$. This pressure is defined, somewhat arbitrarily, as the Minimum Audible Pressure or Threshold of Hearing, although it actually only holds true for the middle frequencies, and for young adults. If the sound pressure is increased, eventually another threshold is reached, the Threshold of Pain, at a pressure in the region of $200 N/m^2$. Thus the dynamic range, or the ratio of the pressure of the loudest sound that can be heard without physical pain to that of the quietest audible sound, of the system is greater than 1 : 1 000 000.

The conventional unit of sound pressure is not the N/m^2, but a logarithmic one, the deciBel (dB), which not only is in line with Fechner's Law which relates response logarithmically to stimulus, but also reduces the length of the scale to manageable size. Actually the deciBel is a logarithmic *ratio*, a dimensionless unit, defined as twenty times the common logarithm of the ratio between two pressures:

$$\text{dB ratio} = 20 \log_{10} \frac{p_1}{p_2}$$

where p_1 and p_2 are the two sound pressures being compared. But if we make p_2 equal to some reference level (conventionally taken to be the threshold pressure of $0.00002 N/m^2$, unless stated otherwise) then we can express p_1 in dB as an *absolute* pressure level:

$$\text{dB level} = 20 \log_{10} \frac{p}{2 \times 10^{-5} \ N/m^2}$$

The relationship between sound pressure level in dB and sound pressure in N/m^2, together with some typical sounds appropriate to various pressure levels, is given in Table 3.1.

Table 3.1 Sound pressures and dB levels

Pressure (N/m^2)	Pressure level (dB reference level 2×10^{-5} N/m^2)	Typical sounds
0.00002	0	Threshold of Hearing
	10	sound-proofed room
0.0002	20	watch ticking
	30	quiet countryside
0.002	40	suburban living room
	50	conversation at 1 m
0.02	60	car passing at 10 m
	70	motorway traffic at 100 m
0.2	80	inside tube train
	90	kerb-side, busy street
2	100	machine shop
	110	weaving shed
20	120	Threshold of Feeling
	130	low jet plane overflight
200	140	Threshold of pain

Human sensitivity to sound

Most sounds in everyday life are made up of a number of different frequencies, and the frequency range of human hearing extends roughly from 20 to 19 000 cycles per second. (The unit of frequency (cycle/second) is now usually given the name hertz, abbreviated to Hz). Human hearing is not equally sensitive to all frequencies in this range, however; the greatest sensitivity is on the range 1000 to 5000 Hz, with a slight peak of sensitivity at about 3000 Hz, due to the air resonance at that frequency of the outer auditory canal. The Threshold of Hearing of 0.00002 N/m^2 only refers in fact to the threshold for a pure tone at 1000 Hz; below this frequency the sensitivity drops progressively, so that a higher physical sound pressure is needed to reach the Threshold of Hearing. Similarly, sensitivity is reduced for frequencies above

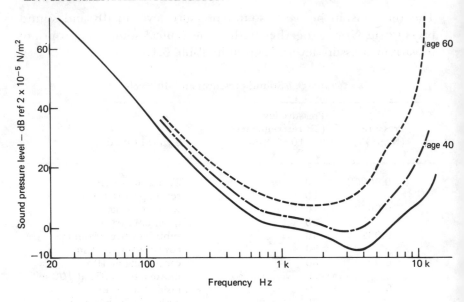

Figure 3.1 Threshold of hearing for pure tones

about 5000 Hz. Figure 3.1 shows (full line) the threshold of hearing for pure tones throughout the audible frequency range. These curves are derived from results published by a number of workers and have been embodied in Recommendation R.226 of the International Standards Organization. It applies to a young adult with normal hearing. The dashed lines show the way in which sensitivity falls off (or in other words the threshold is elevated) with increasing age. This is a normal process, which begins to occur from the twenties onwards, known as presbycusis. If the subject has been exposed for an appreciable time to excessive noise (say 90 dB or more all day in his work situation) the decline in hearing would be more rapid than that predicted by presbycusis alone. Observe that the falling-off in sensitivity is most marked at the higher frequencies; for this reason its earlier development usually passes unnoticed, whether it be age-induced or noise-induced, until it has begun to make noticeable inroads into the region of the speech frequencies (500 to 2000 Hz).

The human auditory system seems to have developed a frequency response tailored primarily to handle human speech; it is in the speech frequencies that its sensitivity is greatest. Above and below these frequencies there is still adequate sensitivity to handle other environmental information, but the attenuation of the ear's response would help to reduce the masking effect of these other sounds on speech. At the lower frequencies particularly there can be much naturally occurring sound of fairly high amplitude, due for example to wind movement; this sound does not usually contain important information, and it would be inconvenient if it were to mask more significant sound occurring at higher frequencies.

It is not always possible to determine whether human hearing performance is being conditioned by the physical properties of the ear or by the way in which the auditory centre of the brain works. For example, it is a matter for common observation that elderly people find difficulty in distinguishing and comprehending conversation, particularly when heard against a background of other sounds. This may well be due in part to the loss of sensitivity associated with presbycusis, a phenomenon which can be measured with considerable precision; but it is probably due also to the progressive loss of cells in the higher brain centres which limits the hearer's ability to analyse and interpret complex sounds.

The dBA scale

Because of the non-linear frequency response of the human ear, special means have to be adopted in making physical measurements of sound level if they are required to have some relationship to the subjective experience of hearing the sound. For this reason, practically all sound measuring equipment is provided in its circuitry with an electrical network, of which the characteristics are internationally standardized; with this network in circuit the response of the meter is made to approximate to the frequency characteristics of human hearing. This network is known as the 'A-weighting' network, and measurements made with it in circuit are given in 'A-weighted deciBels', or dBA. It is a measure used for a wide variety of environmental sounds. Though it is well correlated with subjective loudness, at least for sounds having a wide spectrum of frequencies in them, it must not be thought of as an actual objective measure of loudness as perceived. Though it was first introduced with this aim in mind, it could not match the subtleties of human hearing; to obtain a numerical value of true loudness, it is necessary to perform the laborious task of analysing the noise in question into its constituent octave or third-octave bands and then carrying out an arithmetical or graphical summation to produce the value of loudness, of which the unit is the Phon. The methods generally in use are due to S.S. Stevens and to E. Zwicker; the procedures are fully summarized in British Standard 4198 (British Standards Institution, 1967). An account of the development of the dBA and other scales is given in Harman (1969). Despite the limitations referred to, the dBA measure is adequate for many environmental sounds, and has the advantage of being directly measurable with a meter.

The aural environment

As has already been suggested, aural stimuli of some sort are always present; it is one of the designer's tasks to see that this aural environment is correct for the situation. How is this correctness to be recognized and defined? Clearly people would expect to encounter a different aural environment if they were visiting a cathedral or shopping in a supermarket, reading a book at home or walking in open country. There is no difficulty in calling to mind the aural environments appropriate to these situations, nor in imagining how disturbing an experience it would be if somehow they became mixed up—if the situations acquired the wrong aural environments. Normally this would be an impossibility, because the aural environment of any situation is a direct product of the physical properties of the surroundings and of the activities customarily carried on in them. However, an example is the anechoic chamber, or 'dead' room, to be found in many acoustic laboratories. In such a room, the walls, floor and ceiling are made highly absorbing to sound so that no significant reflections come back from them. Furthermore, they are constructed so that very little sound from outside can penetrate into them. The result is an open-air kind of aural environment, like that of a still night in some remote country district. Yet the visual information which the observer receives describes a moderate-sized rectangular room, and from all past experience this ought to be matched with a very different kind of aural input. The mis-matching of the visual and aural environments, each on its own not especially unfamiliar, can produce in anyone not accustomed to it, a feeling of disorientation amounting to terror; there is at least one University Department of Physics where for this reason it is forbidden for anyone to enter the anechoic room alone.

One aspect of the 'correctness' of an aural environment is thus that it should be matched to the other sensory inputs in a way in which we would, from experience, expect. It will be correct if it is familiar, expected, appropriate to the appearance and function of the place.

This aural environment is not only a product of the sounds produced in a place by the normal activities carried on in or near it, but is also a function of the way in which the surroundings themselves respond to such sounds, especially to sounds made by the observer as he moves about. This property arises from the way in which surrounding surfaces reflect sound: some scatter the sound which falls on them, others reflect it directly, and all absorb a greater or lesser proportion of it according to their physical characteristics. A crude but useful measure for describing this property of environments is the concept of Reverberation Time— the time in seconds for a sound in a space to die away to inaudibility after the source of the sound is stopped. Thus the reverberation time in a cathedral might well be five or six seconds, and in an average living room furnished in a normal manner it would be very close to half a second. Reverberation time is a function of the volume of the enclosed space, the absorptive properties of its bounding surfaces and, to a smaller extent, its shape. Our aural perception seems highly sensitive to this particular variable in the acoustic environment; an unfurnished living room is acutely uncomfortable aurally (as well as in other ways) even though the absence of curtains, carpets and furnishings may have caused the reverberation time to increase by as little as a quarter of a second. We find a living room with a reverberation time of half a second 'comfortable' because the customs and habits of our culture, as concerns the size and furnishing of living rooms, have usually produced living rooms with this characteristic. This concept of familiarity, expectedness, appropriateness is a useful model with which to examine many aspects of human reaction to the aural environment.

A special and most intriguing facet of this particular part of architectural design is the acoustic behaviour of and subjective reaction to auditoria of various kinds.

Auditoria

In an auditorium for speech only the requirements can be stated fairly simply: absence of extraneous masking noise, adequate loudness of the speech sounds and adequate definition of the individual components in the sound. The first is dealt with by proper design of the building envelope to exclude external noise and of the various mechanical and electrical devices needed to service the building. Loudness and definition are both related to the reverberation time of the auditorium, the former varying roughly in direct proportion and the latter in inverse proportion to it. The correct reverberation time can theoretically be arrived at by finding the cross-over point of these two opposing factors, and this point will be found to be related to room volume. As the ideal volume can be derived empirically from the number of seats in the auditorium, it can be seen that the acoustical design of speech rooms can be condensed into an organized set of procedures.

It is quite a different matter with auditoria for music, however. Here the subjective experience of the musical quality is paramount; although there is a general measure of agreement about the quality of various concert halls amongst trained musicians and experienced concert-goers, there is an obvious difficulty in communicating the different subjective dimensions in a manner that will enable them to be related to physical variables. This difficulty is not dissimilar to that encountered in the studies of landscape preferences discussed in Chapter Nine.

Several workers have attempted to identify the subjective dimensions of concert hall acoustics and to assign to them their related physical variables. Beranek (1962) claimed to have identified 18 of them. He further isolated eight of these as being independent, and gave a weighted score to each so that he could, by a rather naive additive procedure, obtain an overall 'goodness' rating for any hall. Beranek's list, with his weighted scoring, is given in the following table.

Attribute	Max Score
Intimacy	40
Liveness	15
Warmth	15
Loudness of direct sound	10
Loudness of reverberant sound	6
Balance and blend	6
Diffusion	4
Ensemble	4
	100

Intimacy seemed to him to be related to the time delay between the arrival of the direct sound and of the first reflection; the shorter this initial time delay the more intimate the hall was judged to be. Liveness is related to the reverberation at the higher frequencies, and warmth to the same phenomenon at the lower frequencies. Diffusion relates to the sensation of reverberant sound coming from every direction simultaneously and is in fact related to exactly that physical characteristic.

In the work referred to, Beranek examines most of the major concert halls of the world, a task he undertook before completing the acoustical design of the Philharmonic Hall in the Lincoln Centre, New York. A weakness of this work is that, though he discussed the characteristics of the halls with many eminent musicians who were well acquainted with them, the results he publishes rest in the end on his own personal experience alone.

A more recent study (Hawkes and Douglas, 1971) carries this sort of investigation a good deal further, in the examination of people's responses to music heard in various seating positions in a hall. Initially the work was done in the Royal Festival Hall, London, but was later extended to three other London concert halls. In this study the authors did not rely on their own judgment, but administered a questionnaire consisting of 16 bi-polar scales derived from Beranek's list. The data produced by this operation were analysed both by factor analysis and by multidimensional scaling. It showed that it is possible to obtain adequate agreement about the meaning of abstract concepts such as 'reverberance', 'proximity', 'definition' and so on, and also to relate these to measurable physical attributes of the hall, attributes which are theoretically within the designer's power to manipulate. It showed also that people are capable of responding to a number of simultaneous psychological experiences when listening to music in a concert hall, each engendered by a different physical property of the space, and that the experience of 'good musical acoustics' is not, as some other workers have suggested (for example Marshall, 1967) the result of a single subjective feeling (albeit under a variety of different names such as 'presence', 'ambience', 'enveloping sound' and the like) attributable to a single physical factor.

Noise

Dealing with the problems of noise constitutes a major part of the designer's work in the aural environment, but so far the term 'noise' has not appeared in this chapter. A general definition of noise would be 'an unwanted signal present in a transmission channel' and as such is not specific to any particular transmission mode. For our purpose we will give it the special meaning of acoustic noise, or sound which is undesired by the hearer. This immediately introduces a problem in the definition of noise, for what is an unwanted sound to one hearer may be carrying important information to another; for a proper definition, the hearer as well as the sound must be taken into account. This has tended to inhibit the development of a general theory of human reaction to noise which could be universally applied in any design situation. Instead, applied research has been directed towards establishing limiting criteria for noise heard in particular situations. Thus there exist criteria for sound insulation of houses against noise from the neighbours, for noise in factories, for industrial noise reaching residential areas, and so on, each taking account of the circumstances in which the noise is heard as well as its absolute level.

Noise can give rise to harmful effects at whatever level it is heard and these can be direct physiological effects or more subtle psychological ones. At the highest levels of noise, such as might occur in warfare, or more exceptionally in industry, conditions can arise which would produce immediate and irreversible deafness in anyone exposed to them: 150 dB is the generally accepted level at or above which noise, even of very short duration as in an explosion, would cause immediate deafness. The risk of this is, however, rare; the danger is understood and precautions to protect people from such noise exposure are normally taken.

It is at somewhat lower levels that a more widespread risk exist, at levels, in fact, which are very common in industrial situations. The generally accepted model of human reaction to noise in a work situation rests on arousal theory: that the presence of noise acts as a stimulus to the hearer which increases his level of arousal. Thus one would expect that up to a certain level his working efficiency particularly for tasks requiring mental alertness would be increased, and this is found to be so, up to levels of about 80 dB or so. At levels higher than this a lowering of efficiency begins to show itself explainable possibly by the subject reaching a state of excessive arousal, or by the noise distracting him from his task, by causing the analytical function of his brain from time to time to shift momentarily from dealing with the relevant inputs to dealing with the irrelevant noise input. This loss of efficiency occurs in a region of sound level in which long term hearing damage is also a risk, a region moreover which would be regarded as perfectly appropriate and acceptable in an industrial situation.

Noise-induced hearing loss occurs as a result of prolonged daily exposure to noise, and is dependent on the frequency content of the noise. As might be expected from a consideration of human frequency response, there is good toleration of the low frequencies, but the ear is more vulnerable in frequencies from 1000 Hz upwards. This long term effect is not due to mechanical damage, such as the rupture of the ear drum or disarticulation of the ossicular chain, as would happen with very intense sounds; it occurs as damage at the neurological scale in the inner ear, and is quite irreparable by any surgical technique yet developed. As the risk is dependent upon the frequency content of the noise, the criterion for maximum safe exposure has to be given in the form of a 'spectrum' in which the greatest permissible sound pressure in each octave-band of frequencies is given. One such criterion is shown in Figure 3.2; it refers to continuous noise throughout an

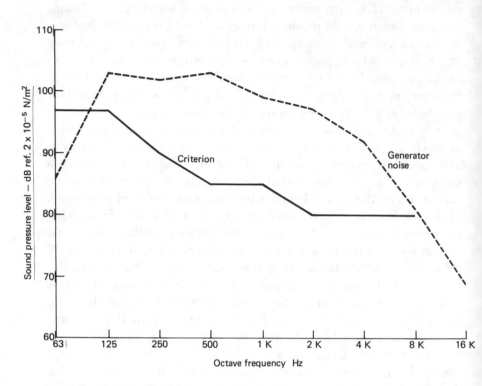

Figure 3.2 Suggested deafness risk criterion, compared with noise measured in Generator House

eight hour working shift every day. On the same graph is plotted the spectrum of noise in a generator house, recently measured by the author. Though this noise is well in excess of the criterion, and is obviously dangerous, the interesting thing about it is that one of the operators of the plant stated that he did not find the noise particularly uncomfortable (even though he was a young man and presumably at the peak of his aural acuity) and did not generally bother to wear the ear-defenders provided by the management. As Edholm (1967) has pointed out, not only do people in such work situations run the risk of the crippling social disability of deafness in later life, but by the time these symptoms begin to show themselves they must also have been working at less than their maximum efficiency for many years through the psychological effects of their working environment. Davies (1968) has made a useful review of the psychological and physiological effects of exposure to high intensity noise.

Noise annoyance

Exposure to high intensity noise, though undoubtedly a serious matter for those exposed, affects only a small proportion of the population. In everyday life, however, we are all exposed to noises of various kinds, many of which we might well describe as excessive. It may be noted in passing that there is a high correlation between the noisiness of a community and its energy use, since a large measure of noise is a waste product of some power-operated activity or other. Transport, industry and mechanized gadgets in the home are all outstanding contributors to the total of environmental noise. This general level of environmental noise is not occurring at a level likely to induce deafness, and is seldom even at a high enough level to produce functional effects such as the interference with speech or the masking of other important acoustic information, but it can frequently produce a general psychological effect, easy to recognize and apprehend, but less easy to define neatly, which has become known as 'annoyance'. The effect can range from the functional interferences referred to, sleep disturbance, distraction from concentration when reading or studying, and so on, down to less precise but undesirable states of mind induced by the noise. Even though people may well put up with having to keep their windows closed in hot weather because of some external noise, or may alter in some other way their pattern of living in order to mitigate the effects of the noise, and may do these things without making any official complaint or protest about the noise, they are nevertheless suffering annoyance as a result of it. It is important for designers of the environment to be aware that latent annoyance can exist widely at levels below which people would make formal complaints, but which nevertheless represent a diminution of the quality of their lives.

What are the physical features in noise which govern its degree of annoyingness? Obviously the noise level, the loudness at which it is heard, is an important factor. But this cannot explain the whole phenomenon; everyone must be familiar with the annoyingness of the small noise in the night, the dripping tap, the window which gives an occasional rattle, the just perceptible sound of conversation in the street: sounds so small that it would be quite a difficult technical problem to make accurate measurements of their sound level, yet which are capable of producing extreme annoyance in someone settling down to sleep. Such sounds are perhaps annoying partly because they are inappropriate to the situation in which they are heard.

We are much more effective as differential analysers of incoming stimuli than as analysers of their absolute level; we are better at detecting a difference or an alteration in a stimulus than in assessing its absolute magnitude. Involved in this is our ability to adapt to varying environmental conditions, within quite wide limits, both physiologically and psychologically. This adaptive process, of course, does not happen instantaneously; anyone who has carried out field research in environmental noise problems will have collected anecdotal evidence of people who have adapted to living for 50 weeks of the year in noisy urban surroundings but who, for the first few nights of their holiday in the country, are unable to sleep because of the absence of the familiar traffic noise. The adaptive process must clearly involve stress at the psychological level, stress which increases as environmental conditions become more extreme until a level is reached at which the individual can no longer adapt. It follows from this that noises which vary in level, or pitch, or in some other physical characteristic are likely to be more annoying than steady noises with the same energy content. As we shall see, in the development of various environmental noise criteria this fact has been demonstrated empirically.

Road traffic noises

With noise from road traffic, it might be hypothesised from the foregoing that the variables most likely to affect its degree of annoyingness would be the actual sound levels produced, and also the fluctuations in sound level due to the passage of individual vehicles, some noisier and some quieter than the average. Road traffic noise, as with many environmental noises, is constantly varying in level, so that a compact physical description of it has to be in statistical form. The mean energy level over a given period of time would be one way of expressing it (a method which is useful in certain applications), or the absolute maximum during the period or the average of the individual peaks. In fact the method which has proved the most useful is to express the noise level in the form of a percentile — the level which is exceeded for a given percentage of the time. Thus the 10th percentile (L_{10} for short) is that level exceeded for only ten per cent of the time under review, and may be taken as representing approximately the average of the separate peaks; L_{50} would be the median level, and L_{90} (the level exceeded for 90 per cent of the time) would represent the average background level. The measurements are made in dBA, and standard laboratory equipment can be used to produce these percentiles from direct readings or calibrated tape recordings of the noise.

A clear correlation between subjective reaction to road traffic noise and a composite physical measure involving noise level and the variability in the noise level has been shown by Griffiths and Langdon (1968). They based their conclusions on the results of a field survey of 893 respondents living in 11 sites in North London at which the L_{10} due to free-flowing major road traffic varied between 61.5 dBA and 75.5 dBA. In addition they took account of 198 respondents living at two other sites which had been used for pilot-testing the survey. The survey consisted of a question-naire dealing with various sorts of disturbance attributable to noise, and a seven-point scale of dissatisfaction with the acoustic environment, in the form:

Definitely satisfactory 1 2 3 4 5 6 7 *Definitely unsatisfactory*

in which respondents were asked to indicate which of the seven points on the scale most closely corresponded to their own feelings about the noise climate at their house. There was also a range of questions covering the way in which the house was used (to detect whether the noise was causing them to use their houses in some unusual way), questions about other environmental noises, a scale of noise susceptibility, and the usual classification questions (age, sex, occupation and so on). This is a fairly typical format for social survey questionnaires of this kind.

The Traffic Noise Index

Griffiths and Langdon (1968) hypothesized that sound level and the variability in level would be significantly correlated with subjective reaction, and that the variability could be described in some expression containing L_{10} and L_{90}. A multiple regression analysis using these two parameters enabled them to put forward an index of noise exposure to free-flowing road traffic noise, called by them the Traffic Noise Index. It is given by the relationship:

$$TNI = 4(L_{10}-L_{90}) + L_{90} - 30$$

The values of L_{10} and L_{90} at each site were defined as the average of the 24 hourly measurements made on a normal weekday, with the measuring microphone fixed one metre clear of the face of the building, at first floor level, facing the noise source. It can be seen that the variability (that is, $L_{10} - L_{90}$) appears as a more potent operator in the equation than the sound level as such. The value of TNI computed for each of the survey sites gave a correlation coefficient of 0.81 with the median dissatisfaction scores of the respondents at each site; this coefficient could be raised to a value of 0.88 if those who gave the response (4) to the dissatisfaction question (that is to say, those with no strong feelings either way) were omitted from the computation. The corresponding values of the correlation coefficient using L_{10} alone instead of TNI were 0.51 and 0.60; the variability of the noise is thus shown to be accounting for a significant amount of the variance in the dissatisfaction response. It was suggested (Langdon and Scholes, 1968) that a TNI of 74 should be taken as a provisional maximum criterion for purposes of discussion; the survey showed that at that level only one person in 40 was dissatisfied with the noise.

Unfortunately, promising though it seemed at the time, TNI has not proved to be capable of more general use; it cannot be applied to noise from traffic which is liable to interruption from traffic lights, road junctions and the like (nor, indeed, did its authors claim that it could); even with free-flowing traffic where the traffic density is high and continuous (the normal urban motorway picture) the value of TNI gives too low a figure, because the difference between L_{10} and L_{90} in these conditions is small. It has one further, and overwhelming, disadvantage, and that is the lack of any technique for predicting it at the design stage. There are at least two well developed methods for predicting the value of L_{10} at any point given the main traffic characteristics and the nature of the space between the road and the site of interest (Scholes and Sargent, 1971; Delany, 1972). No comparable method is possible for L_{90} and the current practice is to use L_{10} alone as the physical correlate in planning involving traffic noise. As already mentioned, Griffiths and Langdon obtained a correlation of 0.60 between L_{10} and the medians of their grouped data on dissatisfaction; though this leaves a fair amount of the variance unexplained by sound level, the correlation is significant at the five per cent level and can form a pragmatic basis for prediction.

Aircraft noise

Aircraft noise exhibits a different kind of variability; instead of the continuous rise and fall of road traffic noises, it consists instead of a number of discrete noise events. The history of aircraft noise units and their relationship to subjective reaction has been a history of the attempt to keep pace with the rapidly evolving pattern of air travel since the 1950s, and with the development of new types of aircraft engine. A new unit of measurement, the Perceived Noise Level unit (PNdB) was devised by Kryter (1959) to take account of the 'noisiness' as well as the loudness of aircraft; this is done by giving extra emphasis to the frequencies above 1000 Hz. It was arrived at purely empirically and there is no satisfactory theoretical explanation why distorting the frequency response in this way produces a measure which is highly correlated with people's reactions to the noise of aircraft. The PNdB merely expresses the noise level of an individual aircraft, but it was realized that the effect of aircraft noise involved exposure to the noise over time and that the frequency of successive overflights had to be taken into account; there followed units

71

based on this concept, such as the Composite Noise Rating (CNR):

$$CNR = PNdB_{average} + 10 \log N - 12$$

where N represents the number of overflights during the period in question (usually 24 hours) (Stevens *et al,* 1957). PNdB itself was developed into Effective Perceived Noise Level (EPNdB) which took account of the duration of the highest 10 dB in the noise of an overflight (Galloway *et al,* 1970).

The Wilson Committee (1963), by means of a simple analysis of the data from a survey carried out around London Airport, put forward the Noise and Number Index (NNI):

$$NNI = PNdB_{average} + 15 \log N - 80$$

The survey indicated that serious annoyance would be likely for people living in locations with an NNI of 50 or higher. This noise and number concept, and the method of calculating the index was incorporated into official regulations governing compensation to local residents and the general planning of residential areas near airports. McKennell (1963) made a more thorough analysis of the survey data and concluded that the best fit of noise to annoyance was given by the equation:

$$NNI = PNdB_{average} + 24 \log N - 70$$

A second survey in 1967 did not succeed in verifying the original NNI concept. Despite the considerable doubt that must exist about the validity of the NNI approach, the original Wilson Committee version is still the officially approved method for planning purposes. Amongst those working professionally in the field of aircraft noise annoyance, the development and official acceptance of a properly validated unit is regarded as an urgent task.

Industrial noise in residential areas

Whereas road traffic and aircraft noise are both constant enough in frequency characteristics to be described by the single number measures of dBA or PNdB, noise emanating from industrial premises could have any frequency characteristic at all, and the more reliable methods of rating such noise in relation to human reaction make use of octave-band frequency analysis of the noise. Perhaps the most fully developed procedure is that due to Kosten and Van Os (1962), prepared under the auspices of the International Organization for Standardization. The 'software' consists of a family of curves of sound pressure level against octave frequency. The noise rating curves represent the maximum recommended levels of intrusive noise for a variety of human activities, and there are special corrections to be applied where the noise is of an irregular or impulsive character, and others to account for the percentage of the time in each 24 hours that the sound is audible. 'Appropriateness' is handled by corrections to be applied according to the character of the district in which the home is situated. The system was validated by social survey, the questionnaire being administered to 69 respondents in their homes; the noises to which they were exposed were mainly of industrial origin (Kosten and Van Os, 1962).

Unification of noise annoyance units

The proliferation of physical units ostensibly related to noise annoyance from different noise sources led Robinson (1969) to put forward the concept of Noise Pollution Level, intended to express noise levels and their variability in a way that would be universally applicable. His hypothesis was that the requirement of universality would be met by expressing a noise in terms of its mean energy level and the standard deviation of the instantaneous levels over the time period under consideration. By re-working the earlier data of Griffiths and Langdon, he produced an equation expressing their physical noise data which showed a good correlation with their psychological dissatisfaction data:

$$\text{Noise Pollution Level } (L_{NP}) = L_{eq} + 2.56\sigma$$

where L_{eq} = the equivalent steady noise level, or mean energy level

and σ = the standard deviation of the instantaneous levels over the relevant time period.

73

This was also found to be a fairly good fit to the NNI data and other sociological data from airports in Britain and in Holland and France. By making adjustments to the value of the constant (which affects the degree to which the variability in the noise affects the result) the L_{NP} unit should be valid for a wide range of environmental noises — road traffic, aircraft, industrial noise and so on. Unfortunately it suffers, like TNI, from the disadvantage that for many common noises such as road traffic noise it is not at present amenable to prediction, simply because not all the necessary physical variables are knowable in advance. There is, of course, tremendous value from the research point of view in expressing a range of environmental noises which actually exist by means of an elegant system of units which are highly correlated with people's reactions to those noises. What is required in the design situation however, is to predict human reaction to noise before the noise itself exists. For all their shortcomings, procedures which rely on L_{10} and NNI do fulfil that basic requirement, even though they operate at a fairly crude level of precision.

Physical factors in noise related to annoyance

Variability with time is a feature, as has been demonstrated, which is present in the majority of noises in the general environment. The frequency and amplitude of this variation has a significant effect on how annoying the noise is, and the way in which this effect works is understood, at least empirically. A general theory of annoyance due to variability in the stimulus is less firmly established. It is possible, however, to hypothesize a model in which our special sensitivity to change in a stimulus is operating combined with an attempt to adapt to the change, an attempt which is bound to be frustrated by the constantly changing level of the noise. Such a model would suggest that noises which fluctuate in a regular and predictable way (such as the noise of railway train movements which recur regularly in accordance with a fixed daily timetable) would be less annoying than noises which fluctuate in a random manner, and there is some slight evidence to support this (Walters, 1970).

It could be deduced from an inspection of the frequency

74

response of human hearing that high-pitched noises would be more annoying than low-pitched ones, and in general this is also borne out by the evidence. It is interesting to note, in passing, that environmental noise, particularly that due to industry and transport, has tended to rise in pitch over the past fifty years or so, due in part to the progressive change from the slow-rotating steam engine as the main all-purpose prime mover to faster running internal combustion and electrical machines. The degree to which this increase has contributed significantly to urban stress, may not be so great, but there is an obvious need to take them into account together with the other aspects of urban stress discussed in Chapter Eight.

Personal factors and individual differences

In addition to physical variables in the noise which affect annoyance there is a variety of factors pertaining to the hearer of the noise which are relevant to annoyance. A few of these can sometimes be taken into account in framing design criteria. For example Kosten and Van Os (1962) in the work already referred to identified one such factor: if the hearer of the noise (in this case industrial noise) was employed in the factory making the noise he would be less susceptible to annoyance from it than if he were not employed there; they computed the value of this 'economic tie' with the noise source at about 5 dB.

Personal factors such as the hearer's previous noise experience, his general state of health including his state of hearing and the like, are of course impossible for the planner or designer to know, as also are personality differences which must be expected to range widely from individual to individual; all that the planner can do is to be aware of the likely range of these differences.

It is a commonplace of research into annoyance from noise that, even in the noisiest situations, there will be found some individuals in the sample who claim not to be perturbed; conversely, where the noise is minimal there will still be a few who complain of annoyance. Such data suggest the existence of two identifiable sub-populations — the 'noise-sensitive' and the 'noise-tolerant'. McKennell (1963) found that these two groups comprized more than one third of his whole sample in the first

London Airport Noise Survey. Similar distributions of annoyance scores were reported by McKennell and Hunt (1966) in the London Noise Survey and they were forced to the conclusion that personal factors were more potent in determining a subject's reaction to noise than the actual level of noise exposure.

These authors made a specific attempt to isolate the effects of personal susceptibility from the results of their survey, constructing a personal susceptibility scale out of six of the questions in their main questionnaire. The uni-dimensionality of this specially constructed scale was verified by the Guttman Scaling technique.

The susceptibility scores were found not to be correlated with individuals' actual noise exposure, and over the whole sample 16 per cent appeared as extremely susceptible and 36 per cent as comparatively unsusceptible. Percentages of respondents who noticed road traffic noise were high in all susceptibility groups, but the percentage *annoyed* by road traffic is correlated with susceptibility — thus, according to these authors, annoyance with the sound of road traffic might well be taken as an index of noise susceptibility.

The effects of noise at work were not so clearly associated with susceptibility as were sounds heard at home and out-of-doors: this the authors attribute to the ability to choose a job that is matched to personal noise susceptibility. This does perhaps seem a little too facile as an explanation; possibly the hypothesis already put forward concerning the appropriateness of noises to specific situations might be a better one.

McKennell and Hunt found non-manual workers significantly more susceptible than manual workers, but that susceptibility was not linearly correlated with age; they did find a tendency for lower susceptibility in the lowest and highest age groups, so the relationship, if indeed there is a real one, would be curvilinear. Anderson (1971) found the same effects in laboratory experiments in noise annoyance, and in field measurements Lawson and Walters (1974) found that the noise-sensitive and noise-tolerant groups tended also to be sensitive to, or tolerant of, other environmental inconveniences. Bryan and Tempest (1973), in the course of a valuable review of the whole problem of individual differences in reaction to noise, indicate some personality traits which are correlated with noise sensitivity. These are based on some work by Moreira and Bryan (unpublished at the time of writing), and suggest that the "type of person who is sensitive to noise is likely to show a fairly high level of empathy, to be creative and to have a relatively high intellectual level". Neuroticism is not shown as in any way determining sensitivity to noise.

Sensitivity to noise

According to Bryan and Tempest (1973) the characteristic of the noise-tolerant person is that, though he may at first be annoyed by a noise, he will be able to adapt psychologically to it, and soon will not be bothered by it all. By contrast, the noise-sensitive subject will be unable to adapt, but will become more and more annoyed as the noise continues. There is little real evidence that noise can actually be a primary cause of mental illness, though noise-sensitive people frequently volunteer the opinion, during interview, that 'they will end up in a mental home if the noise goes on like this'. Abey-Wickrama et al (1969) carried out a retrospective survey of two years' admissions to a psychiatric hospital serving an area around London Airport. The population investigated was exposed to aircraft noise from the airport, about half of it above the 50 NNI criterion and half below; a significantly higher number of admissions were recorded from the noisier part of the sample. However, the majority of the patients were suffering from illnesses which were diagnosed as arising from causes other than noise. The study seems to confirm the generally held view that, though noise cannot be shown to be a significant prime cause of mental illness, people who are already stressed from other causes are at least specially vulnerable to it.

It is, of course, highly unlikely that the population is divided neatly into the three categories — the noise-sensitive, the normal and the noise-tolerant, though some of the research mentioned above might at first glance lead to such a conclusion. It is more probably that everyone has a characteristic adaptation threshold, above which adaptation to the stimulus becomes difficult or impossible. This threshold is likely to be a function of innate psychological factors, previous experience of noise, personal or group attitudes to the source of the noise, and general physical state of health. It could be hypothesized that the levels of personal adaptation thresholds exist as a continuum across the whole population, from very low to very high, and that in any individual the threshold levels for the different sensory modalities will be correlated.

Applying research findings

The Government has recently issued a circular (Department of the Environment, 1973) which, by implication, sets an L_{10} of 70 dBA as the level of road traffic noise at a dwelling at which remedial action at the public expense should take effect; later in 1973 this level was reduced to 68 dBA for the purpose of applying the provisions of the Land Compensation Act. Clearly the sort of research findings that have been referred to were taken into account in this official decision, even though such findings would suggest that perhaps fifty per cent of people would still be suffering annoyance of some sort at an L_{10} of 68 dBA. A more overwhelming consideration must have been how much money the community at large will have to pay for the reduction of 2 dBA, amounting as it must to many millions of pounds for the erection of more noise barriers, the subsidizing of double glazing and similar constructional measures, and in the reduction of rates. In fact, the decision to lower the criterion to 68 dBA must have turned mainly upon the sum which the community as a whole is willing to pay for the benefit of improved motorways and highways generally to compensate the comparatively small number of its members who are disadvantaged by having to live near the improved and noisier roads. The application of environmental noise limiting procedures in an industrial society is a difficult and costly business; criteria are likely to be conditioned more by technical and economic limitations than by established psychological knowledge.

Chapter Four

The Luminous Environment

P.R. Boyce

The visual environment, perception and performance

In any interior an observer looking about will receive an immense amount of information. He will perceive the bounding surfaces of the interior, their colour, texture and lightness: the furnishings, their colour, texture, lightness and arrangement; the relationship, through the windows, of the interior to the exterior and a host of other details. This information will coalesce into an impression of the interior which will vary considerably depending on the social context of the observer and the observed. The stimulus for this impression is the visual environment. Its influence is a huge topic and much of it is unexplored. Furthermore, unlike the thermal and acoustic environments discussed in previous chapters the number of psychologically relevant physical variables is great and the selection of the key human responses is difficult.

This chapter does not attempt to deal with the way people respond to the total visual environment but is concerned with their response to a significant element of it, the luminous environment. By this is meant the way in which the light

81

characteristics of an interior affect the perception of the interior and influence the ability of people to perform work quickly, accurately and easily in it.

Usually perception and performance cannot be separated. In a situation where visual work is required the perception of the interior is likely to be influenced by the ease with which the work can be done. Conversely, it can be suggested that the perception of the interior can influence, at least in part, the motivation of the people towards the work. However, there are some interiors where the division is almost complete. For example, the luminous environment in a boutique, which is typically dark with a few highlights, has little to do with the visual task of examining clothes and everything to do with causing the customers to perceive the interior in a desired way. It is only around the cash desk that visual work, that is, counting money, becomes dominant, and the lighting there is usually much more functional.

The more usual situation can be exemplified by a workshop in which fine engineering is to be done. Here the design of the luminous environment is devoted, first and foremost, to ensuring that the work can be seen easily, but it is usually required that the environment should also be pleasant.

In this chapter these two aspects of the luminous environment will be dealt with separately, thereby reflecting the division in the literature, a division common to studies of job satisfaction in general as expressed in Chapter Six. First, consideration will be given to the effect of the luminous environment on the perform- ance of tasks. Second, its influence on the appearance of interiors, for good or bad, will be assessed. Third, the prospects for the development of a more fundamental and holistic approach to the luminous environment will be discussed. Finally, the relationship of the interior to the exterior will be considered in terms of daylight penetration, window size and view.

The nature of light

Before the effects of the luminous environment can be considered it is necessary to specify the nature of light itself. Light is that part of the electromagnetic spectrum that occurs in the wavelength region, approximately 380 to 760 nm. It is distinguished from the rest of the electromagnetic spectrum by its effect on the retinal photoreceptors of man, through which, by photochemical and subsequent electrical changes, it produces the sensation of seeing. The theoretically fundamental quantity of light is luminous flux. It is a measure of rate of flow of energy.

From luminous flux is derived the quantity characteristic of the light distribution of a source of light, the luminous intensity. Luminous intensity is the luminous flux emitted by the source in a given direction per unit solid angle.

The luminous flux incident on unit area of a surface is the illuminance. The luminous intensity emitted in a given direction per unit area of a source or surface is called the luminance. The ratio of the luminance of a uniformly diffusing surface to the illuminance incident on it is proportional to a characteristic quantity of the surface, its reflectance. For the purpose of lighting design, surfaces are usually assumed to be uniformly diffusing. Table 4.1. gives the most common photometric terms, their definitions, their units of measurement and the relationship between illuminance and luminance (for further explanations see Walsh (1958) and the International Lighting Vocabulary, CIE Publication No. 17).

The physical quantities most commonly used in describing various aspects of the luminous environment are illuminance and luminance. Table 4.2 gives a list of typical illuminances found in various situations and luminances for appropriate materials. It serves to illustrate the enormous range of physical conditions over which human vision can operate and the relatively limited range that is used in the subject of this chapter, the interior luminous environment.

Direct and indirect effects on the performance of tasks

For many interiors the purposeful activity to be carried out in them involves visual work. The luminous environment of the interior can help or hinder the performance of this work in two ways. First, it can directly alter the difficulty of the task, by changing the operating conditions of the visual system through

Table 4.1 Some common photometric quantities

Quantity	Definition	Units
Luminous flux	That quantity of radiant flux which expresses its capacity to produce visual sensation, evaluated according to the standard light adapted eye.	lumen
Luminous intensity	The luminous flux emitted in a very narrow cone containing the given direction divided by the solid angle of the cone i.e. luminous flux/unit solid angle.	candela
Illuminance	The luminous flux/unit area at a point on the surface.	lumens/square metre (lux)
Luminance	The luminous flux emitted in a given direction divided by the product of the projected area of the source element perpendicular to the direction and the solid angle containing that direction, i.e. luminous flux/unit solid angle/unit area.	candelas/square met
Reflectance	The ratio of the luminous flux reflected from a surface to the luminous flux incident on it.	
For a diffuse surface	$\text{Luminance} = \dfrac{\text{illuminance} \times \text{reflectance}}{\pi}$	Luminance in candelas/square met
		Illuminance in lumens/square metr
Luminance factor	The ratio of the luminance of a reflecting surface, viewed in a given direction to that of a perfectly uniform diffusing surface identically illuminated.	
For non-diffuse surface for a specific direction and lighting geometry	$\text{Luminance} = \dfrac{\text{illuminance} \times \text{luminance factor}}{\pi}$	Luminance in candelas/square me
		Illuminance in lumens/square metr

84

Table 4.2 Typical illuminance and luminance values for various situations

Situation	Illuminance on horizontal plane (lux lx)	Typical surface	Luminance (candelas/ square metre cd/m^2)
Clear sky in summer in northern temperate zones	150 000	Grass	2900
Overcast sky in summer in northern temperate zones	16 000	Grass	300
Textile inspection	1500	Light grey cloth	140
Office work	500	White paper	120
Heavy engineering	300	Steel	20
Good street lighting	5	Asphalt road surface	0.1
Moonlight	0.5	Asphalt road surface	0.01

glare and illuminance, by changing the colour contrast of the task and by producing veiling reflections in the task. Second, it seems reasonable to suppose that it can influence the performance of a task indirectly by producing sources of distraction and arousal. This is a similar situation to the other two main environmental variables, heat and noise, discussed in previous chapters. But, whereas heat and noise change the difficulty of few practical tasks directly and have mainly indirect effects, the dominance of vision as a medium for transmitting information is such that direct changes of visual difficulty produced by changes in the luminous environment are much more important than any other effects.

Task illuminance

To examine the effect of changes in task difficulty, the most commonly chosen physical parameter has been the illuminace on the task.

From studies in psychophysics (see Graham (1965) for a

review) it has been found that as the luminance of a two-dimensional visual task increases, the size of detail that can be discriminated or recognized decreases (for example, Stevens and Foxell, 1955). This change in performance is analogous to the Weber—Fechner Law in that at low luminances the initial effect of a given change of luminance on visual acuity, is large. As the luminance increases the change in visual acuity gets smaller for equal luminance increments until at high luminances there is no further change (Figure 4.1). Two further points are worth noting. At very high luminances a decrease in visual acuity occurs for increasing luminance, and secondly, the size of the luminous field surrounding the task has an influence.

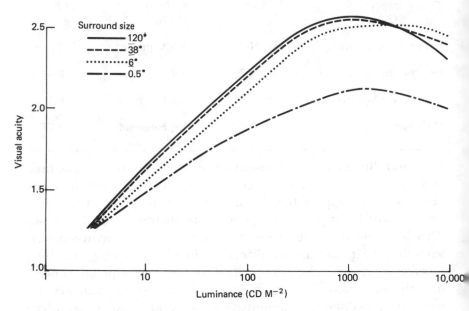

Figure 4.1 A plot of visual acuity (min arc^{-1}) against task luminance for surround fields of different angular subtends. The luminances of the task and surround areas were equal. (From Stevens and Foxell, 1955)

From the above there is reason to expect that a change in the illuminance on the work would effect the ease with which real visual work could be performed. However, before we examine the influence of the luminous environment on the performance of visual tasks, we must describe the method for characterizing the visual difficulty of real tasks.

86

Measuring visual difficulty

Beutell (1934) suggested that most visual tasks could be character-ized by measures of their minimum contrast and minimum size of detail. Physically, the luminance contrast C of the task is usually defined as the ratio of the difference between the task luminance and the background luminance, to the task luminance

$$C = (L_T - L_B)/L_T$$

for a task which is lighter than the background. If the task is darker than the background the roles of the background and task are reversed

$$C = (L_B - L_T)/L_B$$

so that the contrast is always positive. The size is usually measured as the angle subtended by the detail at the eye, in minutes of arc.

Weston (1945) was able to devise a simple task, which was largely visual, and in which the critical size and luminance contrast could easily be changed. Considerations of colour were eliminated by using only shades of grey. This 'ring test' consisted of an array of C shapes with the gap in each C oriented in one of the eight principal directions of the compass. Each of the 15 subjects in Weston's experiment was asked to scan the array and cross off all the Cs with a gap in a specified direction. The speed and accuracy with which this was done was measured. In addition, an estimate of the manual component in the time taken was obtained from the response to ring tests in which those Cs needing to be cancelled had been filled out in red. The speed, accuracy and manual response time measurements were then somewhat dubiously combined to give an index of visual performance (see Fry, 1962, for a comment on this combining of scores).

Four important conclusions can be obtained from these results, shown in Figure 4.2: (1) the effect of an increase of illuminance on visual performance shows, as expected, the 'Weber—Fechner law', in that equal increments of illuminance produce steadily smaller changes in performance for higher base illuminances; (2) the curves of visual performance against illuminance do not cross,

D

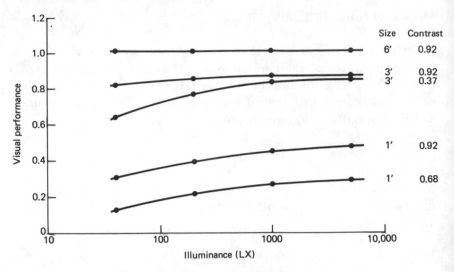

Figure 4.2 A plot of visual performance against illuminance for ring tests of different contrast and angular size of gap. (From Weston, 1945)

hence it is not possible, by increasing illuminance, to make a difficult task be performed as well as an easy one; (3) the influence of a given illuminance change on visual performance is greater for the more difficult visual tasks, that is those with small size and low contrast; and (4) the effects of change in size or contrast are generally more dramatic than a change in illuminance.

The general pattern of Weston's results has been found several times since in different countries and using, in some cases, different but related tasks with different scoring systems (Muck and Bodmann, 1961; Khek and Krivohlavy, 1967; Boyce, 1973).

For many years Weston's results were the performance basis for the illuminance recommendations of the British Illuminating Engineering Society. From practical experience the sizes and contrasts of tasks typical of many different industries were obtained and Weston's results applied to determine the illuminance required for a reasonable visual performance standard. However, the relationship between Weston's results and the recommendations was by no means exact since many other factors, such as the cost of electrical energy, preferred illuminances, acceptability of the recommendations to users, etc. entered into consideration before the standards were finally decided. More recently the recommendations have been less explicitly related to Weston's work but its influence on the final standards is still apparent.

Task movement and duration

As might be expected, the relationship between illuminance and task performance is influenced by task movement and duration. For instance, Blackwell and Smith (1970) have shown that for a very simple threshold task involving detection of a 4 min arc disc the effect of target movement is to make the performance worse by a constant amount but not to change the relationship between performance and illuminance for each rate of working. This conclusion holds for their task for velocities up to 10 detections/second. Presumably for different tasks this breakdown point would be reached at greater or lesser speeds.

Simonson and Brozek (1948) were able to demonstrate the usual change in performance with change in illuminance for a visually easy letter identification task of two hours' duration, together with a decline in performance over the two hours which was greater for lower illuminances. This is not unlikely if one considers that short-duration tests, such as Weston's, reflect the inherent difficulty of the task but the increased duration magnifies the effect of illuminance changes. The problem of the effect of task duration is to know if a subject's knowledge of the duration enables him to pace his performance accordingly. If this is possible then the effect of task duration will be small. Unfortunately, little has been done to examine this possibility.

Effects of age

In his discussion of response to noise in the last chapter David Walters highlighted the influence of age. Similar influences may be expected for response to the luminous environment, since as people age the eye undergoes a number of changes. The three most important here are a reduction in pupil diameter for a given luminance, an increase in the absorption and scattering of light in the eye and a recession of the near point, that is the closest point to the eye where a clear image can be achieved. This last change can be overcome by the use of spectacles.

Boyce (1973) using a battery of visual tasks, including a number of different ring tests, showed that older subjects gave slower visual performance in difficult visual conditions than young subjects. Further he showed that this difference could be largely eliminated by increasing the illuminance on the task. The extent of the increase required varied with the visual difficulty of the task and the age of the people. All the 150 subjects in this experiment had been screened to ensure they had a good standard of vision so the effects of near point recession were largely eliminated. Thus, for work similar to the largely visual tests used, the age of the subject is an important consideration, with older subjects benefitting more from increased illuminances than younger subjects. It is interesting to note that some of the results revealed the necessity of making a simple systems analysis of the complete task to evaluate the importance of the visual component. For some of the tasks which were superficially visual, for example the inspection of discs on a conveyor belt, the performance was limited by the non-visual features of the task and hence no effect of illuminance was found.

Colour rendering

When colour is involved in tasks there exist both luminance contrast and colour contrast. Colour contrast has no strict physical definition but may be taken to exist if the different parts of the task reflect different parts of the visible spectrum. There is some support for the importance of colour contrast from the visibility measurements of Eastmann (1968) using a ten min arc target. He found little influence when luminance contrast was above 0.4. Below that value colour contrast could enhance or detract from the task visibility relative to an achromatic task, but would always enhance it at zero luminance contrast.

When colour contrast is important the spectral emission of the light source is likely to be relevant for the performance of tasks. The most commonly used descriptor of the effect of the spectral emission of a light source is its colour rendering quality. This descriptor expresses the extent to which the source gives colours the same appearance, when seen under the source, as they have under a reference source. Thus if the source has no energy in the red end of the spectrum surfaces which appear as a strong red in daylight will tend to appear black and the source will be said to be of poor colour rendering quality relative to daylight.

There is just a little support for the idea that the colour rendering of light sources is important for the performance of coloured tasks (Rowlands *et al,* 1973; Milova, 1971). However, it is important to note a common confusion of concepts. Colour rendering is relevant to the accuracy of reproduction of colours relative to some standard. Colour contrast, which should influence the performance of chromatic visual tasks, may be enhanced by some *distortion* of the component colours. In other words, colour rendering is important for colour veracity, but colour contrast and hence task performance is related to colour discrimination. Thus, it is not entirely surprising that the colour rendering properties of light sources and performance on chromatic tasks lit by them appear to be ambiguously related. For further progress on this aspect some measure of the extent of colour discrimination possible under different lamps is necessary. In fact, Thornton (1973) has suggested a suitable measure but no work has yet been reported on the way in which lamps that produce different degrees of colour discrimination affect the performance of chromatic visual tasks.

Disability glare

It is now necessary to consider the influence of the luminous environment away from the immediate task area on the performance of the visual task. There is some evidence from psychophysics and ergonomic studies to suggest that provided sudden and extreme changes of luminance are avoided the influence on task performance of the area surrounding the task is slight (Lythgoe, 1932; Stevens and Foxell, 1955; Biesele, 1950). However, there is one feature of the rest of the luminous environment that is important: 'disability glare'. Its existence can be understood by reference to Figure 4.3. This figure shows the range of object luminances over which the visual system can make discriminations.

The dynamic range of the visual system is large but finite. In daylight, luminances below about 1 cd/m² are seen as black, while those above about 500 cd/m² are said to be glaring. The ultimate example of glare is the direct view of the sun.

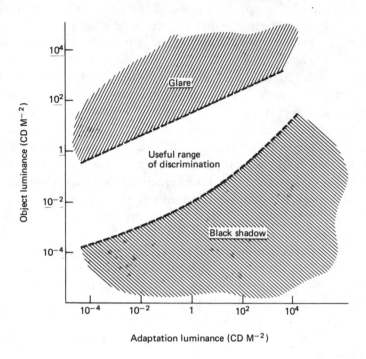

Figure 4.3 A schematic illustration of the range of luminance discrimination against adaptation luminance. The lines are not to be taken as sharp boundaries but merely indicate the regions in which the change to either glare or shadow occur. (From Hopkinson and Collins, 1970)

Figure 4.3. also illustrates another ability of the visual system: 'adaptation'. As the luminances of the surfaces bounding the visual world change, that is, the adaptation luminance changes, the visual system adjusts its sensitivity (greater sensitivity with lower luminances and vice versa). The most common experience of this is on entering a cinema. Initially, the interior appears dark but after several minutes the interior can be perceived with much greater clarity.

If the luminance of part of the visual scene is too high for the

92

state of adaptation of the eye then the source of the high luminance is called a glare source. There are said to be two forms of glare, disability and discomfort glare. The two forms are not mutually exclusive since most forms of disability glare cause some discomfort. They are identified as different because the physical variables influencing each are different. It is disability glare that is of interest here because of its effect on performance. (Holladay, 1926; Stiles, 1928).

The most commonly occurring experience of disability glare is during night driving. Meeting oncoming headlights severely reduces the limits of discrimination on the road ahead, even if the tendency to look directly at the lights is resisted. One explanation of disability glare is that it is caused by the scattering of light in the eye so that a light veil is cast over the retinal area receiving the image of interest. The light veil produces an increase in the local adaptation level and reduces the contrast of the retinal image. The net effect is to make the visual task more difficult.

Fortunately disability glare direct from light sources is a rare occurrence in interiors since control of discomfort glare usually ensures the elimination of disability glare. However, when it does occur, the nearer the glare source is to the line of sight, the greater will be the disability glare effect. It is also worth pointing out that since the number of scattering centres in the eye increases with age, older people should experience more disability glare than the young. This has been found by Christie and Fisher (1966) for a simulated road scene.

The visibility method

The results discussed so far have shown that illuminance, disability glare, and possibly, the spectral emission of the light source can all be important for the performance of visual tasks. However, there is a real limitation on applying these results. This is the rather primitive method of identifying a task solely by its minimum size and luminance contrast. By doing this much information inherent in the visual task is ignored, for example, surface texture or arrangement of various elements of the task.

Fortunately a more complete method of assessing task difficulty and relating it to the visual performance has recently been developed. It is called the 'visibility method' (Blackwell, 1972). The important difference of the visibility approach is that it involves a human being observing the task and visually assessing its difficulty.

The visibility approach can best be explained by describing one use of its physical accompaniment, the visibility meter. A person views the task of interest under what are called reference conditions of uniform, diffuse and unpolarized lighting. The task is viewed from the distance and direction in which it would normally be seen. By optical means, a facility is provided for superimposing a view of the task and that of a field of uniform luminance, a 'veiling field'. The luminance of the task and veiling fields are set to the same value. The combination of these two fields is arranged so that the relative proportion of the total luminance from both can vary but the total luminance is constant and hence the adaptation level is unchanged. Then, starting from a position of zero, the veiling field luminance is increased and the task luminance proportionally decreased until the detail of the task that it is required to detect disappears. The proportion of the total field luminance that comes from the task luminance is used to form a measure of the task visibility, called the *relative visibility*.

This measurement is specific to each observer because of the individual variation in sensitivity in making the 'threshold' setting at which the detail to be detected disappears. To overcome this problem the observer then views a reference 4 min arc disc task at the same task luminance and establishes the contrast of the reference task that is reduced to the threshold condition by the same veiling luminance. He thus establishes the *equivalent contrast* of the task of interest. This is an absolute measure of task visibility and can be used as an estimate of the visual difficulty of the task.

For any particular task luminance the extent of visibility of the task can be quantified by taking the ratio of the equivalent contrast and the threshold contrast of the reference task. This ratio is called the *visibility level*.

In making his judgements the observer is presumably influenced by the luminance of the task, the contrast, size of detail, the colour differences and all the other features, such as surface texture that constitute a visual task. The incorporation of all these features into one measurement made by a human observer is the great advantage of the visibility approach. It is also worth noting that equivalent contrast measured under the same lighting conditions can be used to scale the visual difficulty of a number of different tasks.

Visibility level and task performance

Blackwell (1972), who has been largely responsible for developing the visibility approach, has shown that the actual ergonomic performance of some visual tasks can be related to the visibility level of the task, as indeed it should be. By examining the results of Weston (1945), Muck and Bodmann (1961), Boynton and Boss (1970) and Scott and Blackwell (1970) and assuming that the experiments were carried out under reference lighting conditions, he produced the result shown in Figure 4.4. A similar result has been found by Uitterhoeve and

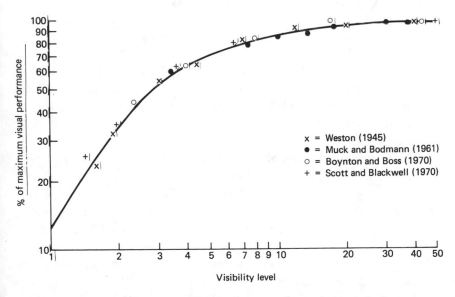

Figure 4.4 A plot of percentage maximum visual performance against visibility level for a number of studies of visual performance. (From Blackwell, 1972)

95

Kebschull (1973) for visual performance of a ring test. There is a clear relationship between increasing visibility level and the percentage of maximum task performance obtained.

These results contradict only one of the conclusions from Weston's results, that is, that a difficult visual task can never be made to be performed as well as an easy visual task by increasing the illuminance on it. Blackwell's results imply that given an equal visibility level, the performance of tasks of the same type but different difficulty level, for example different size and contrast ring tests, can reach the same level of performance whatever the variations in size and contrast. Increases of task illuminance and hence task luminance are one way in which visibility level can be increased. From the viewpoint of the visibility approach it would be argued that Weston's tasks of different size and contrast at the same illuminance, were at different visibility levels. The curve in Figure 4.4 can be used as a basis for calculating the luminance required for a given level of performance.

Allowing for veiling reflections

It is important to note that so far all the various measurements have been obtained under *reference* lighting conditions. Hence any luminance calculated for a given level of performance assumes similar lighting conditions. In practice, a lighting installation rarely produces completely diffuse, uniform and unpolarized lighting. Thus some method for modifying the conclusions as regards task luminance is necessary for practical application.

The most serious departure from reference conditions occurs because most surfaces are not completely diffuse reflectors. They usually have an element of specular reflectance in them which produces localized highlights. If the lighting is not completely diffuse then depending on the relative positions of light source, task and observer it is possible for these specular reflectances to change the contrast of the task drastically and hence its visibility. Some of these effects can be seen in Figure 4.5.

The occurrence of these specular reflections is called veiling reflections. The method necessary to allow for these veiling reflections is to measure the relative visibility of the task of

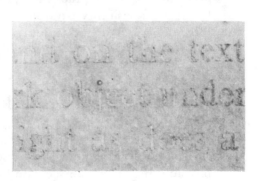

1 2

some parts o   some parts o
e activity sul   le activity sul
organisation (organisation (

actions invol   actions invol
possible effe   possible effe
uch as would   such as would

d on the text   d on the text
k object under   k object under
ght as does a   ght as does a

Figure 4.5 A demonstration of the effect of veiling reflections. The first row consists of a matt ink on matt paper lit from behind the observer (column 1) and from in front and above the observer (column 2). The former situation is designed to minimize the veiling reflections, the latter to maximize them. The second row consists of semi-matt ink on a gloss paper, lit in the same way. Note the reduction in contrast due to veiling reflections. The third row consists of gloss ink on gloss paper lit in the same way as before. Note the reversal of contrast due to veiling reflections

interest under both actual and reference lighting conditions and express the former as a ratio of the latter. If this ratio, the 'contrast rendering factor', is much less than 1, then the actual lighting installation is producing many veiling reflections and a higher luminance than predicted from reference conditions will be needed. If the ratio is equal to unity then there is no difference between the actual and reference conditions and the calculated task luminance can be used. If the ratio is greater than 1 the actual installation is enhancing the contrast above that obtained from the diffuse lighting installation and a lower task luminance can be used. By a similar method any disability· glare in the region surrounding the task can be allowed for.

There are a number of advantages of the visibility approach over the piecemeal approach that has been common in the past. From people's observations, measures of the visibility of the task are obtained. These measures can be used to make estimates of the relative difficulty of a number of tasks or provide an index of merit for particular types of lighting installation in terms of contrast rendering factor. In addition, from data relating levels of performance of a number of different tasks to visibility level, it is possible to estimate the task luminance needed for a given level of performance in a practical lighting installation. Indeed, in the future, the visibility approach may well be applied to moving, three-dimensional and coloured tasks and allowances made for observers' ages.

Indirect effects on task performance

It is now necessary to consider the possibility of the luminous environment influencing task performance indirectly. It seems probable that if such effects do occur the features of the luminous environment most likely to be important are those which can be obtrusive without causing direct changes in task difficulty. Therefore, the most probable effective features are (a) the other form of glare, discomfort glare and (b) lamp flicker.

Discomfort glare is said to occur when a part of the visual world has a luminance which is too high compared with the rest of the scene and causes discomfort but, unlike disability glare, does not affect the psycho-physical measures of performance. However, Stone and Groves (1968) found that the level of discomfort glare did not affect the performance of a ring test even when the glare was considered to be 'intolerable'. This nil result is possibly due to the short duration of this test, of the order of two minutes. For the moment, the possible indirect effects of discomfort glare on performance must remain just that — a possibility.

As for lamp flicker there is again no evidence as to which sort of effect would be prevalent, if any. For the large and unpredictable oscillation occurring in a fluorescent lamp with a faulty control circuit it seems probable that distraction would be dominant. After all a flickering stimulus is used in some visual data display units to attract attention to a reading outside a set of limits. For the more usual lamp flicker, that produced from the operation of lamps on a 50 Hz AC electricity supply, when this is visible it will be predictable and hence any distraction or overload effect is likely to be small, unless the flicker modulation is large, such as occurs in lamps nearing the end of their life.

Overall the indirect effects of the luminous environment have hardly begun to be explored and cannot by any means be said to be established.

Until some work is done on this, discussion of the indirect effects must remain largely speculative.

Summary of effects on task performance

To summarize the work on the effect of the luminous environment on task performance, it is known that for matt two-dimensional tasks with a large visual component the main features of the luminous environment that influence task performance are illuminance and disability glare. The general form of the relationship between illuminance and task performance for achromatic task has been well established. However, when luminance contrast is low but colour contrast is present the usual relation between illuminance and performance for a given luminance contrast may be changed. In this situation the effect of the spectral emission of the light source is important since it can influence the ability to discriminate the colours and hence can enhance the task contrast.

If it is required to obtain quantitative estimates of the effect of the luminous environment on task performance the best approach is to measure the visibility of the task. This takes account of the illuminance on the task, the colour contrast, luminance contrast, size of detail and all the other visual characteristics. Using the visibility approach the required task illuminance for a given level of performance can be calculated (or vice versa) and the influence of any particular lighting installation allowed for. Unfortunately the visibility approach is at present only applicable to some printed and handwritten materials. Until this approach has been more widely developed and the means of measurement are more widely available the best that anyone who wishes to establish the effect of the luminous environment on the performance of a specific task can do, is to (a) identify the minimum size and contrast of the task and use Weston's (1945) results or something similar, to obtain an estimate of the level of performance possible for the illuminance given; (b) check on the extent of disability glare to ensure that it is negligible and (c) consider the possible effect of colour contrast if luminance contrast is low.

The appearance of the luminous environment

It is now necessary to turn to the changes the luminous environment can produce in the perception of an interior. We will find ourselves facing problems which become even more dominant as we proceed through this book. The great difficulty is that assessments which relate to preferences depend very much on the context in which they are made. There are no completely general rules; what is desirable for a working interior is definitely undesirable for a restaurant in which a secluded atmosphere is required. First we shall deal with what is known about preferred conditions for visual work in terms of illuminance and uniformity and then move on to the more general requirements for a pleasant luminous environment, as regards glare, flicker, colour appearance and colour rendering. This will be followed by a review of the attempts that have been made to extend the range of descriptors of the luminous environment and to ensure a more fundamental approach to identifying the relevant factors.

Preferred illuminance

The information available on the desired luminous environment for work is almost entirely related to the office situation. The results most often quoted concern the preferred illuminance, measured on a horizontal plane at desk level. It is usually assumed that illuminance is the most important physical correlate of the subjective assessment although there is little reason for this. In fact, this assumption is probably based on the consideration that illuminance is a prime design criterion. It is possible and indeed likely, that other components of the luminous environment are equally or more important to the observer. Nonetheless, illuminance does influence the difficulty of visual tasks so there is some *a priori* reason to expect it to be at least a relevant variable in the assessment of the luminous environment of a working interior.

There are two major sets of studies: (a) those undertaken in a laboratory situation and in which a special lighting installation is used (Balder, 1957); and (b) those undertaken in the field (Van Ierland, 1967) or in a simulated interior, where commercially available luminaires are used (Saunders, 1969). These two approaches lead to very different conclusions.

The laboratory study, using 296 people rating various aspects of the office interior on a three-point rating scale, shows that the proportion of people who think the illuminance on the plane of the desks is good at 500 1x is about ten per cent but that this percentage steadily rises to a peak of approximately 75 per cent 'good' at about 1800 1x and then declines as the illuminance continues to increase.

The field and simulation studies, the former with approximately 2000 subjects and the latter with 20, both show a reasonable level of satisfaction with the lighting at about 500 1x with only a small increase in the proportion satisfied as the illuminance increases up to 1000 to 1500 1x which is as far as these studies go. The field study used a five-point rating scale referred to the level of lighting on the desk, and the simulation study a ten-point scale with the extremes identified as 'very bad', and 'very good' lighting. The difference in the results between these two approaches highlights the difficulties of simulating the environment discussed in Chapter One.

The immediate problem is to discover which of these two basic approaches is correct. In the laboratory (Balder, 1957) great care was taken to avoid any glare from the light sources. In contrast Van Ierland (1967) had to use the lighting installations, with all their faults, including glare, which were in the offices he investigated. Similarly, Saunders (1969) used commercially available luminaires, which control luminaire luminance to a lesser extent than those available in Balder's experiment. The implication is that it is not so much what you do in providing illuminance that is important to the assessment but the way in which you do it.

Lowest acceptable illuminance

It is worth noting another feature of Saunders' (1969) results. He constructed a five-point scale from his subjects' replies to questions about the suitability of the lighting for reading. Whilst a reasonable approach to the 'very satisfactory' end of the scale occurred for illuminances of 600 to 1500 lx, the mid-point, which is identified as being 'satisfactory', was passed by the mean curve at about 300 lx (Figure 4.6). This curve was very similar to the

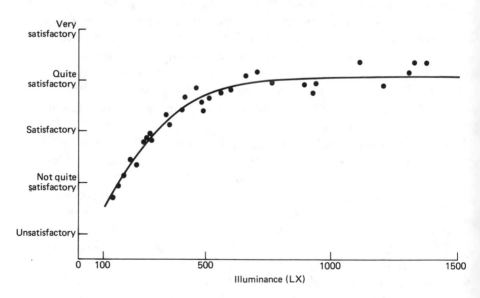

Figure 4.6 A plot of ratings of the satisfaction felt with the illuminance for reading in an office situation, against illuminance. (From Saunders, 1969)

102

curve he obtained from the ten-point rating scale. In these days of energy conservation it may well be that the luminous environment will have to be considered in terms of the lowest illuminance that is acceptable rather than the best that is available. If so, these results of Saunders are very relevant.

Satisfaction and performance

The results of Balder (1957) and Saunders (1969) discussed above, have been obtained in situations where the work involved was limited to a short period of reading. Boyce (1973) and Muck and Bodmann (1961) have all obtained assessments of satisfaction with the illuminance of more difficult visual tasks after the tasks were performed. In neither case was there an exact correlation between the change in performance with illuminance and the change in the assessment of the satisfaction felt with the illuminance of the task. However it appears that initially, as the increased illuminances decrease the difficulty of the visual task the satisfaction with the illuminance becomes greater. Then, when the improvement in performance ceased but the illuminance continued to increase, Boyce (1973) found that satisfaction continued to increase slowly up to the highest illuminance used, about 1600 lx. However Muck and Bodmann (1961) found that, for a very difficult visual task, the satisfaction felt with the illuminance above 2000 lx decreased although the performance of the task continued to increase and, for an easier task, the decline in satisfaction started above 1000 lx although performance was maintained. There is thus no straightforward equivalence between illuminance for task performance and satisfaction. Presumably the decrement found by Muck and Bodmann is due to the effects produced by high illuminance other than change in task difficulty, for example discomfort glare, radiant heating. From these results it can be suggested that for a conservative task illuminance limit, say <600 lx, easing of task difficulty and greater satisfaction with task illuminance go together, but at higher illuminances this equivalence will break down.

Illuminance uniformity

Saunders (1969) also produced some information on another topic of importance to the design of the luminous environment, the uniformity of the illuminance on a horizontal plane. Using his simulated office he was able to demonstrate that satisfaction with the uniformity of illuminance over the desks, quantified as the uniformity ratio, (minimum over maximum illuminance) markedly decreased as the ratio fell below 0.7. This may be related to the fact that in many offices people can expect to find themselves working at many points in the interior or it may be related to a desire for the preservation of lightness constancy in the interior.

Discomfort glare

Discomfort glare has already been mentioned in relation to indirect effects on performance. For most of the experimental work on discomfort glare (see Hopkinson (1963) for details) a very small, élite group of 'reliable', 'trained' subjects was used, operating as 'human meters'.

The subject viewed a picture of a school scene with the 'lights' in the picture set at a fixed luminance, then each subject adjusted the general luminance of the picture until each of the following glare criteria were met, just imperceptible glare, just acceptable glare, just uncomfortable glare and just intolerable glare. From such settings an equation relating the subjective assessment of discomfort glare to the physical conditions was derived. However, the extent to which this equation is generally applicable must remain open to doubt since when the settings were compared with those from untrained subjects the latter proved to be much less sensitive and more variable than the trained subjects. Nevertheless, the work forms the basis of the British Illuminating Engineering Society's Glare Index system.

The Glare Index is a predictive calculation method intended to measure the extent of discomfort glare arising in any interior with a regular layout of luminaires. In fact Bodmann and Sollner (1965) using assessments of a model office, by 37 subjects, have shown that there is a strong correlation between the calculated Glare Index of an office and the observer's ratings of the extent of glare in it. Nonetheless, more doubts have recently been cast on the stability of discomfort glare assessments. Stone and Harker (1973), in an investigation involving the repeated setting of the luminance of a glare source by 41 untrained subjects, found large differences in the settings to match the above four criteria, both between people and within people over time. This may be due, at least in part, to the lack of a specific context in the experiment. The question of context seems to be the key to understanding discomfort glare. It would seem reasonable to suggest that in interiors where there are specific visual tasks and sources of high luminance which are irrelevant to the task, for example offices, schools, discomfort glare can occur. The conditions which produce this discomfort are likely to vary considerably with different individuals at different times and in different contexts, but a rough and ready relationship should exist. When the sources of high luminance have some information to convey the situation may be modified as is shown by the discomfort glare work undertaken for viewing through windows (Hopkinson, 1970). Interestingly enough it would appear that more extreme luminance conditions are acceptable from windows before they are described as glaring, than is the case for artificial light sources, provided the level of discomfort is not too high. Finally it can be suggested that for situations in which there is no clearly defined visual task, the sources of light themselves could become objects of interest, for example chandeliers in a great house, and although fulfilling the physical requirements of discomfort glare for an artificial lighting situation are considered subjectively desirable and not glaring. It will be apparent from the above discussion that the existence, magnitude and stability of discomfort glare is by no means as universally established as would appear from the existence of a numerical method for its prediction.

Flicker

The other distracting effect mentioned in the performance section was flicker. Again, the desirability of this depends upon context. In a few situations it is used for effect, as in discotheques. However, for virtually all working interiors and most relaxing interiors the occurrence of flicker is disliked. Collins and Hopkinson (1954) examined the visibility of flicker seen over large areas. They used a similar multiple criterion adjustment method to that used for discomfort glare but this time 20 subjects were used; the criteria were: just perceptible; just obvious; just uncomfortable and just intolerable and the adjustment of frequency was made by the experimenter. Large differences in flicker sensitivity were found with some people saying a certain flicker modulation was imperceptible whilst to others it was intolerable.

Psychophysical studies have shown that the visibility of flicker is generally higher when flicker is seen over a large area, at high illuminance (Graham, 1965) and by young people (Brundrett, 1974). Kelly (1961) has shown that the exact waveform of flicker is often immaterial for predicting its visibility. Kelly (1961 a) has provided some further data on the variation of flicker visibility with modulation frequency and amplitude. From such data it is possible to predict if a given waveform from a lamp is likely to be visible in an interior although the wide variations amongst people should be remembered (for a discussion of this approach see Cornsweet, 1970).

Colour appearance and colour rendering

The colour appearance of a source is related solely to the source, not to any surface lit by it.

Subjectively, sources are identified as of warm, intermediate or cool colour appearance. The gradation from warm to cool is associated with an increase in power at the blue end of the visible spectrum and a decrease at the red end. This leads to a convenient approximation method of specifying the colour appearance, derived from the fact that 'black body' radiators at a given temperature have a known spectral power distribution which shifts in emphasis from the red to the blue end of the visible spectrum as the temperature increases. Thus, the colour appearance of any light source intended for use in interiors, and which is hence approximately white, can be conveniently identified by giving it the temperature of the theoretical 'black body' which is nearest in appearance to the source of interest. This temperature is called the *correlated colour temperature* (CCT). It is important to note that the CCT has nothing to do with the actual physical temperature of the light source. Subjectively, cool light sources have high CCT (for example 6500 K) whilst subjectively warm sources have low

CCT (3400 K for a tungsten lamp). It is worth noting that daylight can cover a wide range of colour appearance depending upon the prevailing sky conditions.

Colour appearance, which is concerned solely with the light source, has only a little to do with colour rendering. It is possible to obtain the same CCT for two sources, one with a continuous spectrum and the other made up of a number of spectral lines. For these two sources, the colour appearance will be the same but the rendering of colours by the two sources will be totally different.

Colour appearance is of relevance to the assessment of the luminous environment because there are indications that the preferred condition changes as the illuminance of the interior changes. Kruithof (1941) and Bodmann et al (1963) both found that as the illuminance in an interior increases the preferred colour appearance becomes cooler. More precisely for illuminances on a horizontal plane, at desk level, of about 300 lx a warm colour appearance is preferred (for example, CCT = 3000 K) but a lamp of CCT = 6500 K needs to be associated with an illuminance of 500 lx or more. This may simply be a matter of association between low illuminances and firelight or inefficient tungsten lamps both of which have a warm colour appearance and between high illuminances and daylight which is generally of cool colour appearance. Whatever the reason it remains an empirical fact.

There are also some indications that the preferred illuminance of an interior is related to the colour rendering properties of the lamps used. Aston and Bellchambers (1969) and Bellchambers and Godby (1972), using respectively small display cabinets and full size rooms have shown that for colourful interiors, lamps that provide good colour rendering achieve an equal degree of satisfaction to those with poorer colour rendering at a lower illuminance, typically 20 per cent less. It has been suggested that this is related to the greater saturation of colours produced by the good colour rendering lamps (Lynes, 1971). Recent work (Boyce and Lynes, 1975) has confirmed these results for a model office situation but has revealed that it is the difference between colours in an interior rather than the accuracy with which they are reproduced, that is involved in the trade off between lamp type and illuminance.

Some new descriptors

It will be realized that most of the above work on the subjective assessments of interiors has been aimed at identifying desired conditions of the luminous environment by using some of the already existing physical descriptors of the environment. In the 1960s it began to be appreciated that the addition of some new descriptors to the repertoire would be beneficial. In particular it was realized that illuminance on a plane (planar illuminance), while an adequate descriptor of the luminous environment of two-dimensional objects with matt finishes, was of dubious value for describing the appearance of three-dimensional objects, regardless of the reflectance characteristics. In order to rectify this situation a number of alternative measures were developed. The three best known are:

(a) scalar illuminance, which is the average illuminance on the surface of a small sphere at a point;
(b) illumination vector, which is a vector at a point of magnitude equal to the maximum difference between the illuminances on opposite sides of a plane through the point and of direction perpendicular to the surface of the plane;
(c) cylindrical illuminance, which is the average illuminance on the curved surface of a small cylinder at a point.

All these measures are functions of the point where the measurement is made but whereas scalar illuminance is independent of the direction of the incident light, this is not the case for the illumination vector and cylindrical illuminance.

Epaneshnikov and Sidorova (1965) studied the correlations between the planar, scalar and cylindrical illuminance measures and the percentage satisfied with the illuminance in a number of underground station concourses, exhibition halls, etc. in Moscow, using 25 subjects at each location. They found that both scalar and cylindrical illuminances were better correlated with the proportion of people satisfied (Spearman's r = 0.83 and 0.96 respectively) than planar (r = 0.66). Cuttle et al (1967) showed that for the nine subjects they used, scalar illuminance was more closely related to the overall impression of the brightness of the lighting

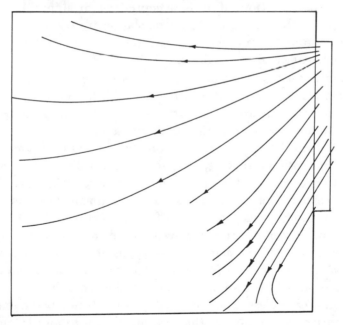

Figure 4.7 Photograph of an interior lit by daylight alone. Under the photograph is the 'flow of light' diagram based on measures of the illumination vector

of three-dimensional objects than was planar or cylindrical illuminance.

Modelling the flow of light

As for the illumination vector, when this is used in a room it is possible to plot the direction of the vector at various points across the room. From these directions it is possible to illustrate perfectly the 'flow of light' (Lynes *et al*, 1966) across the room. Such a representation as the flow of light has no strict physical validity (since light does not flow) and has not been shown experimentally to be related to any of the dimensions on which people assess interiors. Nonetheless, many people who have seen diagrams produced with it state that it relates strongly to their intuitive appreciation of the luminous environment. Figure 4.7. is a photograph and the appropriate flow of light diagram. You can judge the success or failure of the measure yourself. The benefit of this prepresentation, if it is accepted as meaningful, is that it provides a 'Rosetta Stone' for translating from the perception of the luminous environment of the interior by the architect or artist to the language of the engineer.

Another useful descriptor involves a combination of two of the alternative measures. It is the vector/scalar ratio. As its name suggests this measure is the ratio of the magnitude of the illumination vector to the scalar illuminance.

This provides a description of the strength of modelling of three-dimensional objects, and, if the vector direction is given, the direction of the shadows cast can be estimated. Cuttle *et al* (1967) have carried out assessments of the human face, in fact the experimenter's face, under different vector/scalar ratios with different vector directions. It was found that with a high vector/scalar ratio ($>$2.0) the shadowing was considered too harsh, while for low vector/scalar ratio ($<$0.5) the lighting was considered as giving too flat and diffuse an appearance to the face, that is, it was very soft and featureless. The preferred vector altitude was about $30°$ to the horizontal, similar to that produced in a room lit from a side window. Figure 4.8 shows the variations in facial appearance that occur for different vector/scalar ratios for a downward vertical vector direction such as occurs when an interior is lit from the ceiling.

110

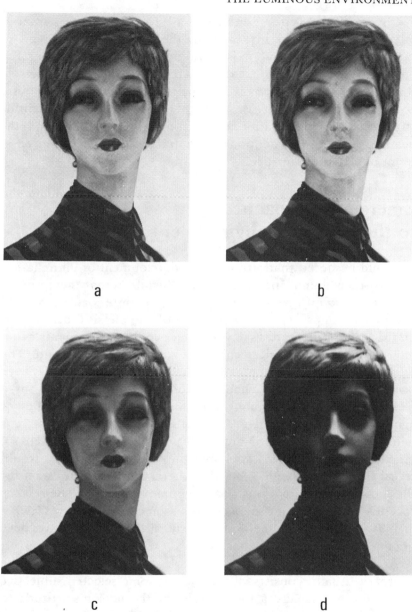

a

b

c

d

Figure 4.8 The changes in the modelling of a face that can be produced by changes in the vector/scalar ratio for a downward vertical vector direction. The values of vector/scalar ratio are (a) 0.0; (b) 0.5; (c) 1.5; (d) 3.0. (Courtesy of C. Cuttle)

Obviously the type of information given by these alternative measures is important in describing the appearance of objects of significance to man, but it is still only a partial description. The problems of highlights, texture, etc. of surfaces still remain (Cuttle, 1971). Guidance on suitable ranges of vector/scalar ratio is now given in the British code of good practice for lighting engineers (the Illuminating Engineering Society Code) and the quantitative recommendations for entrance halls etc. are given in terms of scalar illuminance.

Emerging approaches to the luminous environment

It should be noted that although the development of illumination vector, scalar illuminance etc. are worthwhile in that they provide physical descriptors of some aspects of interiors, they still represent an approach to the problem of the physical description of the significant features involved in people's assessments of an interior from the physical end rather than the people end. The same comment can be applied to all the other variables that have been examined in this chapter. Nonetheless the criteria for a pleasant luminous environment that are given in most codes of lighting practice are derived from the type of data given. It is unlikely that these criteria are totally wrong since if this were so, practical experience in applying the recommendations would reveal the fact. Most probably the criteria so based are inexact for the most specific situations and sometimes irrelevant. The reasons for this conclusion are derived from some criticism by Hawkes (1970) of the basic method by which the criteria have been obtained.

As will be evident from the work described previously the approach usually consists of correlating some selected subjective quantification, usually a rating scale, of the person's attitude to the environment with a chosen physical descriptor of the environment. If the physical quantity correlates well with the ratings it is taken to be the physical index of the psychological variable represented by the scale. It is then used as a criterion for the design of the physical environment. According to Hawkes the first failing of this approach is the assumption that because a high correlation can be obtained between the physical measure and a subjective rating, the psychological variable represented by the scale is significant in people's everyday experience. The second is that the method assumes that the rating scales on which the assessments are usually made are all independent. In recent years a few attempts have been made to improve this situation by examining the dimensions on which people assess interiors. The details of the techniques used in these studies together with an analysis of the different approaches will be dealt with in later chapters, notably Chapters Six and Nine.

Dimensions for the luminous environment

A number of factor analyses have been done on assessments of buildings. Those dealing with the total environment in buildings are dealt with in Chapter Six. However, disappointingly little of immediate relevance to the luminous environment has appeared. This may be due to a lack of difference in the lighting conditions in the interiors used in obtaining the data or the lack of importance of the differences between the luminous environments in people's assessments of the interiors.

The most interesting study has been that of Flynn *et al* (1973) who performed a factor analysis on data collected from 96 subjects who answered a number of semantic differential scales with respect to the same conference room lit in six different ways.

Five dimensions were produced, the first was an evaluative one, the second was called perceptual clarity (or spatial brightness), the third was spatial complexity, the fourth was spaciousness and the fifth was called formality. The luminous environments that were most liked and most pleasant provided a combination of lighting on the conference table and some lighting on the walls. The most unpleasant and disliked environments consisted of diffuse lighting over the table at both a low illuminance (100 lx) and a high illuminance (1000 lx).

The perceptual clarity dimension showed a reasonable relationship with illuminance on the table, the higher the illuminance the greater the brightness, clarity etc. However it is worth pointing out that as would be expected from the results discussed earlier, there is generally more difference in ratings between those interiors with 100 1x and 300 1x than between those with 300 1x and 1000 1x on the table. It is also instructive to note that the spread of scores on some of the scales in this dimension for the four interiors all with 100 1x, is similar in size to the differences between those interiors at 100 and 300 1x. The spatial complexity and the formality factors did not strongly differentiate between the six lighting arrangements but the spaciousness dimension did. Those interiors with lighting only over the table and that at low illuminance were considered to be cramped but the presence of wall lighting alone or the addition of wall lighting or an increase in illuminance on the table alone, all made the interior seem spacious.

Using this sort of results it is possible to answer questions that many a designer would like to ask, for example what happens to people's attitudes to a conference room if I increase the illuminance from an overhead lighting system but do not change the luminous flux distribution? From the work based on the correlation approach all that could be said is that the subjects would be more satisfied. From the above data we can say that such a change will cause people to consider the interior to be more spacious, the detail more clear, but that there will be little change in the perceived pleasantness of the interior. The superiority of such a reply is obvious and reveals, only too clearly, the paucity of the information that has been obtained from much of the previous work. As the authors emphasize, this is a restricted result based on a limited range of lighting conditions. However it does, at least, indicate the dimensions on which the luminous environment in a conference room would be assessed, and demonstrates the possibilities that exist in starting from the people end of the problem.

Multi-dimensional scaling of interiors

Flynn *et al* did not stop at factor analysis, they then collected other ratings on the same room with the same luminous environments using a different set of 46 subjects. These ratings, which formed part of a multi-dimensional scaling procedure

(MDS), required the subject simply to indicate the degree of difference or similarity between pairs of conditions. Unlike factor analysis, when using MDS the experimenter does not have to select any semantic differential scales to be used. From the ratings of difference the number of dimensions needed to explain the differences between the various conditions were obtained, in this case three. From the way in which the dimensions related to the luminous environments the three dimensions were identified as being peripheral/overhead, uniform/non-uniform and bright/dim. Stepwise multiple regressions of the results from semantic differential scales representative of the three most discriminating factor analysis dimensions, (perceptual clarity, evaluation and spaciousness) on the three MDS dimensions were then carried out. Perceptual clarity gave a correlation of 0.99 with the bright/dim dimension of the MDS method on the first step. Evaluation gave a correlation of 0.83 at the first step with the overhead/peripheral dimension and spaciousness gave a correlation of 0.69 with the uniform/non-uniform dimension, again at the first step. Hence it would appear that both factor analysis and MDS produce similar results and can discriminate between various luminous environments in the same room. The use of such an approach over a number of different interiors, each with a different function, and using a wider range of lighting conditions could lead to a much better understanding of the characteristics of the luminous environment which influence people's perception of an interior. Of course, there is the further problem of combining the different dimensions found. This is most acute when trying to put heat, sound and light together.

In themselves the above results are sufficient to suggest a number of general conclusions. First, that the luminous environment can influence people's perception of an interior. Second, that the dimensions upon which interiors are assessed can be clearly related to various physical characteristics and third that the complexity of these dimensions is such that the type of single variable correlation assessment that has been used in much of the earlier work must from now on be considered as lacking in generality and even utility. It is to be hoped that the opportunities revealed by this study are fully exploited in the future.

As an extension of the second conclusion it is interesting to consider an earlier example of MDS applied to lecture theatres (Hawkes, 1970a). In this case four dimensions were found to be necessary to explain the differences. Because it was not obvious from the physical differences between the rooms what the dimensions were Hawkes then performed multiple regressions between the MDS results and a mixture of physical descriptors of the lecture theatres. He found it possible to strongly correlate the dimensions with various combinations of the horizontal illuminance, vector/scalar ratio, scalar illuminance, illumination vector, average luminance and the Glare Index.

This opens up a very attractive route to investigate the physical implications of the way in which people perceive the luminous environment. With MDS the number and sometimes the identity of the dimensions involved in an assessment of an interior can be found. Hawkes has shown that even if they cannot be easily identified the dimensions can be related to the physical characteristics of the interior, which is what the designer needs. It is the physical characteristics that the designer has finally to use since he is designing a physical system but it is the observer's perception of the interior that he is trying to influence. If the dimensions prove difficult to identify by inspection and identification is required, then the Flynn *et al* (1973) results suggest that they can be named by the use of factor analysis.

Blasdel (1972) used a hybrid technique in an examination by 11 subjects of university libraries. The method is to obtain from each subject his assessment of each environment on a number of different rating scales. The analysis is then performed on the difference scores between environments for the same subject using the same scale, that is, an MDS procedure is performed for each scale separately. Then by examining the patterns of the environments on the dimensions discovered by each analysis it is possible to obtain the basic factors to which the rating scales refer.

Using this method Blasdel was able to identify some of the physical features that were either liked or disliked in the libraries. The features included illuminance, wall reflectance, type and arrangement of luminaires, surface colour and finish and reflected glare. Thus, like factor analysis and multi-dimensional scaling, this method offers the possibility of identifying what are the desirable

116

physical features of a luminous environment from assessments of a number of complete real interiors, as opposed to the laboratory approach of varying one feature at a time. However, like factor analysis, the method is somewhat restricted by the need to choose the rating scales initially.

There is clearly a lot of development to be done using these various methods, but at least they offer the possibility of deriving physical criteria and guidelines for luminous environments, suitable for different contexts, based on people's perceptions rather than the engineer's knowledge of what is physically measurable.

Modes of appearance

A completely different but possible future approach is suggested by the existing criteria used for lighting design. Such criteria as illuminance, uniformity, absence of disability glare, and good colour rendering are all considered by lighting designers to be important in producing a luminous environment suitable for most working interiors, and, in practice, the results produced using these criteria are usually satisfactory if not always inspiring. The interesting point suggested by Lynes (1971) is that these criteria also help to preserve colour and lightness constancy.

By constancy, Lynes means that the lightness and colour of objects all appear more constant than they physically should. A wall partly illuminated by daylight and partly by an artificial light source of different colour rendering properties does not appear to be different in colour, provided there is no sharp barrier between the parts lit by the different sources. Further, two surfaces, one of high reflectance and the other of low reflectance, the former with a low illuminance and the latter with a high illuminance, do not look the same even if they have the same luminance. The constancies can also be considered in terms of what are known as the modes of appearance.

Modes of appearance do not describe the object itself but the way in which the objects are experienced. Three modes are of particular interest here, first the *surface mode* in which the stimulus is perceived as the coloured surface of an object, second the *illuminant mode* in which light and colour are perceived as emerging from a self luminous body, and third the *aperture mode*.

117

This last is produced by viewing the object through a reduction tube, that is, a blackened tube with a small aperture, which removes all the spatial cues. The mode of appearance of a surface has important implications for lightness constancy, with the surface mode being the best for preserving constancy.

Now if illuminance is too low, visual acuity is reduced, surface texture is lost, and hence constancy is reduced as the surface changes from the surface mode of appearance to the aperture mode. A change in the mode of appearance also occurs for very high illuminance but this time to the illuminant mode. If uniformity of illuminance is high any changes in luminance can be attributed to a change in reflectance not illuminance, that is, lightness constancy is maintained. This is no longer true if uniformity of illuminance is low. The presence of disability glare destroys lightness descrimination and reduces subjective chroma. The presence of harsh shadows also tends to break down lightness constancy. Finally, poor colour rendering affects subjective hue and chroma, the maintenance of which are necessary for colour constancy.

Lynes (1971) goes into more detail but the above should be sufficient to suggest that the existing criteria for a good luminous environment, which have been derived from limited laboratory work but are justified by practical experience, might well be related to the preservation of constancy. If this is so then knowledge of the way in which constancies operate would be of great relevance to the design of the luminous environment (see Canter (1974) for a discussion on constancies in architecture), for example the importance of ensuring that the light sources can be identified in the interior. However, it should be noted that the preservation of constancy is not always a requirement. Again, it depends upon the context. In situations of display the techniques employed seem to be designed to ensure the breakdown of constancy.

Deficiencies in design recommendations

To summarize this section, there exist recommendations in various national codes of lighting practice as to acceptable illuminances, uniformities, levels of discomfort glare and colour characteristics of lamps, for different interiors. Luminous environments based on these recommendations are not usually disasters, but are they as good as they could be? Regretfully experience tells us the answer must be no. There are a number of possible reasons for this but two that can be suggested from the more fundamental approaches are (a) the fact that the recommendations are an amalgam of criteria, each of which has usually been established independently of the others; (b) most of the criteria have been established in an office situation. There is no justification for assuming that these criteria are readily applicable outside this context.

To pursue an analogy, existing design criteria produce lighting schemes that are like mass-produced furniture, they do the job and that is all. The aim for the future should be to produce the craftsman-made piece with its overtones of quality and suitability for a specific purpose.

Further studies of the type produced by Flynn *et al* in a range of different interiors would help to do this since they would provide a more certain understanding of the important physical features of the luminous environment in each context. Once these are established it should be possible, with the aid of the wider range of physical descriptors available, to provide a physical prescription for the luminous environment of an interior that matches people's expectations.

Windows and the luminous environment

There is one final area which is of relevance to the luminous environment. It is not directly of concern for the performance of visual tasks other than those involving special colour judgment, but it has an important effect on the subjective assessment of an interior. The area of concern is the influence of windows.

The provision of a window in a side wall does two things (a) it provides contact with the exterior and (b) it admits daylight to the interior. In doing the latter it enhances the luminous environment by ensuring that the illumination vector is in the preferred direction, the colour rendering is good, and most importantly, there is a measure of spatial and temporal variety in the luminous environment that is dependent on external conditions. This

E

section will start with the interior effects of daylight, then consider the window itself and conclude with an examination of the importance and preferred nature of the external contact.

Daylight and sunlight

The choice between the dominance of natural or artificial light in an interior is probably one of the most important to be made when designing the luminous environment. There can be little doubt that given a choice people prefer daylight to be dominant in both office and home interiors (Markus, 1965; Bitter and Van Ierland, 1965). However, whilst daylight, which is light scattered in the atmosphere, is almost universally desired, sunlight, which is light direct from the sun is a different matter. In a recent survey Ne'eman (1974) showed that the desire for direct sunlight penetration in interiors was related to the implications it had for the respondents. Thus, in a hospital the patients almost unanimously regarded sunlight as very desirable whilst the nurses, for whom it presumably meant extra work, shielding patients from glare, removing blankets, etc. found it much less desirable. This is a difference which, interestingly, parallels the general differences found between people who have different roles in an organization as discussed in Chapter Six.

To counter these results, Bitter and Van Ierland (1965) in a survey of approximately 1000 Dutch housewives, found that they had a strong desire for sunlight penetration into rooms at the times they occupied them, that is, kitchens in the morning, living rooms in the afternoon. This desire for sunlight was strong enough to suggest that a majority of housewives preferred a house with a living room which had good sunlight penetration but a poor view to one with a good view but no sunlight. These results indicate the difficulty that bedevils much of the work on the luminous environment, the problem of generalizing from one specific context to another. Even the desirability of daylight is limited since large amounts of daylight are usually associated with summer overheating and solar glare, so that people who sit near windows are less enthusiastic about them than people who sit further away. Probably daylight and sunlight, like most things, are desired in moderation.

120

Window size and shape

Until about 15 years ago there was little doubt that the admission of daylight was the primary purpose of a window. However, the uncomfortable experiences of large windows in the late 50s and early 60s led to a reassessment of this role. The consensus of opinion was that with the cheap energy then available the provision of light was better fulfilled by artificial means, with the window's role being to provide contact with the exterior. This was thought to be important, particularly in small interiors. This conclusion led to a steady reduction in window sizes on economic and insulation grounds, until glazing/wall area percentages as low as ten per cent were occurring. This trend produced a number of studies of minimum window size and shape.

Ne'eman and Hopkinson (1970) used a model office through the window of which the observers looked at a number of real views. By adjusting the position of the window sides estimates of the minimum acceptable window width were obtained from a large number of subjects. It was found that this judgment was not much affected by the amount of daylight or sunlight that penetrated the room, by the interior illuminance or the position of viewing the window. The main determinant of the critical window size was the amount of visual information provided by the view. Windows which gave views of close objects needed larger widths to be acceptable than those which revealed distant views.

Keighley (1973a and b) has also examined people's reactions to windows to determine the effects of decreasing window size and of dividing the glazed area into different patterns of apertures. In the first study Keighley used a model office through which the 30 subjects looked out at a number of largely horizontal views, provided by means of film. The subjects were asked to adjust a variable window occupying some 20 per cent of the window wall until it was in the preferred position and of the preferred proportions. It was found that the most frequently preferred condition was a central horizontal aperture with the elevation being determined by the skyline of the view.

In a second study, Keighley used the same model but this time a range of window areas (11—65 per cent of window wall area) were presented with different areas being divided into a number of

121

different apertures. The 40 subjects again saw a number of different views but this time they were asked to assess them for satisfaction on a five-point rating scale. The most preferred situation was one in which a large horizontal aperture was used occupying some 25–30 per cent of the window wall area. Multiple regression equations were developed for each view to relate the level of satisfaction to the variables that influenced it such as mullion width, number of apertures, window height and area. Separate equations were initially calculated for each view for the dependence of satisfaction on window area alone but little difference was apparent between the equations so a combined equation for all three views was finally produced. This showed that above about 30 per cent window/wall area satisfaction was high and remained so up to the 65 per cent maximum area used.

The elimination of the effect of view is in conflict with Ne'eman and Hopkinson's main conclusions. It may be due to the limited range and static nature of the views employed by Keighley. It may also be relevant that Ne'eman and Hopkinson were searching for the minimum acceptable width whilst Keighley was looking for the preferred situation. Possibly the particular view becomes more important as the window size approaches a minimum acceptable dimension. Regardless of this there can be little doubt that windows arranged in a symmetrical pattern which occupy at least 25 per cent of the wall area are desired by people.

View

Of course the provision of a window not only admits light to the interior it also establishes contact between the interior and the exterior, but how important is this? Cooper *et al* (1974) asked the occupants of a number of tower office blocks to rank the important environmental features of the office from a list of 12. The respondents placed good lighting at the top of the list and a good view out in twelfth and last position. Similar results were obtained by Markus (1965) in a similar situation. This positioning of the importance of view was confirmed by a study of Van Der Ryn and Boie (1963) who obtained judgments, from 75 subjects, of which of a pair of views they would prefer from their house and how much extra rent they would be prepared to pay for it. Whilst there was no difficulty in establishing the preferred views, very few of the 75 subjects expressed a willingness to pay more for them. Thus view, whilst most people will say it is important, appears to be not as important as environmental conditions that impinge more directly on the occupant, for example heating, lighting and noise.

Assuming that a view out is possible, what makes a desirable view? This appears, again, to depend upon context. Clamp (1973) in an interesting review paper concludes that for the old or housebound a view with an element of activity in it is desired for its interest but for other groups the preferred view is one that reflects their status in society. Both groups have a common preference for the 'natural' but the intrusion of activities into such a view will be valued very differently.

There is at present no science of view but some results from two factor analyses of views (Building Performance Research Unit, 1972; Clamp, 1973) using student subjects have produced three common factors of assessment of views: (1) evaluation; (2) interest/complexity; (3) privacy. If such studies could be extended to cover a range of different subjects and different contexts then the possibility of classifying views by their suitability for various types of activity is apparent.

Daylight, sunlight and view

In summary, it has been established: (a) that people prefer daylight and sunlight to artificial light; (b) that windows are desirable for the contact they provide with the exterior and should constitute at least 25 per cent of the window wall; and (c) that a good view, whilst pleasant, is less important than other more immediately effective environmental features, such as temperature, noise and lighting. Whilst the existence of these conclusions shows that some progress has been made in this field it seems likely, given the multiple effect of windows, that a more holistic approach to their contribution to the luminous environment will be needed in the future.

123

Conclusion

The study of the luminous environment is, at the moment, going through a period of rapid change. The basic laboratory methods using a limited number of variables have taken us some way with some success. From such studies the effects of illuminance and disability glare on the performance of visual tasks have been established. Similarly, the influence of task illuminance, discomfort glare, colour appearance, colour rendering, and flicker on the satisfaction felt with the luminous environment for work have been investigated. Most of these variables have been used in the studies because they were of relevance to the design process for the luminous environment rather than because they were known to be of importance to the situation under investigation. In spite of this failing, the interiors obtained by designing luminous environments using the available criteria have not generally been catastrophies.

However, over recent years a desire for a more fundamental approach has become evident. The suggestion of new measures of illuminance to describe the appearance of three-dimensional objects was the beginning. This was followed by the emphasis on visibility as a correlate of visual task performance rather than planar illuminance. It has culminated in the use of factor analysis and MDS to examine the basic dimensions by which observers describe the luminous environments for various interiors. This last work is in a very early state but it offers the possibility of explaining some of the differences that occur with context for the luminous environment, and of deriving more soundly based procedures for identifying relevant criteria. If this possibility can be realized then the design procedures for the luminous environment should be able to move from the somewhat negative position of avoiding disasters, which they occupy at present, to the more positive stance of producing interiors that are pleasant, satisfying and suited to their purpose.

Chapter Five

The Spatial Environment

David Canter and Cheryl Kenny

Introduction

In previous chapters the environmental variables of heat, sound and light have been examined for their psychological implications. It was demonstrated that many important relationships exist between these physical variables and human responses. These relationships were in part delimited by the physiology, and indeed the physics, of the organs involved; but a rudimentary continuum is present. As we move from heat to sound to light it is increasingly essential to bring to bear purely psychological factors such as expectations and individual differences in order to account for the established relationships.

This sequence makes distinct sense. Our abilities to discriminate between stimuli within the environment, the amount of information we may apprehend at any point in time, is decidedly weak for thermal stimuli. For acoustic stimuli it is much better as we can distinguish across a range of qualitative differences as well as quantitative ones. When it comes to visual stimuli our capacities are enormous both in the range of wavelengths we can discriminate between and in the range of intensities to which we are sensitive. J.J. Gibson's (1966) insistence that the visual mode of attention is the dominant one fits well into our sequence.

However, besides heat, sound and light there is one other crucial way in which environments vary, in size and shape. Following our simple sequence it would appear that the spatial environment is the one for which we have least room for manoeuvre. After all, although we can cope with different temperatures, light levels and so on, we are not at liberty to change the size and shape of our body. For this reason we may well expect the relationships between the spatial environment and human response to be the most distinct. We may anticipate that human spatial responses are the most environmentally determined of all.

Invalid expectations

It is the naive and invalid expectation of a close fit between space and responses which probably underlies the confused thinking and bizarre theories of human spatial behaviour. This expectancy also fits well with the environmental designer's belief (especially the architect's) that his chief skill and main task is to manipulate spaces. As a result there is pressure on the psychologist to produce theories and results which may be easily assimilated into these expectancies and beliefs. Few psychologists have succumbed but their weaker brethren in biology, anthropology and other behavioural sciences all too often have.

The intricacies of human spatial behaviour thus have important implications for the consideration of all aspects of people's interactions with their environments. If we understand how it is that spatial behaviour is *not* simply a function of the space available then we will come to understand much about the degrees of environmental determinancy in other areas.

The starting point for demonstrating how unrewarding is the expectation of distinct, simple relationships between human response and the spatial environment, is that we are not, of course, concerned with the shape and size of the human body in relation to the environment, but with that of human *behaviour*. This distinction is as fundamental as that between plants and animals. The extent of our activities is enormous and clearly open to massive adaptations, but here again it is easy to fall into the trap of the early human engineers (ergonomists) and to assume that if all the human activities appropriate to a given space can be listed, an appropriate space may be readily produced. Such may be the case for the design of environments in which the person is performing as an extension of a machine, in a similarly mechanical fashion; but in fact, it is difficult to provide many examples, apart from spacecraft, in which this is strictly the case. Caravans, tents and other forms of mobile homes, for example, although ostensibly as small and compact as possible, usually have many spatial aspects which go beyond those necessary for strict reasons of human engineering. Windows and their location, the division of spaces and their overall sizes are just a few examples of these, strictly speaking, 'non-functional' aspects. Indeed, we may refer back, as further support for our argument, to one of the quotes from Churchill with which we opened this book on the *need* for over-crowding in the House of Commons.

When considering more conventional environments such as houses, it is obvious that there are great areas of space into which human behaviour never intrudes, for example the two or three feet below the ceiling. A consideration of the great cultural differences (and differences over time in the same culture) in the spaces considered appropriate, despite minimal differences in the anthropometric qualities of the individuals, testifies to the fact that *space has meaning* over and above the activities it is large enough to literally accommodate.

As a consequence of the range of human activities and the apparent use of space beyond simple functional requirements, any discussion of the spatial environment leads us into consideration of the psychological mechanisms underlying space utilization. It is in relation to these mechanisms that analogies such as those drawn from animal behaviour have had widespread currency. However, as will be demonstrated in detail later, there is a subtle confusion present.

However, for the moment, the significance of this discussion is to highlight the reason for our chapter on the spatial environment appearing at the present point in the book. This is because it contributes to the developing sequence from those man/ environment interactions which have distinct physical and physiological roots to those that may be understood most readily in terms of human cognitive processes. In this role the present chapter also helps to prepare the scene for our move from the consideration of single aspects of the environment to the physical environment in total.

People and objects

To facilitate the consideration of space utilization it is convenient to examine, in turn, the relationships between various combinations of spatial interactions; people in relation to physical artifacts, people in relation to other people, groups in relation to physical artifacts and groups in relation to other groups. Like most categorizing systems this one has a considerable degree of arbitrariness. It does have the advantage of pinpointing the types of psychological difficulties to be faced. For instance, the explanation of the behaviour of individuals in relation to objects would not, on the face of it, be expected to have much in common with the explanation of spatial interaction between groups. It is paradoxical precisely because such explanations do have much in common and thus lead to a disintegration of this category system that it is such a useful educational device.

Let us examine some examples of human behaviour in relation to physical objects. Figure 5.1 shows people waiting for a bus in Glasgow. The question it raises relates to the distance between the bus stop and the people waiting. Does such a distance commonly occur? What are its pattern of variations, amongst people or locations? How does it differ from the distances people place between each other at bus stops? More generally, the question may be asked: what processes underlie the ways in which people consistently locate themselves in relation to physical artifacts? These questions are not about how much space people *need* but rather how they *use* space.

With the example of waiting at bus stops the simplicity of the process makes it seem almost frivolous. After all bus stops are put there to be waited at! The learnt social processes of bus waiting has given rise to a somewhat formalized activity. It would not be surprising if, built into this activity, there were fairly specific moves concerning spacing distances. The distance from the stop

Figure 5.1 Interpersonal distance reviewed at a bus stop

you may stand before other people think that you do not want a bus but are about to cross the road; the space you leave so as to be able to move or look for the bus and many other relatively straightforward processes may be postulated.

In other instances explanation may be a little more difficult. The location people sit on a park bench; the seats people select in a restaurant or the places people choose when waiting in railway stations all have distinct patterns to them. These patterns are not obviously functional. Yet they have implications, both for the practical design of such spaces so that they will be effectively used, and also for the role of space in behaviour.

131

The social context

Another example will help to clarify the theoretical importance of these questions. Altman (Altman and Taylor, 1973) carried out a number of experiments with isolated dyads of sailors. He observed these dyads, taking particular note of the degree to which each individual regularly used the same pieces of furniture. He found that over time increasingly exclusive use was made of beds, chairs and sides of the table. Altman further found that the degree to which furniture was used exclusively related both to whether their needs for dominance and affiliation were compatible and also to the length of time the dyads were prepared to tolerate being in isolation.

In the Altman studies it is clear that the consistent relations which emerge linking people to locations cannot be comprehended without reference to the other people in those situations. They contrast with the bus stop in which the individual and the physical object appear to be the only components present. The observation of men in isolation is similar to the bus stop situation in that interpretation of spatial behaviour is only possible by considering the *social* context of that behaviour. It is necessary to understand the role of the other people actually present or implied in the situation under consideration in order to give a full account of the human spatial behaviour observed. In restaurants it is the other diners and the staff who provide a context for table selection. In railway waiting areas it is, similarly, the other waiters and station users who set the scene for the waiting point selection of any individual.

This self evident state of affairs sometimes leads to some confusions. The first confusion is the merging of ergonomic and social considerations. The amount and shape of space *necessary* to perform certain tasks, a quantity determined in the main by the physical properties of the human body, has to be distinguished from the *use* of space by people during the course of their daily interactions. The blurring of this distinction has led some (notably Hall, 1966) to believe that the specific requirements which may be established across a wide range of problems in human engineering (ergonomics), may have parallels in the human social use of space. This confusion may be highlighted by contrasting the ergonomic

132

calculations of, say, McCormick (1970) with the distances Hall quotes (to the nearest inch) for social interaction. The processes underlying spatial activities is so different in these two cases that it would be surprising if recommendations following the study of them took the same form.

The second confusion is really the other extreme to this first one. It emphasizes the social component of space use so much that the physical context is ignored. Thus, Pedersen and Shears (1973) have produced a detailed theoretical consideration of 'personal space' with hardly any reference at all to aspects of the physical environment which may influence, or be influenced by, space use. This confusion ignores the many consistent patterns in the use of the physical environment, examples of which have been given. The details of these consistent patterns have been presented elsewhere (Canter, 1974) but for the present we may emphasize these consistencies in space use by reference to waiting behaviour in railway stations. Separate studies on three continents, Kamino (1968) in Japan, Stilitz (1970) in Britain and Winkel and Hayward (1974) in America have all reported that the locations people select to wait are (a) close to structural pillars, (b) out of the direct line of movement and (c) in a position from which there is good general visibility. These and many other frequently occurring patterns demonstrate that the physical environment, its shape and size, does play a significant role in space use. This role, however, is neither of the mechanical form found in human engineering, nor is it of the form of something to be manipulated, accepted in many social psychological studies. What then is its role? How do people use space?

Animal analogies

Many authors have tried to answer these questions by reference to animal behaviour. The most frequently occurring concept being the one of 'territoriality'. This takes on many meanings but for human behaviour it has been most consistently used by Altman (1970). In his isolation studies he took the consistent exclusive use of any piece of furniture by one member of the dyad to be 'territorial behaviour'. How does this compare with animal

133

behaviour, for the concept was first used in relation to animals (Howard, 1920)?

Howard was an ornithologist who had observed the claiming and defending of an area of land by a bird. He called this territoriality, claiming it to be motivationally based, being an *inherited* disposition to defend an area.

As territoriality came to be observed in other birds so its definition became more vague. The area concerned varied from a small mobile territory (Hinde, 1956) to a large diffuse area of land (Jourdain, 1921). There was also disagreement about the amount of hostility shown to other birds and about attachment to a particular plot of land before it could be considered as territorial behaviour. The length of time that the land was 'held' also appears to vary between species (Tinbergen, 1957).

However, although there is considerable variation in the observable behaviour involved in territoriality it all seems to satisfy the same functions. It keeps the species spread out to prevent destruction of the feeding grounds, to control populations; it protects the nest and the young, and probably reduces the general level of conflict by keeping each individual in its own plot.

Once attention is turned from birds to animals higher up the phylogenetic scale the notion of territoriality becomes even more difficult to apply or describe. Indeed, Carpenter (1958) detailed no less than thirty-two different meanings for territory and territoriality. As a consequence, a number of terms, usually less precise, have been introduced. For instance, in mammals 'home range', a diffuse area with overlapping boundaries is usually more adequate to describe an area within which the animal may consistently be found. Domestic cats provide a good example of a home range (Leyhausen, 1970). There is extensive overlap of territorial boundaries, but contact is avoided by temporal spacing.

Dominance hierarchies

In primates it is often found most appropriate to describe the processes of spatial regulation in the species by means of dominance hierarchies and personal spacing. Marsden (1971), for example, in observing rhesus monkeys concluded that competition for the use of space was determined by dominance. A subordinate monkey could be dislocated from any area of the compound by a monkey higher in the dominance hierarchy. Distinctly territorial behaviour only appeared to emerge when the dominance hierarchy was disturbed by the addition of strange members to the group. This group defence of the enclosure against the stranger serves to illustrate that the behavioural 'rules' governing space usage vary depending on the specific context.

Although territoriality and its associated concepts take on many forms and meanings in studies of animals, there is general agreement on the functions of these mechanisms. Hediger (1962) summarizes these functions as follows:

"Propagation is insured by protecting the respective animals from the two extremes of either too many or too few mates. This spatial organization of individual animals, however, also insures sufficiently close confinement for each animal to see and hear what the others are doing — say, for example, in a group of monkeys. Then there is imitation and the transfer of mood or emotion. In this manner, a minimum of communication is already achieved, which often resembles or equals the 'optimum'. It may, for example, prevent some of the animals from dozing instead of feeding and then being hungry when the rest of the group is ready to move on. The animals will use the same source of water at the same time, and care of the body, escape from enemies, etc., are also synchronized. This does not require any complicated language".

Hediger's most significant point is highlighted when he says:

"Territory and social distance are important factors in holding the units together, so the power of imitation and transfer of mood can act as 'speech saving' devices".

Description or explanation

In extrapolating from animal studies to the activities of homo sapiens there is an important distinction to keep in mind. This is the distinction between the *description* of behaviour and giving an account of its *function*, or the processes which underlie it.

As we have seen, there are many examples of the consistent, exclusive, use of spaces or locations by people. Altman and Haythorn (1967) were happy to label this 'territoriality'. In other studies more detailed parallels to animal behaviour have been observed. Esser (1970) in his studies of schizophrenic patients found that the individuals he identified as more dominant had access to all the areas under study but that those more subordinate confined themselves to smaller and relatively less desirable sections of the total space available. Lipman's (1968) observations in residences for the elderly revealed behaviour patterns which had even closer similarities to some animal behaviour. He observed old people defending their chairs with acts of physical aggression!

Yet in all these cases, and the many others which may be found in the various literature reviews (Vine, 1974; Klopfer, 1969), the value of using terminology drawn from animal studies is in providing a succinct summary description of the behaviour of concern. Put at its simplest, it is more convenient to speak of 'territory' than those locations in which specific pieces of behaviour are consistently seen to be performed by particular individuals. However, the trap into which many writers have fallen (notably Morris (1967) and Ardrey (1966)) is to move effortlessly from these descriptions to implied functions and mechanisms. They have been particularly incautious by assuming that the mechanisms of innate instincts so predominant in animals may be assumed to function on a similar scale in people.

Weaknesses of animal analogies

There are many reasons why these extrapolations of functional isomorphism from man to animals may be invalid.

The first of these may be taken from our quote from Hediger; territory in animals is a 'speech saving' device. Thus it would be expected that it could only be considered as performing a similar function in humans when the possibilities of using speech are absent, or at least not very great. Lipman's examples in old people's homes provide an example of this.

This point may be taken a stage further by suggesting that in circumstances in which all sources of satisfaction are limited to a particular area, then, mechanisms such as the control of access to those resources, through for example dominance hierarchy, may serve a directly analogous function to similar animal activities. In other words, if we put people in situations in which, for whatever reason, they are encouraged or only permitted to function as animals, then we should not be surprised to find parallels between their behaviours and those of animals! However, because of the great variety of means available to people for communicating, obtaining satisfaction and influencing social interaction, the occasions on which animal-like behaviour will occur may be expected to be very rare.

A second major reason why animal analogies are very weak, may be related to the fact that major changes in animal behaviour depend upon the evolution of physical and behavioural characteristics through natural selection. This is an extremely slow and conservative process, binding the particular animal or group of animals to a limited physical and social environment. Although this process is restrictive, it does ensure harmony between an animal and its environment.

Although we are suggesting that most aspects of animal spatial behaviour are genetically coded, this does not rule out the influences of social convention through learning. Zoological anecdotes of the ejection of young male elephants from the group serve to illustrate this point. It would appear that the animal must *learn* that it can no longer return; but even though this rejection must be learned by the males, the motivation of the females is almost certainly *instinctive*.

Man's ability for associative learning provides him with a versatility and freedom to make decisions. With the ability to conceptualize a situation before it arises he escapes the inevitability of behavioural heredity. Above all, the development of speech and the facility it provides for communicating learned information both between and within generations provides a context for spatial behaviour quite different from that for animals. No two animals, for example, in conflict over territory could agree to submit their differences to legal arbitration. It is similarly frivolous to suggest that the existence of private property has been produced by innate territorial mechanisms.

The third reason for caution when extrapolating to humans from animals is that, although both tend to form groups, the form and function of these groups is very different. People belong to many different groups and the groupings themselves are not static. Furthermore, human groups may exist conceptually even when the members are not in proximity to one another. A woman waiting at a bus stop on her own is nonetheless likely to be in a different sub-cultural milieu from a man waiting at the same bus stop on his own. The various roles which she performs and groups to which she belongs may be different (at least until the Women's Liberation Movement has achieved its goals). These differences will be a factor in the behaviour she produces.

The purposes, goals and norms of different human groups are also much more varied than any which exist among animals. So, any processes present to facilitate group activities may be expected to be equally varied. Even the most potent primary group, the family exists over a longer period of time and serves a wider range of functions than any analogous animal group. The most notable difference being, of course, the provision of a context within which speech may develop.

Defensible space

In concluding this examination of the general difficulties of working from animal analogies we shall consider the work of Newman (1972). He argues that clearly defined boundaries between public space, semi-private areas and private territory are essential for the wellbeing of inhabitants. The most important element is the semi-private area which includes the foyer and halls and the grounds immediately surrounding the building. Through design and surveillance these can be made to appear the exclusive property of the tenants, to reduce crime and provide a sense of security.

Newman is, rightly, careful to avoid direct citation of animal analogies (although he does list the main exponent of these, Ardrey as a general reference) but instead implies that 'territorial definition' is a basic recurrent theme throughout the history of human settlements. On the basis of this he is able to build the edifice of a model of 'defensible space' and suggest that it is a fundamental prerequisite for secure buildings in modern American cities.

138

Without this 'territorial' basis Newman's arguments have an elegantly simple logic, the same logic which enables any child to understand how and why cavalry forts protected soldiers from rampaging Red Indians or ancient Roman castles kept the barbarians at bay. These buildings truly are defensible in precisely the sense Newman means. They kept out those invaders likely to carry out 'crimes'. If Newman's analysis of the state of affairs in American cities is correct, then perhaps he is also correct in suggesting that turning a citizen's home into his castle is the only solution to this. A simple ecological perspective would suggest that putting up barriers will make crime 'go away' but where it may go to is not clear from Newman's account. What is clear is that by drawing upon a concept rich with animal associations Newman masks the central, purely functional, theme of his argument.

In Chapter Eight we shall return to the problem of urban areas which may be aggravated by the absence of 'semi-private' spaces. There we shall see that the *social* implications of urban spatial arrangements may indeed be very great.

'Privacy': an alternative viewpoint

If we are to deal with human spatial behaviour and all its subtleties without the ready shorthand which may be drawn from animal studies, what concepts of models may we put in their place? The concept of 'privacy' may partially fill this role. It is certainly exceptionally free of animal connotations, so much so that reference to animal requirements for privacy smacks of the heinous sin of anthropomorphism! Indeed, Pastalan (1970) has tied privacy to territoriality by suggesting that the former is an expression of the latter; but since we have found little value in the latter, privacy must suffice on its own.

The importance of privacy as an explanation of human spatial behaviour may be seen with relation to control over access to an area which affords some degree of personal solitude. Thus in the strictest sense privacy may be the establishment of a physical barrier against the outside world. This is the type of activity sometimes referred to as territoriality yet, as noted earlier, no instinctive mediating process is needed to explain why people own and protect their property in Western society.

However, we may use the concept of privacy in a more general sense to help explain much of man's spatial manipulations. Taking Westin's (1967) definition of privacy as "the right of an individual to decide what information about himself should be communicated to others and under what conditions", it is meaningful to include the control of interpersonal relationships under the heading of privacy. Thus, we are dealing with preferences to take certain actions in regard to communication with others. Viewed in this manner, privacy encompasses more than the mere separation from others by the use of physical barriers. It includes all behaviour designed to set the individual apart. We are dealing with a sophisticated social process which provides the opportunity of communication with others at varying levels of intensity. As a consequence, it takes into account the relationships between people, their personalities, the social situation and the cultural and physical setting.

The viewpoint expressed here has been most succinctly expressed by Ittelson *et al.* (1974).

"We have indicated two dimensions of privacy that are relevant to environmental design: freedom from unwanted intrusion and freedom to determine the time and place of communication".

However, we wish to take the process further than they have. For if privacy is taken as an optimum balance (or at least 'freedom' to achieve that balance) between 'information' which comes to a person and that which he puts out, then we may see this process as the basis of most human spatial behaviour. With this broader definition we may hypothesize that human spatial behaviour is, in essence, a quest for 'privacy'.

Privacy as part of a system

To emphasize that we are now using the concept of privacy as a technical term with a more precise definition than in its common everyday usage, we may resort to systems theory language. Pedersen and Shears (1973) make this particularly appropriate because of their review of research into personal space from the viewpoint of general systems theory. In effect, they argue that interpersonal spatial behaviour communicates information about feelings and attitudes. They further state that in order for this information processing to be effective one product is that "the person system is equipped with a repertoire to control the influence of its surroundings on its own inner state".

Putting this another way, it is apparent that the ecological distribution of stimuli, or information, of relevance to any given individual is far from randomly distributed. Thus, in any given physical setting a variety of options may be open to the person as to how he locates himself in relation to the existing, developing or potential stimuli in the setting. This is true not only of the stimuli he receives but also of those he puts out. The person in a restaurant or railway station wishes to see without being conspicuous. They wish to achieve an appropriate level of privacy for the particular setting.

As we have observed, the stimuli of relevance emanate, in the main from other people. Thus even in a dyadic situation we must conceive of a dynamic system in which each individual is reacting to the attempts on the part of the other to obtain an acceptable level of privacy. The consistent use of certain aspects of the physical environment, as in Altman's (1971) studies, clearly has the role of producing a balance more efficiently. It is, as a consequence, not surprising that those dyads which did not develop a stable balance in the use of their surroundings were the most likely to give up (abort) before the completion of their time.

As in any comparison of theoretical stands the crucial test lies in the data. It is part of the argument so far, that animal analogies lead to the prediction of specific, relatively invariant patterns of spatial behaviour. For our privacy model we have suggested that the use of space will relate to many aspects of the situation. We must, therefore, now consider the evidence for this variability and the conditions under which it occurs.

In using the notion of an information balance, then we have indicated that this balance will be part of a dynamic process which will achieve different levels in different settings and under different conditions. We must, therefore, now consider those variables which contribute to these differences.

People and people

There have now been many studies of spacing. Studies in which many characteristics of the situation have been varied and controlled. These studies have been reviewed by Sommer (1969) and more recently by Vine (1974). For the sake of clarity we will draw out for discussion those which appear to us as most pertinent; cultural norms, personal characteristics, roles and interpersonal relationships, the activities engaged in and the physical setting. These characteristics do not exist independently in the real world, nor are they completely conceptually distinct. However, a discussion of each separately may clarify the important features involved in spatial behaviour.

Cultural differences

The effects of culture on the use of space is most clearly illustrated by Rapoport and Watson (1972). They examine the published building standards of Western nations, India and Japan, and show that even in these supposedly 'hard-edged' situations, where there are 'Design Codes' etc., there is a great deal of variation which cannot be due to anatomical or physiological differences. Even within cultures they show that standards differ depending on the social context within which the facility is used. Although this may be surprising to designers, who may believe in the biological (not to say innate) basis of their standards, given the viewpoint that spatial behaviour is learned we may expect different behaviours to develop in different cultural contexts. Hall (1963; 1966), an anthropologist, has gone to some pains to point out the differences in the use of space between cultures. He rather confuses the argument by detailed categorizations of the spatial zones whilst still insisting that there are large cultural and, presumably, sub-cultural variations. Large individual differences combined with large sub-cultural variations could easily find two people using similar spatial distances in quite different ways. This makes the notion of tying distances to zones of space (or 'proxemic' behaviour, as Hall calls it) quite inappropriate.

However, in a laboratory context it is possible to establish a setting for social interaction in which most of the variables with

142

which we deal in this chapter are removed, except for cultural differences. Watson and Graves (1966) carried out such a study. They observed 32 students in pairs in seated conversation in front of a one-way screen. Half of their pairs were made up of Arab students and half of Americans.

The observer scored the individuals on five aspects of proxemic behaviour. There were clear differences between the two groups on each aspect, the angle they maintained between one another and the distance they kept from one another being some of the most notable differences. The Arabs were consistently facing in the direction of their partner and closer. They also tended to touch more often, look more directly at each other and talk more loudly.

Outside of the laboratory such distinct differences may not occur so readily but this study does raise the question of the forms of spatial behaviour which may exist. In terms of the privacy concept we may ask what cues are of importance to the various cultures, what types of information about themselves do they wish to give out and how is this mediated by spatial factors in interactions?

Personal characteristics

The use of space in social interaction has proved to be a remarkably subtle form of behaviour. Consequently, cultural differences are not sufficient criteria to predict the variation of which people are capable. To clarify the situation somewhat we have chosen three characteristics (personality, age and sex) that help to explain what is involved in the relationship between spatial behaviour and social interaction.

Although little work has been done on the influence of personality differences on the use of space, there is evidence to suggest that it is a small but contributing factor. The most dramatic results have been obtained from the extreme cases of personality disorders, in particular schizophrenia. People diagnosed as such tend to display an erratic spatial behaviour pattern, either sitting too close (beside) or too far away from others, according to normal patterns for that particular situation (Sommer 1959; Horowitz *et al*, 1964). Schizophrenics' spatial behaviour

143

provides an excellent example of what we mean by the use of space for mediating information flow. Rather than their behaviour being irregular, it shows remarkable consistency, in that the positions chosen allowed for the least communication. This expresses one of the basic characteristics of schizophrenia which is the withdrawal from social relationships.

While other personality studies are less impressive, a recurring result (Patterson, 1966; Williams, 1963) is that people who are classified as introverts prefer to have a greater distance between themselves and strangers than do those considered as extroverts. This suggests that introverts have different preferences than do extroverts in terms of privacy and that they differ in space usage to attain these ends. However, as was previously stated the interpretation of spatial manipulations is only possible by considering the social context of that behaviour. In order to achieve this more information is needed than just personality characteristics. At present it is not possible to ascertain if this difference is constant for different settings and activities as well as for relationships with people other than strangers.

Age effects

There are several studies that illustrate that distancing relates to chronological age. Argyle and Dean (1965) demonstrated an age factor. Children approached a researcher more closely than did adults. A recent study by Aiello and Aiello (1974) reveals the details of this developmental process. They observed dyads of children from six to sixteen years of age and found a steady increase in interpersonal distancing with age. By early adolescence the children showed adult proxemic behaviour, with boys standing farther apart and at greater angles than girls. The explanation for these age differences may lie in the socialization process, part of which is the establishing of independence as the child matures. This is somewhat reminiscent of the male elephant illustration cited earlier, with reinforcement (either positive or negative) from other people attributing to this learning. Such an explanation for human behaviour is, of course, incomplete because it assumes the learner is a passive organism. Further examples are necessary to illustrate possible alternatives.

144

Delong (1970) has approached this area from the other end of the chronological scale. His concern lies with the problems involved in the interaction of elderly people with younger populations particularly in the context of institutional settings. The specific problem appears to be the stereotyping of people according to age. The elderly patients are considered childlike, confused and overbearing by the younger groups that make up the staff and in turn the staff is considered to be distant and uninvolved. While these 'types' may be close to the truth the situation is exacerbated by the clash of two very different styles of communication.

Because of the physiological deterioration of the sensory equipment of the elderly individual, he comes to rely on different types of cues. An example from spatial behaviour is that the elderly tend to position themselves close to and at least at right angles to the other person and at times even side-by-side when interacting. Part of the explanation is the increase of tactile stimulation as a means of communication. Whilst this behaviour might be interpreted as anti-social by younger adults it does illustrate that as people age, they learn to use space in part to compensate for this decrease in abilities.

There are two problems with Delong's study. The first is that the most important means of communication is speech for the human adult. It would not be surprising to find a conflict of interest in the contents of the verbal communication between two extreme age groups. The other problem is that one would expect the institutionalized elderly to have undergone more physical deterioration than those living in normal settings and this may mask additional explanations.

Heshka and Nelson (1972) have carried out a field study that bridges the gap between children and the infirm old. They unobtrusively measured naturally occurring dyadic distancing during casual conversations. These measurements were followed by questionnaires about personal characteristics. Based on this information this study supports the notion that the relationship between age and interpersonal distancing is curvilinear that is, both the younger and older age groups maintain a smaller space between themselves than did the middle age groups). The important point is the range of ages of the dyads. None· of the

145

individual dyads had an age difference between members greater than seven years with the ages extending from 19 years to 75 years. The greatest distances were maintained around the 40 year old mark.

Inadequate learning or dependency does not appear to be a sufficient explanation of smaller distancing in young adults. A more profitable approach is that spatial behaviour is learned as a part of the active acquisition of social roles. This is not a piecemeal operation but rather the learning of the entire role set; behaviour relating to the role itself, the complementary roles and expectations that is, the norms of the group formed by the role set (Sarbin and Allen, 1968). Thus, age represents a sub-cultural characteristic in spatial behaviour with the different age groups using space differently. The role expectations for a person of a particular age, for example, his position and responsibilities emphasize that it is not just a variation in the presentation of information that is important but that this difference may result from the type of information that is revealed.

Previous mention has been made of another sub-cultural characteristic—the sex of the participant. In the bus stop example, observations show that women stand closer to other people than do men and both sexes stand closer to same sexed individuals (Canter, 1974). Leibman (1970) has recorded similar results in that females, given a choice, will sit next to a female stranger rather than a male stranger.

Roles and relationships

Although the effect of roles has been touched upon in the above section, it merits additional attention because interpersonal distancing is a social phenomenon. It derives from the social relationship that exists between people. The first work to consider the relationship between people as an influence on distancing was Little's (1965) experimental manipulation of actors. The subjects were to arrange the characters according to certain criteria, one of which was their degree of involvement—friend, acquaintance or stranger. As expected, the actors designated as friends were put closer together than acquaintances, with strangers being placed the furthest apart.

Heshka and Nelson's (1972) field study illustrated that naturally occurring interactions are somewhat more complex than

146

suggested by this experimental setting. They found the relationship (acquaintance versus stranger) modified the effects produced by the sex of the participant. In all male dyads the personal relationship made no difference to the spacing between them. This was not the case for interactions involving women. When the relationship was at least an 'acquaintance' for all female dyads and male/female dyads the distance was less than that of the male/male interactions. However, if the relationship was that of strangers, a much larger distance was maintained if one of the participants was a women. This suggests that women use spatial manipulation for the control of interpersonal relationships to a greater extent than do men.

Relationships can also be characterized by dominant and subordinate roles. People shown silent films of managers entering other managers' offices could correctly identify the friendliness of the situation and who held the more superior position by their orientation, that is the angle at which, and the distance to which they approached (Hutte and Cohen, 1964). Space is a precious commodity and people who have the most power to control the interaction use space to facilitate this control. It also appears that people in the role of subordinates prefer a greater distance between themselves and those characterized as being in a dominant role than between peers.

Barash (1973) used the role concept by varying the attire of the confederate who would sit closely beside a student studying in the library. Lecturer dress (jacket and tie) produced more avoidance responses and flight than did blue jeans and shirt (student dress). The same response would not be expected at a party. Only when roles are considered together with the activities taking place, and their physical setting can a prediction be made about the spatial behavioural techniques that will be used. Altman's (1971) studies of isolated sailors illustrate the problems that arise when complementary roles along this dimension cannot be established. When the environment could not be effectively used to compensate for the incompatibility, 'aborting the mission' became necessary.

Personal space

Sommer (1969) has utilized the situation of distancing which is

147

incongruent with the relationship, to explore how people restore the balance. An extreme example of this was his field experiment in a mental hospital where he would sit next to a patient who was sitting alone. The most common action to restore balance was flight. Sommer postulates that this situation was an invasion of 'personal space'. He regards this as a bubble of space that surrounds a person and is a part of 'a person's self-boundaries', existing independently of other people.

The greatest contribution of the personal space concept is that it emphasizes that space has meaning. However, spatial behaviour is a social process that has a greater flexibility than can be explained by a rigid individual bubble. An example of this is pre-school children during free play. Hudson *et al* (1971) found that a constancy of distance was maintained, that is, a low variance occurred with both high and low mean distances. The children were regulating themselves and attending to the distance between each other even though they were not engaged in one specific group activity. Also, these distances were well beyond that which could be considered 'personal space'.

We have emphasized that spatial behaviour is a means of controlling interpersonal relationships. Yet the nature of this control has not been specified. One possible explanation is that proximity is a form of non-verbal communication. That is, distancing in and of itself functions as a transmitter of information, indicating our attitude and feelings towards other people and the relationship and activities in which we intend to engage. In animal research this has proven to be one of the prime functions of spacing and much of the work on the use of space by humans has assumed this as a basic premise (Hall, 1966; Delong, 1970a). This is an easy conclusion to draw because of the numerous studies that relate spatial behaviour to personal and interpersonal characteristics. For example, the distancing of actors according to personal involvement (Little, 1965). However, all these have been concerned with the determination of distancing. Research directed specifically at the influence of space on the evaluation of people has produced conflicting results. Porter *et al* (1970) found it was not possible to show that anything was signalled by interpersonal proximity, while several personal characteristics appear to have been affected in a similar experiment (Patterson and Sechrest, 1970).

These investigations were similar in their format in that the subjects were to interview and rate confederates on a series of traits with only the distance between them being varied. There are, however, three important variations which may account for the differences in results. Firstly, the measurement was of distance *per se* in Porter's experiment, with the confederate placing his chair either two, four or eight feet from the subject. Patterson's confederates were to sit at one of four desks either two, four, six or eight feet away. This suggests that the characteristic of the setting may have played an important part in these findings since in the case of Patterson's studies the situation appears to be one of choice, with the other alternatives being obviously visible. In addition, the evaluation took place immediately after sitting. In the first study it occurred after the interview. The sterility and obviousness of the Patterson setting leads one to question whether such findings would generalize to a normal interactive situation.

Cheyne and Efran (1972) have approached this question from a somewhat different angle. Their interests were in the reluctance of people to invade group shared space. The method consisted of two people standing in a corridor at a distance of 41 inches apart, leaving 33 inches between the back of one person and the wall. In one condition the confederates put their hands to their sides and maintained verbal conversation and eye contact, while in the other they turned 30 degrees so that they faced opposite directions. The difference in the number of people who walked between the confederates in these two conditions was significant at the 0.001 level. It appears, therefore, that proximity alone does not signal the existence of an interactive group.

Eye contact and space use

Research by Argyle (1969) has thrown further light on aspects of interpersonal distancing. They have explored the non-verbal components involved in interactions between people. Their emphasis has not been on behaviour patterns that replace speech (as has often been the case of models derived from animal analogies) but rather on non-verbal activities related to space use which supplement the verbal content and ensure the comfortable flow of conversation. Specifically, they have found mutual eye

149

contact to be particularly important in controlling the mood and tempo of a conversation between two people. It is used as a source of information (people look more when listening than when speaking), for feedback (people look at the end of a statement) and also as a social technique (people look at each other more if they like each other). This suggests that there are many factors which contribute to the effect of distancing on the way a conversation may proceed.

Consideration of orientation of the body is also necessary when exploring the relevance of eye contact. Sommer (1969) established that people prefer a face-to-face orientation during informal conversation to a side-by-side position. This is given further support by Mehrabian and Diamond (1971) who found that 180 degree orientations were clearly detrimental to conversation. This adds to the growing evidence that locational behaviour is one of the mechanisms for controlling social interactions. The use of space is instrumental in optimizing or minimizing eye contact. It can be regarded as an orientating act that leads to, maintains and also terminates both non-verbal communications such as eye contact and verbal communications.

Throughout this chapter we have emphasized the importance of balance in the flow of information. In a situation where positive interaction was required it was found that eye contact increased with distance (Argyle and Dean, 1965). This leads us to argue that space use, especially in the dyadic situation, is interrelated to such other non-verbal aspects of the situation as eye contact. This is because both relate to the use of available information. Hence the linking of spatial behaviour to angle and eye contact to distance.

Activities

Variations in spatial behaviour are not confined to different group compositions but also vary from situation to situation. Clearly defined activities produce the most consistent results and consequently provide the best opportunity for clarifying the nature of interpersonal distances.

Sommer (1969) has explored the spatial limits in which comfortable conversation can take place. Two couches were placed facing each other providing the option for the subject of either face-to-face or side-by-side sitting arrangements. The distance was systematically varied with the results being that up to a distance of three feet six inches the preference was for face-to-face conversation. Beyond this the subjects would sit together on the same couch. This study has subsequently been repeated by Canter (1974) who obtained a face-to-face limit of three feet two inches, thus illustrating considerable consistency in this particular form of spatial behaviour. The early studies by Little (1965), previously discussed, also demonstrate the influence of particular activity on the form which spatial behaviour takes.

Arrangement, in space as well as distance, is determined by activity. Using both field experiments, in which people were observed sitting in different places and questioned on the most suitable arrangements for different activities, Sommer (1969) found both distance and angle to be important. At a rectangular table a corner-to-corner or face-to-face arrangement was preferred for casual conversation. For cooperative work a side-by-side position was most frequently used and a distance face-to-face location was maintained for competitive situations. In clearly defined activities such as these, research (Canter, 1974) has failed to show large cultural differences as suggested by Hall. The only variation that occurred was in the competitive arrangement where Japanese students still maintained a side-by-side orientation. This was possibly due to the fact that they did not really compete in the western sense but rather cooperated in the way that they would produce differing results. These studies emphasized that in order to appreciate the role of spatial behaviour it is necessary to evaluate the content of the information as defined in this situation by the activities in which the people were engaged.

Physical setting

Putting together all the components we have considered in portraying the use of space is best achieved by defining the situation in which it occurs. The concept of a 'behaviour setting' will be used to establish the boundaries of the situation and the appropriateness of the behaviour displayed within it. This is a somewhat richer use of the term than was intended by its creators (Barker and Wright, 1955) in that it includes not only the physical

F

setting but also the roles, relationships and activities of the individual contained within it.

An example of the interactive nature of a behaviour setting is a study by Canter (1969) designed to clarify the relationships between distancing and angles. This study has the additional advantage of a successful application of the principles developed in this chapter to a larger group than the dyadic interactions, with which we have so far been concerned. The format was an observational study of the seating preference of students in a seminar room. As we will see the roles, activities and physical environment all interacted. The earlier studies on location behaviour (Stilitz, 1970; Kamino, 1968) established that the most potent stimuli in the environment were other people; this is also the case in the present study. However, the role of the lecturer led to him being the most significant object of interaction.

The students were asked in groups of eight to go into a seminar room in order to take part in an experiment. They were given a questionnaire and asked to take a seat. The manipulated variables were the distance the lecturer stood from the first row of chairs (three metres and one and a half metres) and the arrangement of the chairs either in straight lines or in a semi-circle. When the lecturer stood three metres away in the rectilinear setting the students tended to use the first three rows of seats; but at one and a half metres from the first row the students used only the last three rows. In the semi-circular formation the position of the lecturer had no effect on the distance between himself and the students. The results are illustrated in Figure 5.2. It appears, therefore, that the physical setting of a semi-circular formation and the increased variation in angle that it provides counteracts the distance preference which occurred in the rectilinear situation.

In the previous experimental examples of angles and distances it was apparent that these reflected the type of behaviour which people expected to be engaged in (for example competitive or cooperative). These expectations are also reflected in a classroom setting where it was found that the amount of participation decreased as the seating positions moved towards the sides and the back of the room (Sommer, 1969). This raises the question of whether or not the physical setting can provide cues that would alter not only the flow of information but the content of the

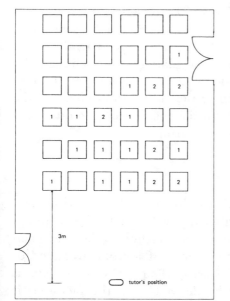

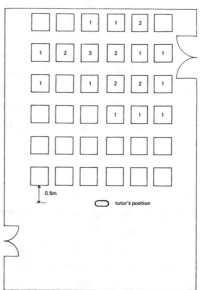

Figure 5.2(a) Frequency of seat selection in rectangular furniture layout in three sessions when tutor was far

Figure 5.2(b) Frequency of seat selection in rectangular furniture layout in three sessions when tutor was near

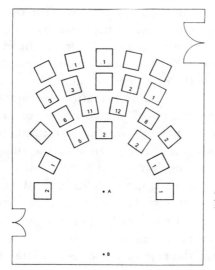

A = 'near' position of lecturer

B = 'far' position of lecturer

Figure 5.2(c) Total frequency of each seat being occupied by a student over four trials with tutor at 'near' position and four trials with tutor at 'far' position

communication. Research by Wools (1970) suggests that this may well be possible in that small changes in the type and arrangement of furniture resulted in large variations in the rated friendliness of a room. From this it is possible to speculate that the semi-circular arrangement, perhaps by providing angles commonly used in informal conversations, may change the entire atmosphere of the classroom necessitating different distancing to accommodate the new balance in the interpersonal relationships.

Leadership and location

Another area in which this relationship of roles, activities and spatial behaviour is quite specific, is the leadership of a group. There appears to be specific significance attached to the head chair of a rectangular table in that the leader of a group will tend to consistently use that position (Hearn, 1957). The higher status associated with that chair may be derived from the fact that it offers the most advantageous position for maximum eye contact with the rest of the group, due to the decrease in angles.

Alliance with a leader is also related to spatial location. In a seminar setting (Delong, 1970a) two sub-groups were naturally formed on the basis of conflicting opinions with the leaders at opposite ends of a rectangular table. The division of the group was along a left/right dimension with the people at the right of the leader siding with him with the commitment decreasing as the positions moved towards the other end of the table.

The importance of access to information is further demonstrated by the classic studies of networks of communication (Leavitt, 1951). Typically, two groups are arranged, one with a circular network of possible interactions and the other like the spokes of a wheel, all having contact with one central individual. While no particular person was appointed leader in the circle, most people could name one although he could occur anywhere within the group. In the wheel formation 92 per cent of the subjects named the person at the hub as leader.

If it is accepted that the role of leader is a desirable position, then it is possible to explain these findings in terms of the model of privacy (a preference to control the intensity of interpersonal relationships). It would appear that the optimum level of

154

interaction for this group was most nearly attained by the person at the centre.

Density and space use

That the most important source of information is other people, provides us with the opportunity of applying many of the principles of location behaviour to diverse situations. For example, the amount of indulgence granted a child is determined not only by cultural variations but also by the density of occupancy of the child's home (Munroe and Munroe, 1971). The larger the household the more frequently the child was held and the more quickly he was responded to when crying, that is, the greater the number of people in the defined space of the home, the greater the stimulation provided for the child. Murray (1974) develops a parallel argument for the influence of crowding on aggression in children.

Increased information flow is not, of course, necessarily the direction desired to guarantee the preferred balance. Therein lies the distinction between the physical entity of density and the psychological concept of crowding. As was established earlier, a discussion of human spatial behaviour in terms of innate needs or desires could not accommodate the complexity of human behaviour. A more fruitful approach is to specify the activities in which people intend to engage. Then crowding, either due to a high density of people or restricted space, is the situation where (as is proposed by Saegert, 1974) "fewer and fewer activities can be successfully and easily carried out".

Returning to the example of child rearing, it is apparent that high density in this situation does not restrict but facilitates the activities of the child. Again, it is necessary to emphasize that it is the quality as well as the amount of information presented to the individual that is crucial in understanding how a person will act in a given situation. Saegert found that high densities necessitated varied and alternative strategies to carry out an activity. They also reduced the amount of information obtained from the physical environment itself. A crowded situation exists when "activities that require the person to assess the environment, plan, test and then reorganize behaviour on the basis of feedback would be difficult".

Temporary crowded conditions are commonplace, as anyone who has travelled on public transport during rush hours can testify. In these situations where space cannot be used as a control in interactions, compensatory actions are taken to reduce intimacy. The most common is leaning or turning away, blocking with the arms or using a barrier between self and others (Patterson and Sechrest, 1970; Russo, 1969). Another behaviour used which is more extreme and probably occurs more frequently is what Goffman (1963) calls dehumanization. By averting their eyes, pulling themselves in and reducing contact to a minimum, people virtually turn others into non-persons. If they are merely objects there is no necessity to relate. Some researchers, notably Milgram (1970), have suggested that this is part of a general syndrome for coping with cities. We shall therefore return to this topic when dealing with the urban environment in Chapter Eight.

One of man's essential features is his proactive nature; he anticipates events and acts accordingly. This dynamic nature provides him with an enormous repertoire of behaviour to cope with situations such as overcrowding. The concern is not that man cannot adapt but rather that adaptation may be at too high a price. If activities are continually frustrated by the presence of others, what does it do to the interpersonal relationship that develops? When spatial distancing is allowed to fluctuate, it becomes a useful resource in preventing disruption of activities.

The library

A behaviour setting designed to avoid over-stimulation from other people is the library. Sommer (1966) found stable patterns in how people spaced themselves. As the library filled, people sat one to a table. When this was no longer possible the next chair occupied was the one furthest from the original occupant. There were also two different tactics used to ensure privacy. One was retreat when the student located himself at an end chair, preferably near a wall and at the back of the room. The other was offensive behaviour characterized by occupation of the middle-most chair and spreading out his belongings thus trying to preserve the entire table.

The physical environment does not determine the structure of the social interactions but rather it sets the limits to the possible variations that may occur. In the case of the traditional library setting, Sommer is of the opinion that these boundaries are too narrow to adequately accommodate the diversity of activities in which the users, given the opportunity, would be involved. These limits are set by the physical restraints of the environment but also by the concept of the particular setting and the norms of the group. Within these limits there are still considerable variations in the techniques used to actively regulate interpersonal relationships with spatial behaviour being an integral part in facilitating this balance.

Groups and buildings

The principles developed in the previous sections provide the basis for at least a partial understanding of social behaviour on a much larger scale. There is, however, one important distinction to be made. In face-to-face interactions, space was actively *manipulated* to ensure appropriate levels of communication. When the behaviour setting is expanded to include entire buildings, space use becomes more static. At this level the importance lies in the range and types of behaviour either facilitated or inhibited by the spatial arrangements incorporated into the design.

The success of a behaviour setting in optimizing the appropriate level of privacy is of course dependent upon the definition of appropriateness. Studies in institutional settings have been particularly successful because the participants are continually placed in reactive positions, with the objectives of the setting determined at a higher level of the organization. An example is provided by one of Sommer's (1969) field experiments. Sommer's setting was a wing, for elderly women, of a state mental institution which had recently undergone renovation in an attempt to improve the general satisfaction of the ward. The results were not successful according to the criteria of greater communication between the patients and a generally higher activity level. This failure was contributed to by the furniture arrangement and the type of people involved. Sommer described the setting as sociofugal in that the chairs were placed side-by-side around the periphery of the room thus inhibiting communication.

157

The predominant behaviour of the women was just sitting and watching people walk by. This was encouraged by the wide corridors providing for the easy movement of staff and equipment through the ward. The setting also contained the basic requirements for waiting behaviour, as presented by Stilitz (1970), of a place with structural support (the wall) which is just outside the flow of traffic. This limited range of activities also reflected the lack of attempts on the part of the patients to modify their environment. This was emphasized by the visitors who more readily repositioned the chairs, presumably to improve the general flow of conversation. Behaviour modification in the form of greater communication was achieved by regrouping the chairs around small tables. This was to be expected in the light of the extremity of the prevailing situation and the previous discussion on spatial behaviour, eye contact and communication. If the increased communication was within each group as is implied, then individual isolation was replaced by small group interaction.

Location of rooms in buildings

Moving from furniture arrangements to the location of rooms within a building, similar tendencies are apparent. The initial friendship patterns in student housing are highly dependent upon proximity. However, this is gradually replaced by similarities in attitudes (Newcomb, 1956) or personality (Duck, 1973) as the most important determinants of lasting relationships. There are, however, situations where proximity continues to play an important part in communication within a building. For example, the Building Performance Research Unit (1972) found six rooms within one school were habitually used for coffee breaks by specific teachers. One of the most important factors appears to have been the actual distance between the coffee room and the teachers' own classrooms.

Within the context of a particular setting, it is necessary to assess the merit of both behaviour that is encouraged by space location and also that which is restrained. In the instance of the school, the arrangement may have encouraged small group interaction; however, the isolation of the group may have had deleterious effects on the teaching staff as a complete unit. If, as was suggested, the more sensitive issues that arise in the teaching situation are best discussed in informal conversations, this fragmentation by spatial division may result in reduced exposure of ideas and fewer opportunities for ironing out grievances.

Location of buildings

The preceeding examples illustrate that the privacy model's applicability extends beyond the small group, direct contact, situation. Risking the claim of excessive repetition, its basic principles are the control of interpersonal relationships through the optimum balance between the flow of information from an individual and that received. The integral role of spatial location within this model may also be demonstrated at the level of interaction between activities and building layout.

The classic study which illustrates our viewpoint is that of Festinger, Schacter and Back (1950), in their sociometric analysis of the relationship between friendship formation and the location of homes. The setting was student housing on the MIT campus occupied by returning veterans and their families. The establishment of intense relationships between families developed through a process of casual, accidental contact. The more frequently these occurred, the greater the possibility of forming deeper friendships.

As previously emphasized, information is not evenly distributed throughout a setting thus necessitating the use of space to achieve the balance in the flow which satisfies the preferences of the individual. In this case the spatial location was held constant, that is, the location of the houses. The two most important factors in friendship formation proved to be firstly, the actual distance between front doors. The second was the functional distance, such as whether the front door faced towards the centre of the estate or outward to the street. Greatest contact occurred within each individual court of the estates, this was not only a good indicator of who would be friends with whom but also what would be the opinions of the residents on certain communal issues. These small isolated pockets of interactive groups displayed considerable internal consistency in attitudes yet were quite different to the attitudes of other groups.

As the housing was assigned by chance alone, this determined who would have the optimum balance in the flow of information. In this situation it was most closely attained by the people who had the greatest contact with others, that is the people most centrally located had the highest number of friends within the estate. Those most peripheral were not only physically separated but also socially isolated from the rest of the community either by sheer distance from others or by the direction the house was facing.

Greatest access to information is, of course, not necessarily the most appropriate level of stimulation to be consistent with individual preferences. For example, Kuper (1953) found that people often expressed dissatisfaction with living in cul-de-sacs because of the lack of privacy. More exposure to information also meant more information from the individual was available to others. On certain occasions this appeared to produce the psychological state of crowding. People felt uncomfortable about carrying out certain activities, although similar sentiments were not found in people living in rows of terraced houses.

One would expect of course that balance at this level would be related to the individual characteristics of the residents. Herein lies one of the greatest difficulties in the Festinger *et al* study. They themselves readily recognize the problem in their description of the population. "The people living in these projects are highly homogeneous along the dimensions of occupations, age, class and family background, education, interests, aspirations and attitudes towards the community in which they lived." One may question whether propinquity would have such a strange effect if the whole population had been less similar.

Estates as institutions

Another problem with the setting was that it was relatively isolated from the rest of the community with all the residents having recently arrived and knowing few people in the town. Thus, most sources of information were contained within this project. In other words this novel group of people lack many of the dynamic characteristics of human groups such as multiple group membership and variation within groups.

The somewhat static situation of Festinger *et al* is reminiscent of the studies on institutionalized people, all of whose needs are provided for by resources contained within that setting. Here spatial behaviour assumes a disproportionate degree of importance to that of more normal settings.

A more complete understanding of the relationship between location and individual characteristics is provided by a recent study based on the principles developed by Festinger and his colleagues. Carey and Mapes (1971) studied more heterogeneous groups in the form of six private housing estates in Britain. The results suggest that, while spatial location in and of itself is sufficient for forming acquaintanceships, it must be considered in conjunction with more positive features in friendships.

Carey and Mapes found that if a woman was to achieve a reasonable level of reciprocal visiting within these new estates two conditions must be satisfied. They are that she finds people who are similar to herself, especially in respect to age and the age of their children, and who are also within reasonably close proximity to her. Without both factors the woman simply did not develop many friendships within the estate.

The problems of high rise

Returning to Newman's discussion of public housing in America, it is informative to contrast the two types of housing with which he was concerned. The first was a high rise block characterized by one main foyer with the area between the entrance to the block and the flat door used only as a pathway. The other was a set of low rise walk-ups with a common lobby for only a small number of families. This style not only fits more readily into the texture of the existing community but also appears to facilitate interaction between the inhabitants and greater use of the space available.

If it is accepted that the psychological state of crowding is the frustration of activities by information from others, either by increasing the complexity of the situation making strategy formation more difficult, or by inhibiting the variation of activities possible, then it may be suggested that the high rise blocks help to maintain a continual state of crowding. The quantity of information from the amorphous mass of neighbours reduces the quality of interaction necessary to form workable

161

friendships. The physical form does not, of course, negate the possibility of positive interaction occurring but limits the opportunities for this to happen. For example, the use of the foyer by 130 families, the journey to the flats in slow moving elevators (a naturally occurring dehumanizing behaviour setting) and the safety risk of extensive use of the corridors all contribute to a preference for a greater degree of privacy than would other settings.

These effects of high rise are not exclusively the problems of the lower class. However, this isolation is probably less detrimental to the middle classes because of their greater access to resources and most probably their stronger affiliation with the larger community. This ensures them a greater degree of control over their environment.

While much of what Newman presents is speculation and requires empirical verification; it does illustrate the necessity for a thorough investigation of the spatial aspects of life in these 'up-ended cul-de-sacs'. Throughout this chapter we have emphasized the importance of the content of the information available. The differences between occupants of public housing and other groups on this aspect is obvious. It is ludicrous to assume that all the communication problems between these people can be attributed to the physical form. While it may aggravate the difficulties, it is neither the cause nor the cure of the plight of the under-privileged who occupy this housing. It is also certain that the use of animal analogies can only serve to reduce our comprehension of these matters.

Space use and the self

In a discussion of the role of spatial location at the scale of building layouts, it is apparent that all environments restrict activities or, at least on occasions, require alternative modes of behaviour in order to achieve a satisfactory balance in information. The types of activities thwarted and the extent and frequency with which this occurs becomes the criteria for the success or failure of that environment. Cast in this light, descriptive concepts such as crowding, isolation and even urban stress can be represented as a restriction of activities due to an imbalance in, or loss of control over, the sources of stimulation presented to the individual. This is, of course, a much broader use of the concept of 'privacy' than can be accommodated by a purely spatial model. It does illustrate, however, even with these more global issues, that the analysis must be at the level of the individual person.

Privacy is a personal matter. It encompasses all behaviour that sets the individual apart. Only through examining the preferences and expectations of the individual can a meaningful understanding of the dynamic interactive role of space usage be achieved. For example, given free choice one person may choose a site for their home which would encourage a high level of social interactions, while others may regard such an environment as intrusive. Such differences in behaviour cannot be accommodated by the simple functional requirements of the ergonomists.

The mechanical relationship between man and his environment assumes that man is a passive organism, responding to his environment in a simple and direct way. A more appropriate picture is that of man as an adaptive, goal orientated being. For our purpose the goal has been defined as 'privacy' — the preferred level of interaction with other people. The ultimate function of this goal lies in controlling the relationship between the 'self' and the environment (Stratton *et al*, 1973). This experience of identity, while being an elusive concept, is essential to our sane existence. All interactions between people involve at least a partial exposure of the qualities of the self. The use of space, as an integral part of the control of both verbal and non-verbal communications, facilitates the successful presentation of the self to the people who make up an individual's world.

Chapter Six

Buildings in Use

David Canter

The total environment

The emphasis in previous chapters has been on the relationship of one set of physical variables to a few, readily defined psychological variables. Temperature has been related to comfort, light intensity to visual acuity and so on. The value of this work is clearly apparent. Guidelines and principles regarding the most satisfactory levels of any given aspects of the environment can be drawn up to assist the decision maker. For the psychologist relationships, of a form direct enough to test the hypotheses generated from his theories, can be established.

However, there is one major problem which reduces the utility of these studies. It is that in the world outside the laboratory, the environment with which most decision makers must grapple, heat, light, sound and space do not exist independently of one another. One very simple example will illustrate this. Buildings are sometimes too *hot* because of their proximity to *noisy* roads, the reason being that people will not open their windows and ventilate their rooms, because the traffic noise will disturb them. It would thus only be possible to explain the heat problems by looking at the *total environment* in the actual situation.

Although of course knowledge of reactions to, say, noise and heat on their own would help to unravel the field problem.

This is not simply an aspect of applying fundamental research. A number of fresh, but nonetheless basic, psychological issues are raised by our example. These are questions such as: what do people notice? This question also raises the query: along what dimensions do people think of (or describe) the things they notice? A third question is the relationship between the different dimensions, particularly in terms of their relative importance or salience. For instance, people may not notice heat but feel that lack of distraction is the most important thing to have in their environment.

There are two further reasons for going beyond the research of the previous four chapters. First, many problems concerning people's interactions with their physical environment cannot be put under one of the four main environmental aspects or studies in the laboratory; the best size for an office or the most satisfactory layout for a hospital ward are two examples. However, many fundamental questions associated with these practical problems have, as we shall see, been investigated in controlled, sometimes experimental, psychological studies.

The second reason has much more in the way of political roots. There is a need to know what people want, or at least how happy they are with what they have got. This in its turn raises some intriguing psychological questions such as how groups differ and how such factors as familiarity or amount of personal control influence people's satisfaction.

All the above reasons have spawned a mass of studies; user surveys, user requirement studies, building appraisals, building evaluations and even a 'psychological analysis' of buildings. It would be impossible to review them all in the present volume. Many of them are private studies or have been published in obscure journals. They certainly exist in the French, German, Dutch, Swedish, Japanese, Hebrew, English and North American literature and probably in most other major languages. All that may be done therefore, in the present chapter, is to look at some of the most prominent examples of this research and thus give the flavour of the possibilities it raises and its deficiencies. With such a variety of work available some bias in its selection is inevitable.

166

The author makes no apologies for this but hopes the reader will accept the warning!

Difficulties and approaches

Before examining the actual research it is well to pause and consider the problems facing the researcher and the procedures which have been developed for overcoming them (or at least circumscribing them).

The first and most obvious difficulty is the one of scale. Real world environments are, because of their very size, difficult and expensive to measure or control for experimental purposes. As we have seen in earlier chapters, even when examining the relatively simple dimensions of environmental variations such as heat, sound or light, the creation of an experimental situation which approximates reasonably to an actual room or building requires a surprisingly large amount of complex equipment. The thermally controlled chambers, referred to in Chapter Two, for instance, need to be remarkably sophisticated to control just radiant temperature and air temperature. Thus, the traditional experimental psychology approach of taking stimuli into a labroatory and measuring subtle responses to minute modifications of them is often impossible if we are to deal with the built environment and still maintain some of its most significant aspects.

Besides the spatial scale of the built environment there are difficulties introduced by the temporal scale over which people interact with it. This time scale also requires approaches different from those frequently used in psychology, in which, typically, immediate responses to existing stimuli are recorded. Thus, there is the apparent paradox that many of the studies of the real world environment draw more heavily upon social psychological techniques than upon techniques from perceptual psychology. The reason is, however, that in the realm of social psychology the central concern is usually with attitudes and behaviour which have developed over time in response to complex stimuli. Thus, our interactions with buildings may have much more in common with our interactions with other people than they ever do to our responses to perceptual stimuli of the form explored in the laboratory. Another, and possibly more profound difficulty which emerges in environmental psychology is that the major applications are sought for in relation to the future. Architects want to know how people *will* react to their buildings. Building administrators want to know how patterns of behaviour will be changed by *future* designs. These questions of prediction must be set against the problems of scale and complexity, yet psychology is essentially historical in its approach! The major methods examine the background, origins or precursors of existing behaviour, with some attention to its present context. Relatively few studies are concerned with providing accounts of the processes of change underlying behaviour, and as a consequence, have difficulty in contributing to environmental issues.

User surveys

User surveys are one aspect of the most popular approach to the problems and difficulties we have mentioned. The survey in its many forms has been used for a wide variety of buildings and aspects of buildings. Indeed, some of the earliest social research directly oriented to environmental decision making consisted of a survey of the reactions of housewives to the daylight and sunlight in their homes (Chapman and Thomas, 1944). On the basis of this, standards in many countries have been determined. The apparent value of the survey is that it provides information about people's reactions, presumably built up over time, to many aspects of their environment. In a country with a firm commitment to democracy such reactions are seen as a necessary base for decision making. However, they contribute more to, and derive their value more from, the existing processes of democratic decision making, than from scientific psychology. In this regard, they are slowly being replaced by the studies of participation discussed in Chapter Eight.

One methodological weakness of most user surveys arises from the fact that to be meaningful many respondents must be approached. Because of limited resources this leads to a relatively limited area of study. Thus, the relationships between the various responses and their links to a variety of aspects of design may not be explored. Furthermore, the pattern of relationships to the original design concepts cannot be readily traced. To deal with these weaknesses, the 'Building Appraisal' approach has been developed.

Appraisals have much in common with the case studies of clinical and organizational psychology. The distinction between the nomothetic and ideographic approach revealed in other case studies is present here. Some deal with each building against a normative background, putting it on to dimensions common to many buildings. Others approach it in a more ideographic way by examining a building's unique characteristics. As we shall see, a combination of these approaches, which have much in common with approaches found in personality research, have emerged in 'psychological appraisals' of buildings.

However, one complication which does not exist in personality research, but which does exist when we try to think of buildings by analogy with people, derives from the fact that we are dealing with *human responses* to buildings. Thus, we have the question of whether it is most meaningful to deal with aggregates of responses from all the people who use any given building, or whether we should be taking into account the details of individual differences existing within a building. As we shall see later, these different approaches will not necessarily give the same results and are, as a consequence, likely to have differing implications for both psychology and design.

Studies of housing behaviour

The review of user studies carried out at the Building Research Station, produced by Hole and Attenburrow (1966) exemplifies research into 'people's need and desires' in housing. (Interestingly, the majority of research into user requirements has been carried out in relation to domestic buildings).

The main concern of the studies discussed by Hole and Attenburrow is with describing how people use their houses. From the psychological viewpoint this provides intriguing information, unrelated to any existing theoretical formulations (with the notable exception of Barker's, 1968), yet is directly concerned with the supposed special concern of psychology, human behav-

169

iour! The main difficulty in finding the contribution of this work to psychology lies in the fact that Hole and Attenburrow take the findings as of direct interest and value in their own right. Thus the furniture found in rooms is recorded to provide an important indication to designers of likely space requirements, but is not examined to show how its layout relates to designers' expectations, as Edwards (1974) has done, or to show the ways in which different types of house layout facilitate a different pattern of activities as did Canter and Lee (1974).

In many cases, of course, these records of building use do reveal patterns not totally in accord with expectations. For example, Hole and Attenburrow (1966) refer to the suggestion that the bedroom was a "suitable place for activities which are thought to require the segregation of some members, particularly children, from the total family group". However, "the way in which furniture was arranged in the bedrooms seen in the surveys gave no indication that bedrooms were used as bed-sitting rooms". From comments expressed by respondents such as "it is better to keep bedrooms as bedrooms" the investigators suggested that most people had a clear concept of the 'proper' use of bedrooms and wished to use them in accordance with it.

The possibility of clear concepts of room usage raises a number of interesting psychological questions about their origin and inter-relationships, especially as they seem to conflict with the views of professional designers. The likely subtlety and variety of these concepts and the behaviour related to them is shown by the observations of Sommer and Gifford (1968) in study bedrooms. Only a small amount of studying took place at the student's desk. Indeed, the impression is formed that, for American students at least, they study on their beds and probably sleep at their desks! Whether studies aimed directly at people's concepts of room usage will facilitate an understanding of the existing patterns and variations remains to be seen, but at least a start at this crucial psychological question has been made (Tagg, 1974).

One recurrent theme of surveys of use which contrasts markedly with most other approaches to man/environment interaction is the large consistencies and the relatively small individual differences. Within any group of families, for instance, at the same stage in the family cycle, there are very similar patterns of usage. For example, "it would seem that the process of serving and eating meals has common design requirements which override cultural and other variations" (Hole and Attenburrow, 1966). Thus the colossal inter- and intra-subject variations typical of psychological studies of perception, learning and the like may well be exploring human behaviour at a level at which differences between people are most exaggerated. If we follow an ecological approach such as Barker's (1968), in which behaviour settings are seen as the best predictors of behaviour, then we may well develop some relatively simple accounts of the effects of the built environment.

One other notable line of research, which historically, if not intellectually, may be seen as a development of the user surveys is the behavioural mapping studies of Ittelson et al (1970). The value of this method has been shown most directly in field experiments so it will be discussed later in that context.

Weaknesses of user surveys

It is interesting to observe that, despite the potential fruitfulness of surveying building use and its early emergence in environmental studies, recent work of the user survey type is rare.

Although there have been a number of recent studies in which space use is a central concern (for example, Canter and Lee, 1974; Akin, 1973; Tagg, 1974; Edwards, 1974; Lawton, 1972; Coates and Sanoff, 1972; Preiser, 1972) none of them is concerned with building up a composite descriptive picture that would give rise to recommendations of the specific design levels to be achieved. Instead, research has turned in the direction of relating uses to preferences and loose theoretical formulations of the effects of the physical environments on the actual uses.

These two developments arose out of weaknesses revealed in user surveys. We have already touched on a number of these but we summarize them here because they may be regarded as hypotheses for future studies.

What people possess or do is determined to a marked degree by their existing environment

Few people would buy a grand piano (or play one in their house) if the largest room was not big enough for it. Thus simply

171

to observe existing patterns is to ignore the possibility of crucial environmental influences on behaviour. Therefore, attempts have been made to uncover the links between environment and standing behaviour patterns (see, for instance, Wicker, 1972; Canter and Lee, 1974).

There is little value in knowing what people have or do unless you know how they feel about their possessions and activities

This viewpoint can be discerned in most comparisons of observations with interview procedures. The fact that students study on their beds may be more an indication of the inadequacy of their desks than the particular suitability of their beds. Only the recorded opinions of the students will help to clarify this. Thus from the earliest studies preferences, stated requirements and evaluations of existing environmental facilities were elicited. These verbal responses gave rise to a further criticism of survey results.

People are unable to give meaningful or accurate answers to questions about environments they have not experienced, especially 'ideal' ones

This weakness (or hypothesis) may be regarded as the verbal corollary of the first point above. In other words, people are only able to make judgements on the basis of their existing experience. Thus the answers to any questions as to preference or ideal are inevitably tied to existing physical environments. Hole and Attenburrow (1966) found for instance, that if local authority tenants aspired to an 'ideal' house "it was usually one occupied by a friend or a relative and, if not another local authority house, was one not very much larger". Again this is a fascinating area for future exploration but has been dealt with, in the main, by asking people to evaluate the spaces they use at the *present* time and where preferences have been examined this has been as a ranking of experienced environments or their attributes.

Building appraisals

As we have seen, even in quite early studies of building use it was found necessary to take into consideration people's preferences.

Thus it is not surprising in the light of the above weaknesses alone that a number of studies have emerged directly concerned with people's evaluations of their existing environments and general preferences.

A particular impetus has been given to the studies from the idea of introducing 'feedback' into design process (Manning, 1965). It is thus important to distinguish feedback oriented studies or 'building appraisals', from preference surveys, which are much more conventionally psychological. In the former the key aim is to evaluate an existing building or aspects of it so as to provide information upon the effectiveness of the principles upon which it was based. The idea of a 'feedback' loop of the cybernetic kind which would modify the original concepts is rather an abstract metaphor for design. As Markus (1969) has suggested, building evaluations may more readily be considered as 'feedforward' to the next building. Thus, their major value is in providing basic psychological data for use in other situations. The form in which the data are collected, the degree to which they can be generalized, that is, questions concerning the methods of psychological measurement, have been a central concern of those engaged in building appraisals. They may be considered 'case studies'. Their contribution is derived from their being able to examine the complexity of *in situ* relationships.

Where appraisals are concerned with establishing *levels,* especially of user satisfaction for existing buildings, preference studies are concerned with revealing the relationships which exist between: (a) environmental variables and psychological responses; (b) preferences for different aspects of the environment; and (c) social and psychological determinants of the results found in (a) and (b). The search in these studies is, as a consequence, for relationships capable of generalization.

Preference for office size

The simplest example of the study of the relationships between preference and some aspect of the physical environment may be drawn from Canter's (1968) study of offices. He asked 1100 office workers the question "Other things being equal, in which size office would you prefer to work?" He then plotted the frequency of

173

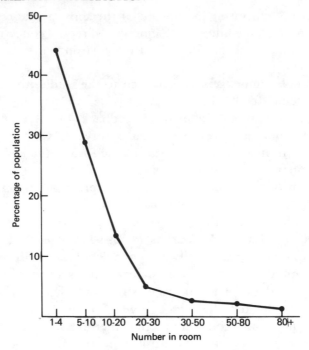

Figure 6.1 Percentage preferring each room size, shown by answers to the question "other things being equal, in which size of office/room would you be happiest working?" Total Sample 1180

each room size being chosen, to produce the graph shown in Figure 6.1. The interesting thing about this relationship is that if the frequencies are adjusted to the normal distribution, as most psychological judgements may be expected to fall on such a distribution (*cf.* Fouilhé, 1960), and the room size adjusted to the logarithmic distribution commonly found as meaningful for physical variables (*cf.* Stevens, 1961) then you obtain the very neat relationship illustrated in Figure 6.2. Such straight line relationships are relatively rare in psychology and thus the demonstration of its existence may be taken to indicate the presence of a distinct attitude towards office size. The larger the office the more likely are people, in principle, to be antagonistic to it.

Because the size of the existing rooms in which the respondents worked was known it was possible to relate preferences to existing

174

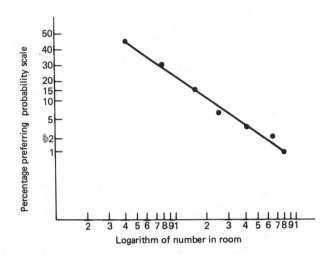

Figure 6.2 As Figure 6.1 but percentage preference is drawn on a probability scale and room size is drawn on a logarithmic scale

room size. Table 6.1 shows this relationship. From that table it is clear that the dislike of larger rooms is common to all workers but that this is tempered by the existing room, workers in larger rooms being more likely to prefer the middle size rooms than those in smaller rooms. This finding would appear to relate to the adaptation levels found in many areas of psychology (*cf.* Helson, 1964). In the office situation these levels are explained in terms of 'status' given by a single room or what is 'expected', but nonetheless the basic relationship is still the one of existing experience acting as an anchor or modifier for preference patterns.

We may continue with the office size example to illustrate further attempts to relate preferences to group differences. Wells (in Manning, 1965) developed a Thurstone scale measuring attitudes towards open offices. Using it he showed that supervisors and workers both had quite different reactions to open offices, the former more in favour than the latter, and that management fell somewhere between the two. Wells thus demonstrated the ways in which role within the organization influences preferences for particular environmental levels. This is a theme to which we shall return.

175

Table 6.1 Frequency of rooms of each size category preferred by respondents, cross-tabulated with frequency with which respondents worked in each room size category

	ROOM SIZE IN WHICH RESPONDENT WORKED							
	4 or less	5 to 10	10 to 20	20 to 30	30 to 50	50 to 80	80 or more	Total
ROOM SIZE PREFERRED								
4 or Less	*302*	70	45	10	11	10	14	462
5 to 10	50	*112*	71	13	28	27	31	332
10 to 20	9	21	*68*	2	14	17	18	149
20 to 30	1	5	21	*4*	13	3	8	55
30 to 50	0	2	0	0	*18*	3	4	27
50 to 80	0	1	1	0	6	*5*	5	18
80 or more	0	1	1	0	3	9	*2*	15
Total	362	212	206	29	93	74	82	1058

Note: Frequencies in italics are those for which the room size in which the respondent worked and the room size preferred are identical.

Satisfaction with school buildings

Another determinant of the relationship between preferences and physical variables may be taken from the study of comprehensive schools in Scotland carried out by the Building Performance Research Unit (BPRU, 1972). They measured teachers' overall satisfaction with their school buildings, obtaining averages for 20 teachers from each of 30 schools. They correlated these average values with a number of variables, but of particular interest was their correlation with 'age'. This was defined as the number of years the school building had been in use. As such it may be thought of as the conceptual age of the school; the time elapsed since its built form was finalized.

The relationship with age is given in Figure 6.3. There is a steep fall in satisfaction in the first three or four years but this levels out after eight or nine years. The BPRU presented evidence to indicate that such factors as the average age of the teachers or how crowded the school was did not account for this relationship.

It would thus seem that some process is taking place which may

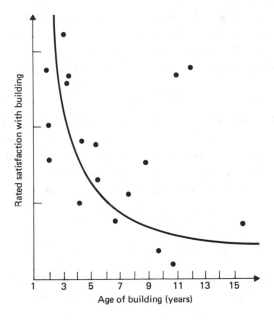

Figure 6.3 Relationship between satisfaction and age of school building (BPRU, 1972)

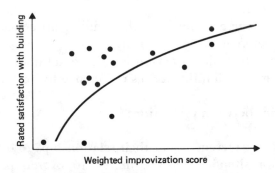

Figure 6.4 Relationship between amount of improvization to and satisfaction with school buildings (BPRU, 1972)

best be thought of as 'obsolescence'. The changes over time in the use of the buildings or in teachers expectations of them are leading to reduction in satisfaction.

Some more light may be thrown on this process by examination of the other key variable to correlate with the teachers' evaluations of their buildings, 'improvization'. This was an intriguing measure

177

made up of a weighted combination of the number of changes in use of spaces and the number of spaces which had multiple usage. The frequency of these changes being derived from a comparison of the architect's plan of a school with observations made in the actual building. The significant relationship found is shown in Figure 6.4.

Although the number of data points is very small the implications of this figure are considerable. The increase in satisfaction with the *increase* in changes to the building suggests that these had some positive quality. They were not simply stop-gaps or coping activities. In that case, at best, a horizontal relationship would have been expected.

Preferences for buildings

We may, tentatively, summarize some of the key processes underlying preferences for aspects of buildings as follows:

1 The existing environmental context has a marked influence upon preferences in the direction of preference for the existing environment.
2 The role of the person within the building influences his environmental preferences.
3 The degree to which a person is able to act upon and modify a building may well influence his preference for it.

Relationships between evaluations

In looking at preferences and their relationships to other variables we have, for simplicity, been limited to overall preference, or evaluation. It is nonetheless, clearly the case that evaluations of the environment do not relate to one single dimension. As discussed earlier, evaluation of the acoustic environment may be high at the expense of a poor thermal environment. As a consequence, a central concern must be to examine the relationships between various environmental evaluations. This examination contains three quite distinct sets of problems, each of which has wide ranging implications for building both theories and environments.

178

Identifying dimensions

The problem here is to uncover the aspects of the environment which are open to independent evaluation. Designers do already have some idea of the dimensions along which to consider buildings, such as cost, amount of heat lost or intricacy of design; but it is quite conceivable that these dimensions are neither independent of one another nor do they bear much relationship to the dimensions underlying the *user's* evaluations of the building. The former deficiency leads to a lack of parsimony in any discussions about the building or attempts to develop an understanding of people's responses to it. The latter serves to aggravate the former deficiency and lead to great difficulty in determining with which user responses to be concerned.

Identifying the underlying dimensions of evaluations of buildings, then, is an important first step to resolving how they are structured. The technology for identification is discussed elsewhere (for instance, Canter, 1974). For our purposes, however, it is necessary to emphasize one point. The words upon which the analysis is based are most appropriately derived from those readily used by the actual building users. Their evaluations in all their richness are collected and collated. In essence, a lengthy questionnaire is produced which asks the users to evaluate many aspects of a building with which they are familiar. This questionnaire is then subjected to dimensional analysis, usually principal component analysis.

The dimensions of building satisfaction

The most detailed example of a study of the dimensions of building satisfaction may be given by referring again to the study by the Building Performance Research Unit (1972). They gave 500 teachers sets of questionnaires dealing with each of the aspects presented in Table 6.2. The aspect groupings had been derived from separate analyses of sections of the questionnaire. Scores were derived from each of these aspects so that there were eighteen scores for each teacher. The 100 or so questions on the original questionnaire had, by this process, been reduced to a more meaningful and manageable set of 18 aspects of the teachers'

179

Table 6.2 Dimensions and rotated factor loadings for teachers' reactions to their school buildings (N=500)

Building Aspect Title	Rotated Factor Loadings (variance)		
	1	2	3
Satisfaction with heating and ventilation	0.92	0.03	0.05
Satisfaction with daylighting and view	0.74	0.02	0.08
Satisfaction with classroom lighting	0.62	0.14	0.09
Satisfaction with classroom overall	0.57	−0.01	0.45
Satisfaction with space in classroom	0.49	0.11	−0.50
Centrality of classroom	0.23	0.97	0.13
Convenience of classroom position	0.25	0.79	0.13
Degree of isolation of classroom	−0.09	0.42	0.06
Distractions from the corridor	−0.03	−0.02	−0.56
Noise from outside the building	−0.06	−0.11	−0.53
Distractions from other classrooms	−0.05	−0.01	−0.44
General satisfaction with school building	0.39	0.16	0.42
Percentage of Common Variance	*56.00*	*25.00*	*19.00*

environment. The question which followed was to find the dimensions underlying these 18 aspects.

Before discussing their results it is necessary to raise an important methodological issue. The teachers came from 33 different schools. It would thus be possible to calculate means for each *school* and to carry out the analysis of those figures. Such an analysis would emphasize the dimensions, influenced by *building* differences. It would thus have some validity for broad architectural considerations. The results of such an analysis are presented in BPRU (1972). The analysis based on scores for *individuals* derived from Canter (1971) will be presented here.

Examination of the factors suggested that three dimensions best explained the structure underlying the 18 aspects. The loadings for these three dimensions, after rotation, are given in Table 6.2.

The first dimension, which accounts for 56 per cent of the common variance, is of a surprizingly general nature. For although is has the overall measure of classroom satisfaction highly loaded on it, it also has questions dealing with heating, view, lighting and classroom size, with noticeable loadings on it. Thus, although the heating and ventilating questions have the highest loadings it is nonetheless, best described as a dimension dealing with overall 'atmospheric' quality. The fact that a general dimension of evaluation consistently emerges in studies of people's reactions is a theme to which we will return. For the present, two points may be noted: the very high loading of the thermal aspects on this dimension and the central role of satisfaction with the classroom itself.

The second dimension (accounting for 25 per cent of the common variance) deals with the position of the classroom: how convenient or central it is. The establishment of a dimension like this raises a number of interesting points. Note that the dimension is derived from questions dealing with how teachers felt about various aspects of the position of their classrooms. Thus, if school plans had been greatly different from one another, correlations between items across teachers would not have been anticipated. Yet the factor demonstrates that even if the configurations of the school buildings were very different, the psychological experience of them was very similar. The potential of using experience as a way of measuring aspects of buildings difficult to assign numbers to, such as their configurations, would as a consequence seem very great.

The third factor accounts for 19 per cent of the common variance and correlates with satisfaction with the building as a whole. That distractions should produce such a distinct factor demonstrates their clear separation from the considerations of overall evaluation. Further, that distractions are related most closely to satisfaction with the building helps to identify the modes teachers use for discriminating between the advantages of buildings as opposed to classrooms.

It is of value to compare this analysis with the analysis published by the BPRU (1972) of the same data. As mentioned, in their analysis the means for *buildings* were employed. The key difference between the two analyses is in the role of the spatial and thermal variables. For whilst the distractions dimension is similar in both analyses, the first dimension in the BPRU analysis lays much more emphasis on spatial aspects. Their second dimension is a combination of the thermal, lighting and convenience aspects.

This makes some sense. What distinguishes *schools* from one another, in terms of how satisfied on average their staff are, would appear to be the spatial qualities of their classrooms. Furthermore, the position of classrooms is confounded with the relative positions of windows (and hence lighting, heating and ventilation), when schools are compared with one another. On the other hand, *teachers* differ from one another in terms of their overall satisfaction with their classrooms which would appear to be especially related to the heating and ventilating properties of those rooms.

This study has been given in some detail to illustrate the possibilities and problems associated with identifying dimensions of building appraisal. Let us move on to even thornier problems.

Relative weightings

Once the dimensions of evaluation which exist independently of one another have been identified, the question which follows is their relative weightings in relation to one another.

The applied relevance of this relates to the fact that, for financial or other reasons, a designer cannot produce an optimum level for all aspects of a building. He may increase acoustic separation, for instance, at the cost of reducing space. As a consequence, knowledge of those aspects of the environment most sensitive to overall satisfaction would enable the designer to determine which aspects should be brought as close to the optimum as possible.

From a more theoretical viewpoint, the relative weightings may be considered as indications of the structure of satisfaction. By uncovering the inter-relationships between different aspects of satisfaction it should be possible to build up a more appropriate model of satisfaction, how it operates and develops.

There are a number of ways of providing weightings for aspects of satisfaction, each of which has different theoretical implications.

The most obvious way of assigning weightings to aspects of the environment is to elicit ratings of their relative importance.

A typical example of this approach is the work of SEF (1972). 363 teachers were presented with a set of ten aspects of the environment and asked to indicate their relative importance in an 'ideal' school. They report that there was considerable agreement amongst the teachers and that of most importance was floor area, layout, noise control and the heating and ventilation. The aspects of least importance were appearance, electrical outlets and visual privacy.

The problem of this information is to know what it means. In one study Canter (1970) correlated satisfaction of various aspects of the environment with how important they were considered to be and found no significant correlations at all. Furthermore, the general feelings on the part of subjects with the degree of importance of the physical environment in general, was not found to relate to their satisfaction with their existing environment, except for a plausible but rather complex pattern which defied statistical description! Further, the SEF study found that the greatest problems with existing buildings were heating and noise control, and that "by comparison the problems in outdoor area, appearance, visual privacy, electrical outlets and furniture affected relatively few people".

Wheeler (1967) took ranks of importance as his central concern in a survey of 1461 students' reactions to their halls of residence. His respondents were required to indicate the relative importance of items in sets dealing with such things as indoor recreation facilities, traffic systems and communication systems. Of particular interest is the ranking derived from importance ratings on "general consideration". At the top of this list are such items as "student-room doors should lock" and "student rooms should be large enough to rearrange furniture", and at the bottom such items as "student rooms; bright, strong colours" and "furniture; period styles".

The degree of overlap (or lack of it) between rated importance and satisfaction, would be expected to relate to that for which the environment was 'important'. If the subject interprets it as importance for his activities, quite different results from importance for 'wellbeing', might be expected; but in both cases the subject is being asked, in essence, to indicate his hypotheses about the results of his environmental interactions. A high degree of sophistication and concious awareness of environmental effects are thus assumed.

Comparison with actual effects, through the slightly less conscious study of satisfaction, may be derived with reference to the inter-correlations between all aspects. Some aspects will correlate highly with many others and thus in some respects may be considered 'neutral'. In terms of principal component analysis, a more general statement of a similar concept emerges from the proportion of variance accounted for by each dimension. This proportion enables us to identify the relative contribution made to the variation in responses, and their inter-correlations, by each dimension.

Proportion of explained variance

The value, or meaningfulness, of the proportion of variance depends to a very large degree on the representativeness of the items upon which the analysis is based. Because the variance which is proportioned is delineated by the sample of items making up the original battery of questionnaires, any imbalance in these items will be reflected in the relative proportions of variance. Thus, it is highly probable that in many cases the relative sizes of the various dimensions reflect some bias in the way the investigator originally selected his items. It is, therefore, particularly important that proportions be compared across investigations and investigators before their generality is accepted.

Once relative proportions gain any general acceptance they would have many theoretical and practical implications. In particular, the reasons why any dimension continually emerges as taking a major proportion of the variance (such as the 'evaluative' dimension, as we shall see later) raises psychological questions about the structure of human judgements of buildings. At the practical level the relative sizes of dimensions may contribute to decisions about design priorities. Although, of course, the underlying mechanisms postulated to explain the proportions may have greater long term implications for decision making.

These points may be clarified with reference to an example. Unfortunately the great majority of studies in which proportions of variance have been published have been those derived from the connotative approach made popular by Osgood *et al* (1956) and thus require discussion from a different perspective which we will consider later in the chapter. We must therefore return to the study by the BPRU which was described above.

In that study it was mentioned that the evaluative dimension accounted for 56 per cent, the position dimension 25 per cent and the distractions dimension 19 per cent of the common variance. We may therefore argue that, insofar as the 18 original measures were representative, these proportions of variance illustrate the relative contribution made by each dimension to the overall appraisal of the building. In the BPRU case one particularly interesting question is why the 'classroom' related dimension should be almost three times the 'size' of the 'school' related dimension. Does this illustrate the relative impact of these aspects in the teachers mind?

Correlation with a criterion

The third way of assigning weightings to aspects of environmental evaluation is by relating them in turn, or together to some overall criterion of evaluation. The degree to which each of the aspects makes a contribution to the criterion is an indication of its importance in the matrix of influences upon overall satisfaction. The key assumption in this case is that the criterion itself is an appropriate and accurate measure of overall evaluation, or in other words, that some such overall response is psychologically meaningful.

Can (and do) people in fact make overall evaluations of their environments in a consistent fashion? Part of the evidence for this may be derived from studies of the other forms of weighting. If, generally, people are not prepared to distinguish between aspects of their 'importance' and a major dimension does emerge relating to evaluation, then we may have confidence that asking people to make overall evaluations is a meaningful task. As yet there is no definitive series of studies to enable a firm answer to be given to this question but those available do lend support to the feasibility and psychological validity of asking people to make overall evaluations of environments. The fact that people will happily answer questions so posed also tends to support their meaningfulness.

The BPRU study (Canter, 1971) to which we have already had cause to refer, also provides information on the relative contribution to overall satisfaction of each of the major aspects measured. We have also already mentioned the problem of aggregation. It is

185

usually the case that application of these studies is made in relation to large buildings which many different people will use. The problem thus arises of whether the functions relating satisfaction should be based upon aggregates for buildings as well as aggregates for subjects. More specifically, whether averages for groups of subjects within a building should be the basis of the analysis or all responses should be dealt with independently of the actual building. As we saw when dealing with the identification of dimensions, these approaches can give rise to results with different emphasis.

The argument in favour of the use of group averages is that a group of users, through interaction in relation to a given building may develop a consensus. The combined properties of such a consensus may, as a consequence, be different from the properties of the population of individuals treated independently. Canter (1971) presents data for this possibility in relation to contributions to overall satisfaction. He showed the correlations between each aspect of the classroom and overall satisfaction, with scores calculated either from all 498 respondents or based on the means for each of 27 schools. Table 6.3 presents the results.

In Table 6.3 it is apparent that apart from increasing the size of

Table 6.3 Correlations with general classroom satisfaction

	ASPECTS OF SATISFACTION			
	Space	Lighting	Position	Distractions
Individuals in Cheshire sample* (N = 98)	0.57	0.43	0.24	−0.43
Individuals in Scottish sample** (N = 498)	0.49	0.43	0.25	−0.12
Scottish school means (N = 27)	0.64	0.60	0.46	−0.18

*there were four schools in this sample located in Cheshire

**this was the main sample described in BPRU (1972)

the correlations (presumably by reducing the variance) there is little relative difference in dealing with school means or individual responses, suggesting that (at this level of generality) it is the school aggregate which is the core determinant of the relationships between specific and general satisfaction. So, although we may be able to reveal dimensional differences between groups and individuals, as discussed earlier, provided we keep our analysis of the relationships between dimensions to the same level, the evidence is that groups and individuals will provide the same results.

Another way of exploring the same problem has been demonstrated by Davis and Roizen (1970). They dealt directly with the percentage of students who expressed different degrees of overall satisfaction with their college halls of residence. For all students who were highly satisfied overall, the relative proportion who had high or low satisfaction to each of 25 aspects of their environments were examined. This is really a crude form of correlational technique, differing from those above in that the criterion is a specifically dichotomized one.

Davis and Roizen were dealing with 950 students in 43 halls of residence and thus quite small difference in percentages related to a significant number of students. However, they concluded that "because of the limited range of differences, none of the variables stood out as being most important to student satisfaction". Their data shout out so loudly for analysis in the form of one of the other studies in this section that it seems a pity to leave it after such a preliminary analysis, but we must content ourselves with a summary of what emerges from the table of percentage differences they present.

Of the students who were highly satisfied with their residences less than five per cent were dissatisfied with the 'size', 'homeliness', 'privacy' or 'freedom to change appearance' of their rooms. On the other hand over nine per cent were dissatisfied with the 'lighting', 'quietness', 'suitability for sleeping', and 'opportunity to develop friendships' of their residences. If we accept the former group as more closely related to overall satisfaction than the latter, the similarities with the results of the BPRU study are apparent: the relative importance of spatial and control aspects and the relative unimportance of acoustic, lighting and other 'functional' aspects.

187

Frequency of complaint

What might be termed the 'bureaucratic' approach to the relative importance of different aspects of design is to examine those aspects about which most complaints are registered. This approach has the great advantages of highlighting environmental deficiencies and putting forward a distinct behavioural criterion for comparison. This criterion of the number of people who complain clearly depends upon the ways in which the complaint is elicited or recorded (calls to an ex-directory number would yield different complaint rates to those achieved by stopping people in the street). Yet this limitation may well derive a rationale from the decision making context within which it is determined. From the psychologist's viewpoint it may be claimed that spontaneous complaint rates may be thought of as non-reactive responses.

However, for the purposes of revealing the structure of evaluations actually asking people what they find irksome has the merit of control over sample characteristics.

An example of this approach is given by the Ministry of Housing (1967) survey of 49 housewives in Coventry. They found that over 50 per cent of the housewives were dissatisfied with the amount of storage space, the size of the garden, room heating and noise from the outside. Whereas, less than 25 per cent were dissatisfied with the size of the living room and the green spaces in front of their houses. As the survey was being carried out in relation to a specific form of system building its potential contribution to decision making is obvious. However, interpretation of the processes underlying the results is difficult because the relative effects of the particular building type are difficult to assess. Many such studies exist, often commissioned by building contractors (for example, Proplan, 1966) but they usually suffer from the fact that a variety of questionnaire forms have been used, each one in only one set of buildings. It is thus impossible to derive any generalizations from them.

A notable exception to the above is the study by Langdon (1966) in which he questioned 2287 people in 2734 rooms, approximately 29 per cent of the occupants of those rooms. As part of a long questionnaire they were asked to indicate which of a series of adjectives were applicable to their own office. "75 per cent ticked 'well-lit', 66 per cent 'warm' and 51 per cent ticked 'well ventilated'. The other favourable adjectives were: 'spacious' (47 per cent) 'free of draughts' (46 per cent), 'quiet' (34 per cent) and 'smart' (24 per cent). The unfavourable adjectives marked most frequently were: 'noisy' (31 per cent) and 'stuffy' (17 per cent)."

Relative effects of environmental variables

One further method for elucidating aspects of the structure of environmental evaluations is to relate each of the different aspects to some physical variable. Bednar (1970) for instance, in an exploratory study, had 94 students in ten laboratories give their evaluation of each of 22 aspects of those laboratories. He then correlated their evaluations with actual physical measures relating to the aspects. He found that the laboratory location and distance of the bench from the window had highly significant correlations with actual measures (0.44 and 0.34 respectively) but that such things as the number of fume hoods and the distance of the instructor had correlations of 0.00.

Bednar himself expresses disappointment with his results. Yet this type of painstaking correlational approach could contribute directly to understanding the pattern of links between psychological and physical variables. Those responses most sensitive to existing physical variables may well be the responses to which designers should pay most attention. They certainly would be the responses which would enable us to understand more fully the evaluation aspects of man/environment interaction.

Another approach to establishing environmental priorities is to introduce environmental changes and observe their relative effects, both before and after study. The difficulty with this approach is usually that the physical variables modified are limited. As a consequence it is not possible to disentangle differences in sensitivity of the respondents' evaluations from differences in degree of the environmental changes. Nonetheless, in three studies comparing open-plan/modern office layouts with older/traditional ones there are indications that general attitudinal changes occur more readily than evaluations of specific aspects of the working environment (Brookes, 1970; Wheeler, 1969; Osbourne, 1971). Many other similar studies now exist, particularly in the area of office design, mostly in private internal documents. A researcher who examined these for their common trends might well find his patience rewarded.

Types of building evaluation

Before moving on to other aspects of the study of the total environment it is of value to consider the types of evaluation which are available and how they might be used. This may be thought of as a cross-sectional view of the variety of verbal measures which are considered in this book.

In essence, people may be asked to evaluate a building which exists as part of their experience. The great majority of building 'appraisals' with which we have been concerned have been of this type. On the other hand people may be asked to evaluate a range of alternatives none of which they have actually experienced. Stringer (1972) has explored in some detail the differences between an abstract indication of relative merit, as for instance in the Peterson *et al* (1969) study and a truly *proleptic* approach. In the latter case the central concern is with finding out, what people (if given the opportunity) would actually prefer to experience. Stringer points out that there is often confusion between examining the structure of people's evaluations and seeking justification for action taken by designers. These confusions have implications for the application of findings from evaluations. A justification approach assumes similar value systems for both designers and users whereas the direct evaluation may well test this assumption amongst others.

From the viewpoint of understanding the nature or structure of environmental evaluations the distinction between appraisals, abstract evaluations and proleptic preferences is a crucial one. Unfortunately there are very few studies of the latter type at the building scale, the study of office size preferences (Canter, 1968) being one of the few. Two distinct sets of studies, however can be identified in relation to our other two types of evaluation. The appraisals have been mentioned above. Their value, as we have seen is to reveal the links between aspects of evaluation, and between those aspects and physical variables, in the context of the user's experience of the building.

190

The more abstract evaluations, to which we shall soon turn our attention facilitates the exploration of psychological environmental responses at a general level, independently of the particular context of the building. They also greatly increase the possibility for control over stimuli to be presented to the subject and thus the possibility of revealing the mechanisms underlying responses to them.

Diagnostic possibilities of *in situ* evaluations

One particular advantage of *in situ* evaluations may be demonstrated with reference to a clinical analogy. By comparing the profiles of evaluations on various aspects it is possible to 'diagnose' strengths or deficiencies in buildings. These diagnoses could contribute both to administrative policies, by identifying areas for attention, and to an understanding of the relative environmental influences in complex real world situations.

Figure 6.5 helps to clarify these implications. It contains profiles for two schools (A, and B) based on the mean scores for 20 teachers in each school. A is a British secondary school of conventional cellular design. B is a new British secondary school built on the principle of interlocking open spaces (Canter, 1971). The scores on each of the four main aspects and on overall classroom satisfaction have been converted into standard scores by comparison with the BPRU sample of schools. Thus comparisons between relative difference on each scale is quite meaningful. These profiles as a consequence have many similarities to the personality profiles frequently encountered in psychology. In looking at these profiles we may form an impression of the aggregated reactions to the school buildings. Many hypotheses may be generated from the profiles but for the sake of illustration a few points will be made. For although the average *classroom* satisfaction is comparable in both schools, being close to the mean for the population, the unconventional school is the most extreme on all *aspects*. Of note in this is that 'distractions' are scored very low indeed in school B; whereas 'space satisfaction' is quite unsatisfactory.

School A was appraised in some detail by BPRU (1972).

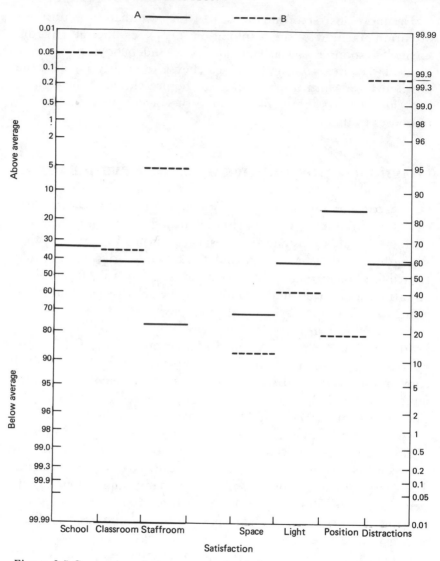

Figure 6.5 Comparison between two schools for teachers' average satisfaction with seven aspects of their school. (Vertical scale is probabilities when compared with 28 other schools)

Yet if B is more typical of newer schools that appraisal might well be out of date. The newer schools, on average may possibly work as well overall but the variations in adequacy for different environmental aspects may be great indeed. In such a situation

192

knowledge of the processes underlying evaluations and their relative weightings becomes of increasing importance. For if we accept some of the weightings uncovered earlier then improvements in the reduction of distractions may be of far less eventual significance than increase in the dissatisfaction with space.

General dimensions

When dealing with the structure of environmental evaluations in the abstract, not surprisingly, most investigators have taken their cue from Osgood *et al* (1956). Osgood's concern was with identifying the underlying dimensions of meaning, that is, he was a psycholinguist. It is possible to explore the description of environments as an aspect of psycholinguistic studies, to reveal those general underlying dimensions which appear to account for the ways in which buildings are described.

The difference between these essentially linguistic studies and the appraisals encountered above must be emphasized. For although there are many apparent similarities they have a crucial difference with regard to the type of psychological interactions with the environment they explore. As a consequence the relationships and dimensions revealed in the two types of study are best considered complimentary, providing different views of familiar areas of concern. Also, the differences between them may reveal some important aspects of how people conceptualize their physical environment.

In the 'appraisal' then, we are concerned with people's descriptions and reactions to buildings of which they have had some experience. The buildings are part of the respondents usual 'life space', even if it is only a building they pass every day. The investigator is thus at great pains to capture these daily reactions in some numerical form and relate them to aspects of the buildings.

Those studies, which we are calling 'abstract evaluations', as a rule *take* people to the environments of interest. Some form of simulation, as discussed in Chapter One, such as slides or models, is not uncommon, but even in cases where the actual buildings are the stimuli, the respondents are taken to them (for example, Vielhauer-Kasmar, 1970; Collins, 1969) and asked to comment on

193

a great range of bi-polar adjectival scales (of the form Osgood called Semantic Differentials). The abstraction this has involved has lead investigators to concentrate on revealing the underlying dimensions, usually through factor analysis, within the bi-polar scales. The search is for those general dimensions which may be shown to exist in all cases. Hershberger (1972) has summarized many of these, Table 6.4 being derived from his summary. He concludes that great confidence may be placed upon "five strong dimensions": (1) aesthetic (unique-common); (2) friendliness (friendly-hostile); (3) organization (ordered-chaotic); (4) potency (rugged-delicate); (5) space (loose-compact). He goes on to suggest

Table 6.4 Summary of five analyses of verbal descriptions of buildings (drawn from Hershberger, 1972)

Building aspect title	ADJECTIVES FROM RESEARCHER				
	Vielhauer -Kasmar (1970)	Canter (1968a)	Craik (1968)	Hershberger (1972)	Collins (1969)
AESTHETIC		impressive unique interesting	dynamic different interesting	exciting unique interesting	expressive unique interesting
FRIENDLINESS	beautiful attractive appealing	soft friendly welcoming	civilized cheerful joyful	soft friendly comfortable	fun happy joyful
ORGANIZED	organized efficient orderly	tidy coherent clear		ordered controlled clear	equipped coordinated complete
POTENCY		rough coarse dark		rugged massive permanent	
SPACE	roomy large wide	spacious changeable flexible		spacious large loose	liveable lived in curtained
ORNATE	bright colourful gay		conservative colourful bizarre	generous rich lavish	textured bright colour flashy
NEAT	clean tidy neat		dirty empty broad		cluttered confined roomy
SIZE	large huge		big huge broad	large formal proud	big large roomy

that there is some evidence for a further ten (colouring, neatness, size, temperature, lighting, privacy, shape, ventilation, noise, rigidity).

Interestingly, no one feels satisfied with Osgood's three dimensions of 'evaluation', 'potency' and 'activity', all investigators requiring more than three and the majority finding little support for anything other than 'evaluation' and possibly 'potency'. This is not too surprising in the light of Osgood's recent (1970) work and the growing awareness that the dimensional structure is closely linked to the stimuli being judged. Yet, that some measure of agreement has been found requires consideration.

Differences between general and particular responses

Possibly the most useful way of examining the semantic dimensions is by comparison with those discussed in the section on building appraisals. The differences are apparent. The large role of acoustics, heating and lighting as well as the dominant position of spatial properties of the environment, in the appraisal studies contrasts markedly with the essentially visual or 'ambient' dimensions of the semantic differential studies. This difference is commonly experienced between architects and laymen. The former are frequently concerned with the subtleties of the visual forms of the underlying structures. Studies which have made direct comparisons between architects and non-architects, however (Canter, 1969; Hershberger, 1972), have not demonstrated the great divergencies in dimensional structure which might have been expected. Thus access to these different, but overlapping, systems may be possible for various groups.

The dominant feature which ties the groups together and the various forms of study is the 'evaluation' dimension. Whether it be overall satisfaction or aesthetic pleasantness the essentially evaluative nature of the major dimension is clear. What this implies is that, as in every other area examined, people's reactions to buildings contain as a significant component their feelings about how good or bad a building is. This is important because it demonstrates not only that people are prepared to evaluate their

195

physical surroundings but that this action may be regarded as a central feature of their environmental perceptions.

No doubt more and more researchers will attempt to produce a 'definitive' set of dimensions. Such an exercise lends itself to post-graduate thesis work and has a clear product not often encountered in psychological research; but there are many reasons to suggest that this approach will now contribute little. First, the sets of dimensions revealed overlap to the degree that it seems plausible that within the limits of the procedure and methodology currently employed, little new will be revealed. Secondly, the assumptions underlying the methodologies employed are now being seriously questioned. In particular it is being asked whether the search for *independent* dimensions is psychologically valid. Many of the reactions we have to buildings appear to be interrelated. As a consequence, forcing on the analysis an orthogonal structure may be an injustice. Indeed, Küller (1973) has begun to explore the relationship between his orthogonal dimensions, thus demonstrating the weakness of a key assumption.

Of possibly more concern is the argument articulated most clearly by the followers of Kelly (1955). They suggest that aggregating data to produce common dimensions across groups of individuals hides many important individual differences. Further, the process of perceiving or evaluating buildings is an active ongoing one and any technique which delineates a given static state loses something of the important changing character of human reactions.

As we saw in an earlier section none of these assumptions is an inevitable part of studying reactions to buildings, or of aggregating those reactions. Satisfaction with a building may be taken as a meaningful index of the existing stage of an ongoing process. Correlations such as those with improvisation and age may be used to *explore* a changing process. Yet in all these cases the message is, as before, that the definition of dimensions is only a first and tenuous step towards understanding judgements of buildings.

Experiments into room friendliness

One way in which the implications of general dimensions may be

196

understood a step further is by relating them to experimentally controlled stimuli. A number of researchers have carried out this type of study (Winkel *et al*, 1968; Sanoff, 1969; Van der Ryn and Boie, 1963; Pyron, 1972) but probably the longest series of experiments of this kind were those which explored the dimensions of 'friendliness' (Canter and Wools, 1970; Wools and Canter, 1970). An example taken from the environmental displays they used is shown in Figure 6.6.

Wools and Canter selected a series of architectural variables as likely to influence the perceived 'friendliness' of a room, 'friendliness' being selected as one of the more intriguing dimensions found in earlier studies. Roof angle, window size and type of furniture were used as the architectural variables. Two levels of each variable (flat or sloping roof, large or small window and office or easy chairs) were then used in all possible combinations to produce eight, factorially designed, rooms. Each room, thus, consisted of a specific combination of one level of each of the three variables. As can be seen in Figure 6.6 each room looks quite realistic, although photographs and slides were taken from one-twelfth scale models. The rooms certainly do not look as if they were 'manufactured' to some overall scheme, yet it is possible to derive the relative effects of each variable on overall response.

Responses were usually obtained by asking people to complete ten-item bi-polar adjectival scales measuring 'friendliness' (see Canter and Wools, 1970 for details).

An analysis of variance on total scores derived from these scales reveals the relative effects of the architectural variables. Table 6.5 presents a summary of three studies carried out with groups of architecture undergraduates. The relative percentage of the explained variance associated with each variable is notably constant across the three groups, the furniture accounting for over 50 per cent the roof angle 35 per cent and the window size around five per cent, little more than the error variance. These relative effects have been repeated with a number of groups, the only changes which occur with any frequency being the relative effects of window size and roof angle.

Another important consistent finding is that significant interactions occur only rarely. In other words, each of the key variables appears to be acting independently. This suggests that, with these

197

(a) An interior created with sloping roof and easy chairs

(b) An interior created with flat roof and easy chairs

(c) An interior created with sloping roof and office furniture

(d) An interior created with flat roof and office furniture

Figure 6.6 Examples of four rooms 'factorially' designed to study effects on room friendliness (after Canter and Wools, 1970)

Table 6.5 Summary of three analyses of variance of 'friendliness' ratings of factorially designed slides similar to those illustrated in Figure 6.6 (after Canter and Wools, 1970)

Percentage of variance accounted for by:	ARCHITECTURE UNDERGRADUATES In Strathclyde		In Nova Scotia	Average for eight other studies
	A	B		
Furniture type	55	55	51	43
Roof angle	35	34	36	33
Window size	4	0	7	11
'Error'	8	11	6	13

variables at least, human response works on a simple additive basis rather than one aspect of the environment distorting the influence of another.

The relative influence of the three architectural variables may be compared with the establishment of relative weightings in responses. For, just as it is crucial to know which of the response variables should be given greatest weight, it is necessary to establish which of the environmental variables has the largest influence. The difficulty of doing the latter with any vigour in the field situation is one reason for carrying out laboratory studies. However, because the major architectural variables may be manipulated through simulations, it has been possible to look at aspects of rooms not studied in any detail in the appraisal literature.

The great difficulty of the experimental approach is that even with sophisticated, computer aided, multivariate, statistical procedures there is still a great limitation to the range and variety of variables which may be dealt with. There are other indications also (Canter, 1971) that once the number of slides a subject is asked to rate in one session increases beyond ten or twelve, motivation and reliability begin to drop noticeably. There is as a consequence a pressing need now, to draw together results and theoretical formulations from the different approaches discussed so that a coherent picture may be developed. That picture would still have many gaps in it if it drew only upon the type of study with which we have been dealing so far. We must now turn our attention to other forms of study uniquely able to provide the basis of an overall framework for the consideration of people in buildings.

Studying the single case

In those professions for which the particular problems of a specific client are a central concern, such as medicine and the law, a major portion of research and teaching is built upon detailed studies of individual cases. If we accept that human behaviour in buildings forms part of a coherent multifaceted system then it is essential to study that behaviour in a way which does not distort the system's qualities. Studying the individual case in detail in its natural setting is one possible way of doing this.

The case we select for study, in this context, may be either a person or a building. To the psychologist, concentrating on a person, observing in detail the same people in a variety of environmental contexts, it should be possible to explore the way the contexts and the people interact.

Probably the most notable study of this kind is that by Tars and Appleby (1973). They observed closely the same child at home and in an institution. They were able to demonstrate that important differences in behaviour occurred which could be clearly linked to the institutional setting. Willems (1973) has put similar problems in a more firmly ecological context, drawing on the language and concepts of Barker's *Ecological Psychology* (1968). The difficulty with the ecological approach, for environmental designers and psychologists alike, has been that the units of study have been at the wrong scale to reveal any effect of the physical milieu. Willems has gone some way to rectifying this deficiency by dealing with such notions as the independence and complexity of patient behaviour. He suggests that "differences

201

between settings account for far more variance in patient independence than do differences between patients". More recently these notions have been taken even further by exploring the 'social ecology' of an institution (Moos and Insel, 1974), but to do this it has been necessary to draw upon detailed accounts of the functioning of the institution which unfortunately takes this significant research beyond the scope of the present book.

In emphasizing the structure of people's behaviour there has been a reduction in the examination of the building and its creation. In particular, two sets of contributions to the environment may be underestimated, the designer's and the 'managment's'. Case studies of *buildings* are uniquely able to reveal these aspects. It is only by examining the whole building in the context of its production, administration and use that a full understanding of the environmental contingencies of behaviour may be understood.

Two major detailed case studies have been published. One of a comprehensive school in Scotland (BPRU, 1972), the other of a children's hospital (Canter, 1972). The former study included the responses of the teachers as part of a detailed examination of the costs and performance of the fabric of the building. From this it emerged that decisions often made at a level of central government, about the costing and production of the building may well leave their mark in important ways on the use of the building. Of far greater importance, however, is the administration of the building's use and the structure of the organization which it houses. Possibly the most notable finding was that although the school proved to be psychologically average, studies of its fabric and utilization demonstrated many weaknesses. Thus, this provides ways of clarifying the 'average' responses to physical and administrative artefacts.

Case studies of children's hospitals

The case study of the Royal Hospital for Sick Children at Yorkhill was solely concerned with responses to the building but attempted to examine these and the influences upon them as widely as possible. Not only were the results of repertory grid studies with the architect and senior nursing officers reported but also the results of interviews with members of the public who regularly passed the building. Between these two extremes were detailed surveys of the reactions of the various staff groups to parts of the building and to parts of the hospital wards.

Two central themes emerge from this study, both relating response to the building to the organizational role of the person under study, and to their conceptualizations of the building and its use.

(a) Roles

The first theme is most simply illustrated with reference to the study of the 'public at large'. Figure 6.7 shows the mean rating on

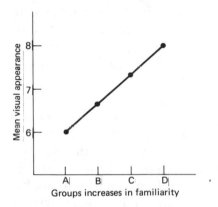

Figure 6.7 Relationship between familiarity with a children's hospital and evaluations of photographs of it

'visual appearance' of the building for each of four groups. Groups A and B did not recognize the building, groups C and D did. Group B was told what the building was, Group A was not. Group C had neither been inside the building nor knew anybody who had, whereas Group D had. Thus the groups are in a sequence of increasing familiarity with the building *as a children's hospital.* Further, the more 'familiar' people were with the building, the more highly they thought of its visual appearance. This, it should be noted, included the experimentally produced 'familiarity' of telling subjects the type of building it was.

203

It may be of value to substitute for the concept of familiarity that of the *type of interaction* a person has with a building. This would appear to be the significant component of 'familiarity'. It allows us to consider in a similar way the differing groups within the hospital, all of whom, because of their roles, will have differing interactions with each other and the building. From an extensive questionnaire with these groups it was possible to demonstrate that quite different patterns of responses were obtained from different role groups. Three main groupings emerged, administrators, consultants and nursing personnel. The indications were that the architect's views were closest to those of the administrators', the group with whom he had had most contact. The only other comparable study in the literature (Denton *et al*, 1973) which looked at group differences in reactions to student halls of residence, also demonstrated that role differences produced notable differences in reactions. We may also refer back to our earlier examination of Hole and Attenburrow's (1966) studies, where familiarity (or 'stranger' versus 'resident' roles) also had a marked effect.

(b) Concepts

The second theme is the influence of the conceptualizations of the senior (architect and administrator) groups on the form of the building produced. Canter presents the details of a repertory grid carried out with the architect. He argues that its main dimensions and simple structure is reflected in the strengths and weaknesses of the building. Thus, the emphasis on aspects of the nursing situation in the architects's conceptual system, is reflected in the success of the central ward areas at the expense of the administrative spaces and the cubicles for mothers staying with their children. Other viewpoints such as, for example, the essentially domestic one put forward by the hospital cleaners, finds no expression either in the architect's concepts or in the building he produced.

The importance of conceptualizations is further illustrated by the comparison of the nurses 'conceptual structure' of the wards with actual behaviour on them. For although the wards were conceived by architects and administrators as essentially open-plan the analysis of the nurses' view of them showed three distinct areas. This distinction was reflected in the use of the ward revealed through detailed observations.

204

(c) Interactions over time

One great weakness of Canter's study was that it really examined the hospital at a particular point in its history, for only a brief period. No attempt is made to examine the process of interaction with the building over time. The study of a children's psychiatric hospital by Rivlin and Wolfe (1972) takes this process as its central concern. They elaborate the crucial role of the administration, and the conceptualizations of the administration, for mediating the influence of the building on the behaviour within it. They show how over time, the administration changes the use and effects of the building to fit their own concepts of its influence, by for example, locking doors and placing sanctions on room use.

Putting the themes which emerge from these case studies together, highlights the potential for recurrent conflict in effective building use. If concepts and reactions are very different for people in different roles, yet if designers and administrators have a major impact on the way the building functions, it is likely that the people in junior positions will normally be less satisfied with buildings than their seniors. It may be very significant for the application of psychological ideas, that only by studying buildings in their full, real-world context do we derive psychological formulations which have clear implications for the structure of the design procedure. As we shall soon see they also have strong implications for the processes on which building evaluation is based. Before turning to these summary formulations we must consider the other form of study, the field experiment.

Field experiments in offices

The great advantage of any experimental procedure is that it is the experimenter who introduces the change and observes its effects. Thus, the direction of the causal links may be established. The chief disadvantage of the experiment is that, to fully understand the causal processes, the controls of the laboratory are usually considered necessary. This leads to precisely those concerns for real world richness, which have been central considerations in this chapter and which we argued in Chapter One were so crucial to research, in environmental psychology. However, no end of case studies will unravel the complex causal relationships underlying building influences. As a consequence, those studies which attempt to introduce an element of experimental control into an ongoing, real world situation may be of considerable theoretical significance. These studies are those in which a change is introduced into an existing situation and any resultant effects compared with a comparable situation of no change. Such studies may best be considered as field experiments (see Seashore, 1963). Field experiments may be usefully considered as a type of case study because the change is introduced into an existing context, and thus many of the relationships between the change and the existing context are open to examination.

Field experiments themselves can, of course, vary from those which are still closely linked to the laboratory procedures, in which subjects are required to perform tests, to those more closely linked to ecological research, in which observations are made of the effect of the change. We shall briefly consider one study from each end of this continuum.

In his study of the effects of office size Canter (1968) wished to establish whether changes in clerical performance were in any way influenced by the size of the room in which a person worked. He therefore gave clerical performance tests to two randomly selected groups of people in large offices (100 people in any one room), medium sized offices (30 people per room) and small offices (four or five people per room). One group were tested in their usual offices, but at other desks. The other group were taken from their normal offices and tested at desks in offices of a different size. In effect, the researcher introduced two potentially influential changes, moving people from their desks and moving people to offices of a different size. The first change, however, occurred for both groups, so it was only possible to examine the effect of the change of room size on the overall effects of room size. A control group tested at their own desks would have greatly improved this experiment, but presumably the limitations imposed on the investigator by the office organization did not make this possible.

Figure 6.8 shows the results of the analysis of variance of the clerical performance scores. Because of the experimental changes it is possible to relate the two groups to 'long term' and 'short

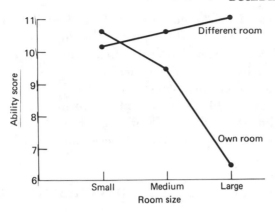

Figure 6.8 Relationship between room size and general ability for two groups

term' effects of office size. The measurable influences on those who were moved to different offices derived from the immediate context of the office, in which they were studied, whereas those tested in their own offices were influenced by a process of longer duration. From Figure 6.8 it is apparent that there is no difference in the effects of office size on those moved to other rooms for the testing. On the other hand, there is a relationship (also shown by other forms of analysis) between room size and performance for those tested in their own room, performance decreasing as room size increases.

The experiment thus enables us to be sceptical of the possibility that the existing environmental conditions in offices, such as the noise level or visual distractions, have a direct influence on performance. This fits in well with the discussion in Chapter Three. However, Figure 6.8 does suggest that other, longer term processes, may be in operation. The nature of these processes is difficult to determine; it may be a long term debilitating effect or an aspect of selection not identified by the investigator. Canter himself argues that the latter is more likely than the former, but presents no data on the effects of length of stay in the office which might have helped clarify the issue.

From the viewpoint of the general theme of this chapter, the importance of this experiment lies in the nature of the processes it explores. The conglomerate influence of a total environment over longer or shorter periods is examined. In doing this other organizational issues come to the fore especially how and by whom it is determined which people should occupy which room. The experiment, whilst giving reasonably clear results is nonetheless confused by the 'testing situation'. The subjects were being *tested* (their typical behaviour was not being recorded) and this may well have hidden much useful information. In the second field experiment we shall look at, the form of measurement was a central concern, being essentially observational.

Before/after study of a psychiatric ward

Ittelson *et al* (1970) carried out a series of observational studies in psychiatric hospitals. The essence of these studies was to produce 'maps' of behaviour throughout the hospital wards. These 'behavioural maps' provide a numerical picture of the patterns of activity taking place. In one of the hospitals they found a solarium which was rarely used. They hypothesized that the causes for its lack of use were its location at the far end of the corridor and "the inadequate and uncomfortable facilities it offered". The investigators, as a consequence, "decided to study the effect on the use of the solarium of providing comfortable, attractive and carefully laid out seating arrangements". The change in furnishing was introduced immediately after the first mapping and two months later a second mapping was carried out.

By comparing the mappings before and after the change the authors came to the conclusion that:

> "It is clear that what occurred was not merely an increase in the solarium's share of behaviour with proportional drops in the other public areas, but rather a marked alteration of the entire patterning of activities among the public areas".

They illustrate this by showing that, whilst the proportion of active behaviour in the dayroom dropped from 28 to 11 per cent, in the corridor it dropped only from 39 to 34 per cent, the solarium increasing from 33 to 55 per cent. Isolated passive behaviour increased in the solarium from 32 to 49 per cent and in the dayroom from 36 to 46 per cent but it dropped in the corridor from 32 to five per cent. Thus by recording a total environment Ittelson *et al* are able to demonstrate the effects of their introduced change throughout the whole ward area. They can trace the ripples produced by their pebble as well as measuring the size of its splash!

For the reader who likes categories, the study by Ittelson *et al* (1970) may be thought of as a member of the 'before/after' sub-section of the 'field experiment' variety of 'case study'. This particular sub-section is an increasingly popular one. Canter (1972a) has summarized a number of such studies of the effects of office layout. The great difficulty of such studies is that many things change over time in any organization and thus the before and after measures may be influenced by much besides the change introduced by the experimenter. One way of coping with this is a control group who do not suffer the change. The difficulties made famous by the Hawthorne investigators (Roethlisberger and Dickson, 1939) then intrude upon interpreting differences between the groups. However, with adequate control groups this method of research design may prove very fruitful.

Studying environmental change as it happens

One further sub-category may be identified, which has considerable theoretical interest. This is the observation of the effect of changes occurring independently of the investigator. For instance, Ittelson *et al* (1970) report that between their observations the number of patients on the ward increased and that it had an effect on patterns of social interaction beyond the simple arithmetic of the increase. In a study carried out at the University of Surrey (Bycroft and Wolff, 1974) during the Winter 1973 energy crisis, secretaries completed job description scales on days when they were allowed lighting and on days when they were not. The results suggested that no discernible effect was present, but the weaknesses of the study, in part brought about by the difficulties of carrying it out, preclude generalization.

The interest of this type of study is twofold, although there are many difficulties in interpreting the results. First, the change is part of the course of events and therefore is more integrally linked to the system of which the built environment is a part, than any experimental change. Not surprisingly, therefore, what such studies serve to illustrate is the fact that environmental effects are interrelated and are part of an interrelated system. Results produced by isolating these effects must, therefore, be examined with caution.

The second interest lies in the close relationship between this type of research and the process of environmental design. All buildings are changes introduced into an ongoing system. Thus, the study of a situation before and after some environmental modification could, quite feasibly, become a recurrent aspect of the design process. Indeed, if the designer and researcher work closely together, we may move towards the day when architecture and planning may be treated as large scale field experiments.

A summary model

In this chapter we have taken as our central concern the study of the total environment of buildings in use. Because of this we have, inevitably, paid more attention to the problems underlying the study of the total environment in buildings, and the methods available for solving those problems, than to any answers or theoretical overview. By way of summarizing this chapter therefore, we shall conclude with the exploratory outline of a model for considering people's behaviour in relation to their physical environment. This model will thus draw more heavily on the results of the studies discussed in this chapter than the method on which we have focussed our attention so far.

1 The evaluation of the central interaction
At the core of our tentative model is the interaction between the user and his environment. By interaction we mean that the building may inhibit or facilitate the actions which people wish to perform or the meanings which they wish to demonstrate. That is the 'building influencing action' aspect of the interaction. The 'behaviour modifying the building' counteraction has tended to be missed by psychologists (for example Lee, 1971) and emphasized very strongly by designers (for example BPRU, 1972). This is not

surprising as the latter is the essence of design, whereas the former underlies the process of much psychological, laboratory research.

By postulating that this two-way process is central to our model, we must also assume that building evaluation is, in some sense, an estimation of the success of this interaction. The definition of success requires a detailed consideration of the costs and benefits involved in the interaction which cannot be derived from the existing literature. All we may speculate at the moment is that (as a number of studies have suggested) a positive ability to modify the environment is an asset. As a consequence we may expect the interaction equation to be quite complex.

2 The structure of evaluation

The next aspect of our model is that evaluation is structured. We may identify interrelated, yet distinct, aspects of it. We also have clear evidence that these aspects may be ordered, by a variety of means in terms of their contribution to satisfaction. A consistent aspect of this ordering is that, typically, some overall response predominates. Yet the relative contribution of satisfaction to specific aspects of the environment is more difficult to determine. Many matters appear to influence which aspect has the most significant contribution to make. Aspects of the spatial environment do tend to recur at the top of many lists with lighting and heating frequently placed lower down. It is quite common for aspects of the acoustic environment to be very low on any ordering of the relative weights of different aspects of the environment.

As we are postulating that evaluation is derived from some assessment of interactions with the environment, it is plausible that the relative weights which contribute to this assessment are themselves influenced by the interaction process. Weightings might change with different environmental levels or with any of the other factors to which we turn our attention. Nonetheless, the demonstration, in a wide variety of ways, of the patterning of environmental reactions is possibly the most significant contribution of the work discussed in this chapter.

3 The effects of role

A number of studies have shown that quite different reactions

211

may be obtained from people who perform different roles within any given environment. This is a point which is readily extended to the natural environment as discussed in Chapter Nine. Role is a variable which may be expected to influence directly the demands which a person makes of his environment, and hence the interaction he has with it. It follows that the effects of role fit squarely within our model. We may even put forward an hypothesis for future testing derived from the role effects:

"The more disparate the environmental interactions of two or more roles the greater the difference in the structure of their environmental evaluations".

4 Influence of administrators

One role which may be usefully separated from the others is that of the building administrators. This group is significant in that they can influence the form of interaction between other users and their environment.

Although they may well have an evaluation structure which is different from all other users, they will further influence the pattern of evaluations which other users may produce. In the hospital which Rivlin and Wolfe (1972) studied, for example, the locking of doors by the hospital administrators may well have led the patients to think differently about the building.

The complex series of interactions being sketched here is, more than likely, the key reason for the disparity in relative weightings from study to study. Few studies to date have attempted to identify role differences in evaluation or the influence of administrators. Nonetheless the effects of these variables has been clearly apparent in a number of the studies reported.

5 Change with time

Our model is a dynamic one. Nowhere within it do we postulate a static process. Those studies which have paid attention to temporal variables have been able readily to demonstrate their influence. Yet the most frequent research paradigms have been static ones. The examination of changes over time have usually been incidental, but as findings accumulate it is inevitable that

212

more attention will be paid to the all important *processes* and less to given *levels* at a point in time.

The dynamic aspect of evaluations has two further implications. First, it throws into relief the importance of environmental experiences *prior* to those in the building being evaluated. We must assume that previous interactions with buildings leave an important mark on people if we are assuming that evaluation is based on interactive processes. The second implication is that examination of a building and its users independently of their context, the broader framework in which they exist, may leave crucial explanatory variables out of the picture. The case studies described earlier serve to illustrate these two implications particularly well. They show, for instance, that comparisons with previous buildings and the urgency with which moves to new buildings were made, both contributed significantly to evaluations.

Finally, we may consider why it is that evaluation plays such a central role in all the research of this chapter. The chapter has dealt with research distinguished by two qualities. First the total environment and the interrelationship of its parts was the concern. Secondly, the researchers wished to contribute to design decision making. It was 'applied' research. In order to make design decisions a designer must aim to produce a total building, but he also has to produce the 'best' he can. Thus, he has to evaluate the likely interaction of his potential users with his proposed environment. We can see, then, with hindsight, that the psychological information which the designer requires is also the theoretical question the answer to which the environmental psychologist requires: "How do people evaluate buildings?"

Chapter Seven

Understanding the City

Peter Stringer

In the last chapter our attention was focussed on the study of large and complex buildings. The next three chapters increase the scale of environmental concern to an even more macroscopic level. We shall be discussing the built environment in terms of whole towns and cities, as well as in terms of their constituent parts. Two main topics will be introduced: the way in which people 'make sense' of their urban environments; and some of the environmental sources of satisfaction and dissatisfaction which they experience in urban life. In Chapter Nine the natural environment is considered. This may serve as a complement to our otherwise rather persistent concern with built form.

Three dominant themes underlie Chapters Seven, Eight and Nine, independently of their particular subject matter. Criticism of methodology, and particularly of the instruments used, is one recurrent theme. Too often we find that techniques are taken from mainstream psychology and applied without due regard to their suitability for the problem in hand. This is inevitably more common when the researcher is not a psychologist (*cf.* the work on wilderness evaluation in Chapter Nine).

When psychologists are involved, however, they tend to provide examples of our second theme — the frequent failure to explore what might be psychologically interesting in environmental psychology. One demand that should be made of any branch of psychology, however newly sprung, is that it should attempt to throw new light on traditional and mainstream psychological issues. Generally this requires that studies should have a firm basis in psychological theory, or be actually developing a new one. A good suggestive example of how this demand might be met is given by Kirkby's (1973) approach to man-made environmental hazards, described in Chapter Nine.

An even sterner test, especially for psychologists, is that the results of investigations should contain clear implications for any practical questions which may be relevant. Many of the studies discussed in this volume arise from a practical problem for which policy and decision makers are seeking a solution. Sometimes the issue is treated as no more than a convenient reference point with everyday life, to bolster an academic's belief that he can do relevant research. If the search for a solution is taken seriously, the research must have at least two unusual characteristics. The research must be designed in such a way that the general shape in which the results are cast enable them to be fairly directly translated into practical policies or decisions. This is not an easy task. It is made very difficult when one does not have a tight specification of the research question, and thoughtlessly grabs the most familiar or fashionable techniques available. Secondly, the research must be carried out in a context where there is some commitment to use the results.

Coming to make sense of urban environments is normally a process simultaneous with using them. If it is convenient to separate it in this chapter, one may also remark that this separation is a regrettable feature of much of the research on urban environments which is described here.

Basic to understanding any environment is an ability to find one's way around. Orientation and route-finding, and the rather more specialized matter of distance estimation, have been investigated in a number of studies. Distance estimation is studied on the assumption that it may be an indicator of people's 'images' of the city. There is evidence, for example, that we may 'stretch' or 'compress' the image from an Euclidean base, depending on whether it relates to the city centre or the periphery, to familiar or unfamiliar places.

The 'imageability' of a city is taken to be a source of emotional security to the individual and of collective conciousness to the group. Environmental meaning is studied analytically by examination of a city's physical and social meaning; and in a more evaluatory way, in terms of individuals' impressions recorded on rating scales.

'Mystery' and 'coherence' are two aspects of our response to urban environments which have received particular attention. They have been incorporated in a model of environmental perception and cognition. The model suggests that people do not seek nor prefer certain objects or content in their environment. They gain their main satisfaction from the process of acquiring and using information in the environment.

Different individuals or different groups are likely to vary in the image each has of any given place. The images of children have been studied in particular for the light they may throw on the development of environmental representation. Important racial differences have been described in one investigation. In another study, children's environmental images have been used to explain the relatively poorer adjustment of those who had a long ride to school compared to those who lived within walking distance.

Professional groups who are responsible for planning urban environments, not surprisingly, see them differently from the public which uses them. These differences, and the nature of the public's images, have practical implications for decision makers and need to be charted.

Lynch's image of the city

If one is looking for a single starting point to the recent study of environmental cognition, the strongest claim can probably be made for Lynch (1960). Lynch was interested in the way in which cities are seen, and the implications of city images for their design. His book considered in particular what he called the 'legibility' of the cityscape — "the ease with which its parts can be recognized and organized into a coherent pattern". Although he remarked on the interest some psychologists had taken in how animals and men structure the environment and orientate themselves, and although his scheme for describing city images looks reminiscent of the Gestalt principles of perception, his work is much more firmly rooted in the design disciplines than in psychology. In particular his approach derives from that of Kepes (1956) in rather different fields.

Orientation, route-finding and ease of mobility are important goals of the image for Lynch. At the same time a clearly imageable environment is expected to provide a socially important collective consciousness of the home town, and emotional security to the individual. It "also heightens the potential depth and intensity of human experience" by supplying strong expressive meaning. Mystery combined with coherence are aspects of our pleasure in the city.

The active role of the individual in perceiving the world and creatively developing an image of it is stressed. But although it is possible for individuals to strengthen an image or have their perceptions retrained, Lynch considers the modern city to be too complex for that to be a useful strategy. Our perceptions cannot adapt to the scale and rapidity of environmental changes. We must develop our images of the environment by operating on the external rather than the internal world. We must build more imageable cities. Because city planners are primarily interested in designing environments to be used by many and various people, individual differences are passed over in favour of group images — the "common mental pictures carried by large numbers of a city's inhabitants".

Environmental images are given three components: identity, structure and meaning. A useful image enables one to identify objects or parts, to see their spatial or other relations with oneself or other objects, and includes some practical or emotional meaning. To be valuable in the business of orientation the image must be pragmatically sufficient, easy to 'read', safe, adaptable to change, and communicable to others.

Lynch's main empirical work was an interview study of thirty individuals in Boston (USA), and fifteen each in Jersey City and Los Angeles. Their images of their city were analysed in terms of five elements: paths, edges, districts, modes and landmarks. These are proposed as the building blocks out of which we structure the city, both in perception and in design. They have a number of qualities which the designer may act directly upon, such as

218

figure-ground clarity, simplicity of form, continuity, dominance, clarity of joint, directional differentiation, and so on.

These rather formalistic concerns have not been uppermost in the planning profession in the past fifteen years. There is little evidence that the concept of 'imageability' has had much impact on city design. Lynch's work seems so far to be more of value in providing a scheme for the analysis of environmental perception in existing cities. Despite his disclaimer the scheme is probably more useful as a way of enabling people to understand, and retune their urban 'maps'. It has also had a considerable influence on those psychologists and geographers who have done the greater part of subsequent work on environmental cognition (see, for example, Downs and Stea, 1973).

Orientation

For example, successful orientation as the main goal of mental 'representations' of the environment has often been proposed since Lynch's book appeared. This term will be used hereafter where possible in preference to the over-specific 'image' or 'map', and the often inaccurately used 'perception' or 'cognition'. Zannaras (1973) in a typical study examined the cognitive structures of three cities with different land use patterns in terms of the instructions given to strangers who were trying to find their way through them. She was principally interested in whether differences in land-use distribution were associated with the relative importance of particular types of environmental feature (such as church, stream, shopping centre) in giving route instructions. And at the more theoretical level, Stea's (1969) 'model for studying conceptual spaces' is devoted to accounting for orientation and the way in which we move about the world. However the attention given to orientation processes in the empirical research tends to be rather superficial. What might be involved psychologically in orienting oneself in a city or any other environment is neglected in quick experiments and specialized academic concerns.

Distance estimation

A good example of this kind of neglect is in the literature on

219

'distance estimation'. The earliest work related people's estimates of the distance of capital cities from Stockholm to their imagined emotional involvement in experiencing various events in those cities (Ekman and Bratfisch, 1965; Bratfisch, 1969). It was primarily concerned with technical aspects of scaling, even though the inverse square relationship discovered could have some psychological interest. Indeed, one suspects that much of the subsequent work was motivated largely by the opportunities afforded for high quantification (*cf.* Briggs, 1973; Cadwallader, 1973).

The next reported study was done by geographers (Golledge *et al*, 1969). Geographers are interested in the way in which urban environments are perceived because they believe that behaviour within towns and cities will be found to be related to the perceptions. They hope that the structure of environmental perceptions will conform to the physical models which they have objectively derived from their analysis of urban structure. This would validate the use of the models in planning and decision-making. Distance estimation is studied because it is taken to be one indication of how urban representations are stylized.

In this experiment subjects were asked to estimate the closeness of pairs of points (nine in the vicinity of a university, and two in the downtown area), as well as distances to each from a standard reference point. In both cases estimates were good, but more errors were made for points further from the university. Relative newcomers to the city were less accurate than longer term residents, leading the experimenters to propose a learning model of environmental representation. However, since it was only proposed after the investigation, hypotheses derived from it were not tested.

A psychological approach

Lee (1970), a psychologist, had university students estimate the walking distance from the main entrance to their Students' Union to various distinctive destinations in the city. His main finding was that distances of journeys away from the centre of the city were overestimated significantly more than those towards the centre. The explanation is that people's "schema of the whole city

220

includes a *focal orientation,* built up by the satisfactions of the centre. These satisfactions would have a dynamic effect on the perceptual process, causing a foreshortening of perceived distances in the inward direction, perhaps on an increasing gradient, and affecting judgements and behaviour which might otherwise be quite independent of the city centre"(pp.41-2). If this explanation is to be *psychologically* interesting, the question of 'satisfactions' should be dealt with. As an afterthought Lee did estimate the 'unfamiliarity' of each destination to his students, in terms of the number of them who were unable to judge its distance. He found that estimated distances *toward* the city centre were significantly more in error for the more *unfamiliar* destinations. But to measure their relative familiarity in terms only of subjects' performance on the experimental task, rather than from an independent source of information, is operationally weak. The further aspect of the 'rewardingness' of the various imagined destinations is not dealt with at all. As a result we know little more than that distances for inward and outward journeys are differently estimated by psychology and education students in a laboratory setting.

What is of *environmental* interest in such distance estimates? Lee introduces his study by stating that perceived distance is a cost variable in the "profit-and-loss accounting" which must be involved in every journey.

"It is this measure which is required in equations which attempt to predict the probability of people embarking on a journey. The practical application of such knowledge is to the planning problems of siting for such facilities as shops, leisure buildings, and churches, and for the more general problems of city and regional layout."

From a viewpoint of environmental psychology it may be more important to know whether perceived distance is in fact a cost variable in the anticipation of a journey, than how accurate it is. *Is* the probability of a journey related to its perceived, as distinct from its actual, length? If there are discrepancies between the two sorts of distance, does this matter in any way?

Lee (1962) has earlier suggested that, if distances are under-

221

estimated toward the city centre, shopping centres would be more attractive and used more often if they lay on that side of one's residence. He found that housewives whose nearest shopping centre lay 'outwards' were less likely to make use of it than those whose nearest centre lay 'inwards'. But no data has yet been provided actually relating distance estimates to shopping behaviour. In the 1970 study we learn nothing of the significance for students of the locations whose distance they estimated.

Practical implications

Lowrey (1971) went some way to supplying this defect when he selected as locations a variety of public service facilities (bus stop, library, garage, hospital). He was interested in the extent to which the accuracy of distance estimates varied with different facilities, and from people with differing socio-economic characteristics. A random sample of 138 persons was taken from a large area of Baltimore, Maryland. It was found that people estimated the distance from their home of the ten facilities which they individually used according to a common subjective rule. However, short distances (typically for bus stops, libraries and post offices) were judged in a slightly different way from long ones. Drivers and non-drivers showed a completely different way of thinking about distances. The former made more errors, and the latter were less variable as a group. Men and women had similar ideas about the relative distance of different facilities, but men were more confused than women. Lowrey concluded that "substantial differences in subjective judgement rules exist, whether because of past experience and other motivational factors or because of some discontinuous feature in the stimuli". These variables need to be investigated. He also suggested that because bus stops, schools, libraries, post offices and parks were all judged as being closer to people's home than they were physically, they may act as cues or special features, of the type to which Lynch drew attention, contributing to a commonly held concept of neighbourhood. Lowrey does not go a long way in giving meat to the distance estimation issue, but there are a few more implications in his work for urban planning decisions.

Comparing experimental results

In an experiment following up the earlier one by Golledge, Briggs and Demko (1969), Briggs (1973) found that "for small distances, cognized distances toward downtown were greater than those away from downtown". This had been indicated in the previous study. Before one concludes that this finding contradicts Lee's results, an important difference between the two studies should be pointed out. Although both used student samples who judged distances from a familiar location, the downtown area of Columbus, Ohio and the centre of Dundee, Scotland are not comparable environmentally. The distance of the downtown area from the university is greater in Columbus than in Dundee. The use of the two areas by students probably differed. And more generally the structure of European and North American cities as regards the location and use of 'downtown' areas is crucially different. Added to which Dundee's topography, including its site up from the Firth of Tay, makes it untypical even of most European cities.

There is a similar uninterpretable conflict between Lee's findings and those of Cadwallader (1973), who found no relation between deviations between cognitive and real distances and familiarity with the locations. The attractiveness of the locations and length of residence in the area were equally unrelated to the accuracy of distance estimations. Cadwallader used a sample of households in Los Angeles. They estimated distances from their home to thirty neighbouring towns up to 65 miles away. This study showed that aggregated data obscures important individual differences and to some extent exaggerates relationships. Like Briggs, Cadwallader found that results varied according to whether one asked subjects for absolute mileage judgements or for a ratio estimation.

Research design

The differences and similarities between Briggs and Lee's studies are important over and above one's frustrated wish to compare their results. One of the attractions of environmental studies for psychology is that they represent a more everyday, familiar and

223

significant context for trying to answer psychological questions, than the traditional laboratory. Using student samples in the laboratory is convenient, and can often be justified. But in environmental studies one would hope to see that their use had appropriateness rather than convenience. Either students should be a particularly fitting group in whom to investigate the process in question, or one should show that one is interested in students as such. Is there any reason why distance estimation might be psychologically relevant to students? Is it likely to be more relevant to them than to other groups? Or are they representative of the general population in this respect?

Neither Briggs and his colleagues nor Lee give any justification for using their particular samples. The point is stressed because it is a criticism that can be made of so many investigations in the literature. But it is ironical that in environmental studies students may often be a very appropriate population. A situation of change is frequently a powerful context for examining psychological processes. If one wishes to understand how people perceive and value their dwelling, for example, and how they behave in it one research strategy is to focus on house purchasing behaviour or moving house and settling in. Students are typically involved in a wide range of environmental changes.

This characteristic was used to some purpose by Hudson (1974) in an investigation of shopping behaviour. He was interested in the way in which inter- and intra-urban migrants adapt to their new retailing environment, how environmental representations change over time and the relation of them to changes in behaviour. Shopping records were kept by student samples for the first ten weeks in their new environment, and their environmental representations were elicited by a repertory grid technique. Shopping behaviour could be related to the way in which an individual construed the set of available shops. Postgraduate students moving into the city and undergraduates moving from a hall of residence into private accommodation provided entirely appropriate samples.

In their account of Briggs' work Golledge and Zannaras (1973) suggest that his distance estimation data can be seen as indicative of an environmental learning process, and as a function of the level of information one has about the environment. Much of the other work they describe does have these characteristics; but in Briggs' they are not built into the research design. In the distance estimation work to date one tends to be presented with a bare, quick experiment. The points of real interest in the phenomenon are discussed as an after thought. They should be built into the research design. The hallmark of good research is to be able to incorporate those points that so often never get further than the introduction or discussion sections of a paper.

A remark was made above about the difference between city centres and downtown areas and the peculiar topography of Dundee. Here is a further example of how insufficient forethought robs the work of much of its potential interest. Environmental questions are at issue. The environments that serve as stimuli should be as carefully selected as one's subjects. They should either be sampled representatively, or be clearly seen to be particularly appropriate to answer one's question. In general it is unlikely that one or two environments or locations will be sufficient. If separate studies are to have any chance of being related and compared — and this is highly desirable — they cannot be encapsulated and unique case-studies. Wohlwill (1973) makes a cogent plea for the representative sampling of environmental stimuli. He complains that very little attention is given to this part of the research design. An environmental stimulus should "be defined in objective, physical terms, and analysed into its component variables, as much as possible, via operations that are independent of the subject whose behaviour is under study".

Imageability

Distance estimation work has been discussed as an example, if somewhat misguided, of how environmental representations have been looked at as subserving orientation. Other potential roles, several of which are referred to by Lynch (1960), have been followed up with less persistence but perhaps greater brilliance.

Lynch's idea that a clearly imageable environment may provide a socially important collective consciousness of the home town, and emotional security to the individual is explored by Wood (1971), a geographer, in his thesis on environmental representations of San Cristobal las Casas, Mexico. His refreshingly unpedantic, sensitive and enthusiastic approach to the topic gives one a vivid impression of the idea's potential validity. He likens his own work to that of Lynch as exemplifying a fusion of the 'civic' and 'urban' approaches to the city. Previously the city as 'civitas', analysed in terms of social, religious, political and recreational order, had been considered independently of the city as 'urbs', in its physical aspects. However, he criticizes Lynch as being solely interested in the arrangement of the visual surface of the world. Political, economic and social considerations were ignored.

"Image analysis is valuable, but no matter how legible a living space is, that alone is not enough. Legibility, clarity, without communality is nothing more nor less than sterile sanity. Spatial replication may well be one avenue leading towards a communal, social, if you will living space — a living space, that is, that is not only articulate but human. It is just not enough to walk out of your house onto a street and know where that street goes. It is not even enough to walk onto that street and know that in some way that street is yours. And it will not be enough until you can no longer walk out of your home at all, but simply into larger and larger homes filled with more and more family".

What Wood found particularly exciting and satisfying about San Cristobal was the way in which 'replication' holds the city together, gives a sense of community, and establishes an individual's identity. The inhabitants' representations are integrated across the three levels of home, *barrio* (roughly 'neighbourhood'), and city, because physical structures are repeated from house to house and *barrio* to *barrio,* and 'replicated' from house to *barrio* to city. For example each has an open space common to all inhabitants — the patio, the *barrio plaza,* and the central *zocalo.* There are recreational opportunities at each level; and religion is replicated in the family shrine, the *barrio* church and the Cathedral. Each celebrates its birth and continued existence in *fiestas:* the socio-religious existence of the family in marriages, baptisms and deaths; the professional and craft structure of the *barrio;* and the political, religious and social life of the whole city.

The process of replication is not only physical, but permeates all the varied aspects of the *'civitas'*. Wood's particular contribution is to analyse together the physical and social aspects of urban representation, and draw out of the analysis an underlying principle, replication.

Environmental meaning in the city

A further theme introduced by Lynch was the semantics of environmental representations. He suggested that a clearly image-able environment supplied strong expressive meaning, and "heightens the potential depth and intensity of human experience". If there has been a relatively large number of studies dealing with environmental meaning in recent years, this is probably due less to Lynch's influence than the availability and popularity of the Semantic Differential technique. We shall discuss the technique again in Chapter Nine. Psychology has not been very successful so far in throwing light on such concepts as "the potential depth and intensity of human experience", or on how it might be measured or improved; but a semantic differential does enable one to describe expressive meanings. A particularly thorough example of this sort of approach is offered in a study by Lowenthal and Riel (1972a).

They went further than many other investigators in their attention to stimuli, subjects and task. Their 294 subjects covered a range of ages and occupations. From six to ten environments in each of four American cities were chosen. Although neither sample appears to have been randomly or representatively select-ed, they are much more adequate than the common 'single environment — student subjects' design. These subjects actually walked through the environments before they recorded their impressions, and uniformly in daylight and fine weather. This is an obvious improvement on the more usual methods of stimulus presentation involving drawings, photographs, or verbal reference. Impressions were elicited on 25 bipolar rating scales, such as 'natural — artificial', 'people — things', 'smooth — rough', 'poor — rich', 'self awareness — awareness of surroundings', and 'vivid — drab'. In addition, subjects indicated five words from these scales

227

which best applied to each walk; and described it with four other words which were not in the rating scales.

A descriptive approach

Much of Lowenthal and Riel's data analysis is highly descriptive. For example, the observations collected in New York City (1972b) are differentiated in particular in terms of the three groups of subjects who helped them there — professional architects, female psychology students, and first year student nurses.

> "The words most frequently used to describe all midtown milieus do vary from group to group: thus *tourist, massive,* and *depressed* figure high among architects, whereas *wealthy* (and other words for money) and *busy* topped the list for both groups of women. The nurses stressed *happy, active,* and *variety,* the Hunter students *crowds, colorful, stores,* and *hurry . . . .* The student nurses tended to assess rather than to describe what they saw, and on the whole expressed reactions that were much more favourable than those of other observers. The architects' comments were the most descriptive and their focus emphasized the general or abstract qualities of the environment more than its specific features. The Hunter College students reacted most emotionally to the city environments, and their responses were the most negative, but these are relatively minor variations within a set of generally accordant descriptive terms used by all three groups." (p. 15)

Responses to each of the different walks are similarly described.

> "To summarize responses to Times Square, the architects bemoaned the discrepancy between its night-time glamour and its day-time drabness, the Hunter students were shocked by its sleaziness and evil, and the nurses responded to it as entertainment and excitement". (p.18)

> ". . . all three groups perceived the West Side Tenements as a

228

slum: the architects in terms of drab, unkempt, deteriorating buildings, the Hunter students in terms of danger and filth, and the nurses in terms of poverty, ethnic solidarity, and neglected children". (p. 19)

The differences in the way New York City is seen by these individuals is related to background differences of age, sex, professional interests, residence and general environmental attitudes. The analysis is also extended into a comparison of impressions of New York with Boston, Cambridge Massachusetts, and Columbus Ohio. A range of important variations emerge between the structures of meaning of the different environments. But it is difficult not to feel dissatisfied with this kind of descriptive information, however readable it may be. Even though the experimental design is an improvement on that of other similar studies, and the analysis more sensitive and humane, it does not go far enough. If the cities, walks, and subjects had been sampled representatively, however, or if one knew that the experiment was to be repeated every few years, the results might have formed an invaluable historical document. As it is Lowenthal and Riel turn to two other themes to try to give their work some conceptual generality.

Is the meaning in the environment or in the words used?

From a semantic point of view it is important to establish whether the impressions gained of environments are controlled by the words with which they are recorded (the 25 bipolar ratings scales), or whether they are environmentally induced. If there is a strong correlation between certain attributes in the way in which they are applied to the environment, is this due to the simple connectivity of the words or to actual environmental experience? Lowenthal and Riel (1972c) compared the correlations between environmental rating scales with the strength of association between the same words when they were judged by a different group of subjects for similarity of meaning in a non-environmental context. They found similarities and differences. While the natural structure of language sometimes coincides with and reinforces environmental experience, at other times the two are opposed. Thus, some of the associations between environmental attributes are universal and invariant, while others are determined by environmental experience. In the latter case the associations may be general to all the environments studied, or vary with locale and/or individuals.

This is an important finding, but scientifically the excursion into semantics is weak. To derive the 'natural structure' of the attributes from inferential judgments made without foundation by 97 individuals is not satisfactory. If the ratings scales had been an actual Semantic Differential it would have been possible to draw on much more valid comparative data from a variety of other contexts of their use. It is a failing of most studies of environmental meaning that they are divorced from the substance of relevant psychological and linguistic work, even when they borrow or mutilate their techniques. The lack of common reference points prevents their making a contribution to semantic knowledge, and prevents them benefitting from the achievements of a more well-established field of knowledge.

Practical significance

Such studies should also have some practical significance. Lowenthal and Riel (1972c) in the last two of their 359 pages indicate what they think might be the relevance of some of their findings for environmental design and management. They list six hypotheses and the implications:

"(1) *People often prefer environments whose character they disagree about* . . .
 In designing a building or an environment, clarity of aim and statement may not be the best goal. People often do not like being in places where perception is specifically directed, and where images are clear and straightforward. Their tolerance for ambiguity in environments may be much higher than most planners realize.

"(2) *Most people like 'nature', but associate it with quite different things, often with contradictory things* . . .
 To strive for 'naturalness' because everyone likes it may

230

result in confusion, if no account is taken of its range of connotations to different people in different circumstances. What people *say* natural means is, moreover, radically different from what they actually link it with in any environment.

"(3) *Men and women disagree in their attitudes toward spatial density and emptiness* . . .

The basic concepts of density and emptiness, together with such related elements as open and bounded, are differently defined, perceived, and responded to by the two sexes. In order to satisfy *both* sets of preferences, density and spaciousness should each be given its due.

"(4) *What people are most aware of in the environment is not what they discuss most freely* . . .

Certain key qualities (e.g. chaos, order, diversity, uniformity) may convey the essence of a multitude of feelings about environments. Unfamiliarity with design vocabulary or inability to structure associations and ideas often makes it difficult for people to convey such feelings accurately or adequately in response to direct questions. Underlying but unspoken agreements and disagreements, likes and dislikes, may be crucial in environmental choices.

"(5) *Preconceptions based on names and sterotypes govern many responses to environment* . . .

Judgments about places may be based more on specific or experiential preconceptions than on objective observations and comparisons. This is not a new discovery, but our data indicate that the effect is far greater than is commonly realized. Only knowledge of individual backgrounds can determine how much this needs to be taken into consideration in environmental design.

"(6) *Things that people feel go naturally together in any environment are not all liked — or disliked — to the same degree; some such clusters include both liked and disliked attributes* . . .

Since people feel that 'good' and 'bad' things go together, it

231

may be fruitless to hope for environments pleasing in all respects. To become aware of the common contradictions in public taste may permit planning to be more realistic, less impossibly utopian." (8 pp.44—46)

Much of this adds up to saying that such qualities as ambiguity, contradiction, variety, and unobvious associations should be incorporated into planned environments. But this is scarcely advice for designers. Lowenthal and Riel did not set out to give them advice. Their "aim was to develop ways of studying environmental responses that would: (1) show how people conceive the everyday outdoor milieu; (2) indicate what connections people tend to make among various environmental attributes; (3) ascertain what kinds of environments people prefer; and (4) measure the extent to which differences in personal background and environmental setting affect these judgments, choices and relationships" (Preface, p.iii). But since these four objectives were to be a means to the "enhancement of environmental quality and resources", the results need to be translated into practical terms. It is unrealistic to expect designers to do this. If environmental studies by social scientists are to be practically useful, their implications in concrete terms must be inherent from the outset. They must be reflected in the methodology, and be quite clear in the discussion of results. Far too many investigations, which in the end could only have been worth doing if they did have practical implications, simply tack them on in a footnote.

Mystery and coherence

Let us return again to the themes which Lynch introduced. His book has in the fifteen years since it appeared been heavily criticized. But although it can be found wanting on nearly every score, it has been seminal to much of the most interesting work done since. We mentioned his idea that mystery combined with coherence are aspects of our pleasure in the city. It too has been taken up recently, by Kaplan (1973), in an attempt to provide a more integrated framework for environmental cognition and preference. He claims that only if an integrated model is proposed of how people experience and make sense of the built environment, and of what sorts of human needs must be satisfied by it, can designers use the results of empirical investigations. The integration would contrast with the scattered miscellany of concepts we have today; it would unify concepts and permit generalizations, both of which are essential for design applications. We shall deal with environmental preferences again in the next two chapters. Kaplan's model will serve as a bridge.

"The cognitive map is a construct that has been proposed to explain how individuals know their environment. It assumes that people store information about their environment in a simplified form and in relation to other information they already have. It further assumes that this information is coded in a structure . . . and that this structure corresponds, at least to a reasonable degree, to the environment it represents . . . [But the map] is schematic, sketchy, incomplete, distorted, and otherwise simplified and idiosyncratic. It is . . . a product of experience . . .

" . . . four domains of knowledge must be included in one's mental map: recognition (knowing where you are, being able to identify the common objects of your environment); prediction (knowing what might happen next, being familiar with what leads to what); evaluation (knowing whether these next things are good or bad, being able to anticipate whether alternative actions have favorable or unfavorable probable outcomes); and action (knowing what to do, being able to think of effective alternatives). Through these processes man structures his uncertain environment and makes it livable."(pp.275–6).

Human needs

Kaplan goes on to suggest that these information processing domains also represent human needs. Man needs to interpret new events in familiar and simplified terms; he has interest and enjoyment from resolving uncertainty; delight in evaluative categorizing; and in 'making a difference', exercising choice, making the environment respond.

An evolutionary argument is proposed.

". . . man evolved as a far-ranging organism, able to relate (and thus take advantage of) environments dispersed in space and thus never experienced all at one time . . . a cognitive map of the spatial environment would be essential for survival . . . If the quality of cognitive map were related to the probability of survival, then those who survived would have been those who loved to explore, who craved to know, whose restlessness and eagerness for new sights constantly led them to map-extending experiences . . . [Man] would ideally station himself along the shifting fringe between the known and the unknown." (pp.277–8).

Purposeful curiosity for the four kinds of knowledge makes man "a motivated, dedicated, addicted . . . builder of cognitive maps".

Designers often ask what people's environmental needs are, looking for something akin to hunger or sex-drive, but Kaplan suggests that it is *process* rather than *content* which defines environmental needs. A need for *information* is different from the primary needs. He claims that the process of information acquisition, and of maintaining and using it gives pleasure and from an evolutionary viewpoint is adaptive.

What, then, are the properties of the environment that would allow the expression of these informational needs and so be most suitable to human beings? Three requirements are vital.

"It must be an environment one can make sense of. Making sense, finding order, uncovering rules and relationships are after all the very essence of environmental knowledge, of the cognitive map by which an individual relates himself to his world. *It must offer novelty, challenge, and uncertainty.* As the unknown becomes known, the frontier tamed, the individual is driven to new ground to practice his powerful processes. There must always be new domains to be comprehended, new problems to be solved, new insights to be won." (p.279).

234

The apparent contradiction here is illusory. Lynch was only the first to show that differentiation rather than simplicity and uniformity is necessary for a legible environment. The differentiation, or variety, must have a *coherence,* however, a perceptible pattern or order, which makes it recognizable. The environment must be *mysterious* and uncertain, but there must also be a discoverable underlying order. Lynch's coherence and mystery are thus two properties of the environment that serve our information-processing needs.

The third property is that:

"*It must permit choice*. The bias to act, to be decisive, to make choices is a profound one . . . People wish to be 'origins', not 'pawns' . . . [People] desire that novelty be available, not inescapable.

"As we consider these informational needs it becomes increasingly obvious that curiosity is not a hobby, that such design dimensions as variety and coherence are not decorations. The designer must unavoidably deal with factors that touch deep and ancient human concerns. His role, in terms of this framework, is neither to dazzle nor to create ambiguity, but to respect these concerns through designs that develop and enhance a sense of place.

"It is hard to escape the conclusions that variety can only be appreciated in the context of order and that order is lifeless and useless without such variety. These considerations apply to an internal model of the environment, to a cognitive structure of how the world works, in very much the same way as they apply to the environment itself. Given the difficult task he faces, the designer in particular needs a map of the domain he is struggling with, a model of the processes with which he must contend." (pp. 281–2).

It is possible that a model of this kind may be of more direct use to designers than specific empirical results. Rather than helping them to solve small parts of a problem piecemeal, social scientists can give them a basic framework to inform the whole of their complex design, though from a scientific point of view one could wish that the model had been put to some empirical test.

235

The images of children

Although Lynch believed that it was more important for designers to be aware of group images of the environment than the range of individual differences, his own investigation did not use samples of people who could be taken to represent significant groups. Nor did he take a representative sample of the general population. The role of individual differences within psychology generally is important enough to ensure that attention has been given to it in subsequent environmental studies. Similarly, group differences in environmental representation are being systematically explored.

Two examples of the latter approach of particular interest are the studies which deal with children, and those which contrast professionals' with laymen's representations. The former can have a particular contribution to make to understanding the basic processes which may underlie environmental representations, by studying their development. The latter will often impinge very directly on practical issues, on policy and decision making.

Black, white and brown

Maurer and Baxter (1972) explored children's imagery of their homes, neighbourhoods, journeys to school, city and their favourite and disliked places. Not only did they look at boys and girls from seven to fourteen years of age, but they included black, white and Mexican American children. Their total sample of 96 children enabled them to disentangle some of the effects of sex, age, and race, despite some imbalance; but since they did not control for intelligence, socioeconomic level, or home background, the variations in imagery they found may be as much due to those factors.

The children were interviewed by a young woman of the same race. They were asked to draw a map of their neighbourhood, of where they lived; to show its boundaries and mark their home; to draw a map of the city of Houston; and again to name the items in it; to describe the journey from home to school; and to say what was their favourite place to play, and what place they did not like.

Contrary to expectation, very few effects were found of age on the children's imagery. The only significant difference between

236

groups was that the younger children drew the neighbourhood much smaller than the older ones. The effect of race was very strong. White children's imagery was much more extensive: more of them were able to draw the city map; their neighbourhood maps covered a larger geographic area; and they referred to more preferred play places than the Mexican and particularly the black children. Several additional observations were suggested as factors underlying this enhanced environmental perspective: the white children's friends lived further from their home; they were more likely to ride than walk to school; and they had lived less time in their present residence, which was perhaps an indication of a greater general mobility. The black children emphasized their home. It was often drawn first and took up a larger relative area on the neighbourhood map. Details, such as doors, windows, chimneys and television sets, were elaborated more.

Not only was there a difference between the races in their mode of transportation to school, but it had an independent effect on the style of their imagery.

"Going to school by bus or car resulted in a high incidence of structure (stores, factories, houses) and pathway elements. Children who walked to school made little use of structures other than houses and relied heavily upon natural environment elements — trees, grass, sky, sun, and animals in their descriptions. The children who travelled by bus reported imagery not unlike Lynch's adult subjects." (p.376).

Maurer and Baxter make it clear that their data do not allow one to decide whether the differences between the races are more appropriately described on a general environmental 'complexity-constriction' dimension; or in terms of 'clinging to versus rejecting' the home. But they do throw some light on an argument put forward by Rainwater (1966) and Wilner et al (1962) that interest and investment in a home by adults can only occur when it is seen as a sanctuary. Because the interior of the home and the neighbourhood are seen as one with regard to safety from danger and threat, only when people feel secure at home will they "push out the boundaries of safety into the larger world". Following this argument, one would expect that drawings of home and neighbourhood would show the same degree of elaboration and would correspond to feelings of safety. The children's drawings, however, did not show this similarity. Where the homes were elaborated the neighbourhood appeared constricted, and vice versa. The case may simply be different for adults and children. The latter have no material investment in the environment, are less aware of many sources of danger and threat, and have a different scale of environmental perspective. It is unfortunate that Maurer and Baxter did not incorporate the implications of the Rainwater hypothesis fully into their research design. With some information on the children's feelings of security, a wider meaning could have been given to their performance on the imagery tasks.

Like Lynch, Maurer and Baxter found that flowers, vegetables and water were strong sources of imageability; though the children in the later study were more aware of birds, animals, sun, sky, trees, grass and other children. Like Lynch's adults they often drew and spoke of pathways, and were familiar with street names. However, their accounts are very much more detailed, intricate and vital. These, and the following points, could have distinct implications for the planning of neighbourhoods and design of houses wherever one was particularly concerned with the interests of children and of disadvantaged groups. Ground level railway crossings and main roads invariably acted as boundaries to the child's mapped neighbourhood. There was no consistency within race, age or sex about their preferred or disliked play places. Places liked by some children could be equally disliked by others.

The psychology of bussing

The effects of mode of transportation to school on children's imagery had been touched on in an earlier study by Lee (1957), which in two important respects was considerably more pointed. It used imagery not as the end of the research strategy, but as an intervening explanatory factor. And the investigation set out to throw light directly on a clearly-defined real-life issue — the centralization of rural primary schools in the county of Devon, England. Centralization meant longer journeys to school for many children. Did this have any harmful effect on them?

Children from 57 rural primary schools (883 in all) were assessed by their teachers on dimensions of 'adjustment'. Those who had short and long walking distances to school (under or over one mile), and those who had a short and long ride (under or over fifteen minutes) were compared. For journeys of approximately equal time those who walked were rated as more adjusted than those who rode. Though for both modes of transport longer journeys were associated with lower ratings for 'energy', 'concentration', 'popularity', 'intelligence' and 'absenteeism'. On 'anxiety', 'depression', 'affection' and 'aggressiveness' there were no significant differences. Children who had a long ride to school were seen as significantly more 'withdrawn'.

It still remains to account for these effects.

"Three alternative explanations were considered. The first was that children who make long journeys come from remote homes where the methods of child rearing are different, where there is lack of social contact with other children or where hereditary predisposition to neurotic disorder exists because they come from 'poor stock'. This hypothesis was examined by breaking down the total sample into subgroups according to residence (market town, village, hamlet or solitary farmstead). Within these groups there were still sufficient children making the different types of journey to retest the main thesis, independent of residence. The association between length and type of journey and classroom adjustment was still evident—so this explanatory hypothesis could be dismissed." (Lee, 1971, p.656).

However, there was a sex difference. Not only were boys less well adjusted than girls, generally; but the apparent effect on them of long journeys was more marked. Age also was relevant. The children were all six or seven years old. The effect of long walking journeys which was serious for six year olds decreased with the older children. But this improvement did not occur with long rides to school; if anything the seven year olds showed poorer adjustment. It is unfortunate that the data are not available to trace the effects in yet older children.

"The second hypothesis [sic] was that children are fatigued by the long journey. The main reason for dismissing this explanation is that a child who sits in a bus for a given period is likely to be *less* fatigued than one who walks, but the results indicate the exact opposite. If one postulates a special and esoteric form of 'stress' which might occur in school buses, it then becomes difficult to account for the deterioration that occurs with the long walking journeys unless totally different explanations are invoked for each kind of journey — and this is non-parsimonious.

"The third explanation involves the psychology of space . . . It was postulated that children who journey to school are experiencing intermittent maternal separation. For the past three decades there has been mounting evidence that young children manifest a variety of symptoms of social and emotional maladjustment if they are separated from their mother . . . This applies not only to cases of prolonged absence but also for short periods. Anything which serves to maintain the connection with mother and home, for example, a line of communication or a comfort object, will help to alleviate the symptoms . . .

"In the case of rural infant children it is the perceived *accessibility* of the home territory and the mother that is so very different for walking and bus children. In the former case, the child walks of his own volition over what very soon becomes familiar territory. He forms a schema of the route which unites the home schema with the school schema and he knows that, although the walk constitutes a psychological barrier greater as a function of its length, he can cross at any time during the school day.

"On the other hand, the bus child builds little in the way of a connecting schema. The journey itself is not articulated by action or any form of decision-making on the part of the child nor recorded in his cognitive structure. At best he may register a disconnected set of images but, more important, once the child has been deposited at the gate of the school, the bus disappears for six and a half hours and the main means of home access is removed as surely as the kicking away of a gangplank." (pp. 656-7).

It should be noted that the role of imagery as a mediator between the journey to-and-from school and poor adjustment is only hypothesized. No data were collected from the children, as might have been done, to attempt to invalidate the hypothesis. But at the level of suggestion the third explanation gives a poignant meaning to a child's representation of his environment and has clear implications for decision-makers.

Some work by geographers

Much less clear is the geographical work of Gould and White (1974). In a typical experiment they delineated the mental maps of adolescents in various parts of Britain who were about to leave school. The pupils gave their preference order for the 92 counties of Britain as places to live in; aggregated preferences were translated into 'desirability contours'. Regular and distinct differences between their patterns were found for the twenty-three school locations. What is missing from this and most of their other studies is any evidence as to what the representations might mean for people's behaviour. In the final chapter of their book the authors make a great many very plausible suggestions about the wider meaning of mental maps. But throughout a series of investigations the validity, and particularly the predictive validity, of findings is passed over. Until that is established any attempts to demonstrate the practical significance of such studies is bound to be unconvincing.

However, the more general significance of environmental representation is suggested very powerfully by the developmental work of another team of geographers (Blaut *et al*, 1970). They have shown that "pre-literate children of school-entering age can (1) interpret a vertical aerial photograph, hence perform the mapping transformations of scale reduction and projective rotation, (2) abstract from the photographic image to a system of highly iconic map signs, (3) use the reduced, rotated, abstracted presentation in solving a simulated route-planning problem and, therefore, (4) engage a real, if primitive, form of map-reading, map-making and map use." (p. 346).

The abilities they demonstrated go far beyond any that were expected. In some ways these young children showed skill superior to that of their elders. If 'mapping behaviour' of this kind emerges at so early an age, surely it is an indication that these representations are fundamental and of considerable adaptive importance. Mapping, like drawing and other forms of representation (*cf*. Hochberg and Brooks, 1962) may not be so artificial a medium as we have believed.

Theoretical considerations

The theoretical background to the development of environmental representation takes in several of psychology's most prestigious scientists. Hart and Moore (1971) centre their review of this field around some of the concepts of Werner and of Piaget.

"In the sensorimotor period of development the infant moves in a space of action. His orientation to the larger environment is totally egocentric at this period, and he has no topographical representations.

"As spatial actions become internalized through the dual process of assimilation of impressions from the environment into the sensorimotor schemas and accommodations of the schemas to the environment, the child's first images or iconic representations of space develop. This leads to a major new period, that of preoperational space, the beginning of representational space. During this period, most topological relations are formed and projective and euclidean relations begin to be constructed. Egocentric orientation gives way to the onset of a fixed system of reference, centred first on the home (domocentricity) and later on a small number of uncoordinated routes, landmarks, and/or familiar places. The child no longer operates solely in a space of action for he begins to represent his routes (route-type representations). Generally this is a period of gradual differentiation of the child from his environment, of the child's point of view from that of other people, and of elements and relationships from each other within the environment.

"These differentiated but uncoordinated representations of discrete parts of a total space (e.g. routes, landmarks, barriers etc.) begin to be coordinated with the onset of concrete operations during the early school years. Many other specific developments occur, such as the concept of the straight line,

242

paralleleity, proportional intervals, and angles. As we have shown, the child's understanding of these relations is a result of the grouping of partial structures to be coordinated whole through the equilibration of assimilation and accommodation. The child is now able to coordinate perspectives and construct a euclidean system of reference. Both of these are most important for his understanding of the large scale environment. Furthermore, the child's individual route-type topographical representations become coordinated into a comprehensive survey-type representation.

"Finally with the onset during early adolescence of formal operations, which are a reflective abstraction from concrete operations, the individual is not only able to act in space and mentally coordinate his thoughts about concrete objects and spatial relations, but he is also able to reflect on these accomplishments and consider a theoretical space totally abstracted from any concrete particulars. The concepts of length, distance, area, and volume, all of which depend on the formal concept of infinity, are also able to be constructed and conserved. Thus both a true metric space and a totally abstract space are possible for the adolescent.

"It seems from the research literature on the autogenetic development of spatial cognition that there are five domains of parallel development: levels of organization of spatial cognition (sensorimotor, preoperational, concrete operational, and formal operational); types of spatial relations (topological, projective, and euclidean), modes of representation (enactive, ikonic and symbolic); systems of reference (egocentric, fixed, and co-ordinated); and types of topographical representations (route and survey). Each of these developments in turn parallels the four periods of general intellectual development discovered by Piaget and the orthogenetic principle and developmental progressions elucidated by Werner . . . [There] seem to be certain direct correspondences and explanatory relations between the different domains of the development of spatial cognition." (pp. 63-4).

However suggestive these explanatory ideas may be very little empirical work to test them has been done specifically in the field of environmental studies. But this is undoubtedly an area in which environmental psychology could make a significant contribution to issues more in the mainstream of psychology.

Planners and their public

An early study which looked at both professional and lay people's representations of the environment compared the central city images of Rotterdam, Amsterdam and The Hague as elicited from twenty architects and planners and approximately twenty-five inhabitants of each city (de Jonge, 1962). In common with Lynch he identified paths, nodes, edges, districts and landmarks as the main elements of the image, and concluded that most variation in the images was attributable to variations in the form of the cities themselves rather than to his subjects. His sample, however, was very small. When Heinemeyer (1967) interviewed a more carefully structured sample of 320 people from twelve socially and spatially diverse areas of Amsterdam he found considerable variation in the image of the city centre. An individual's age, sex, social status and patterns of use of the city could all make a difference to his representation of it. It seems likely that both social and psychological characteristics and variations in environmental form and attributes will affect its representation.

A comprehensive perception study in Venezuela

The different images held by different groups takes on a more vital meaning when they are considered in the light of design or policy-making. And it is in this context that the images of professionals can be particularly important. In the new Venezuelan city of Ciudad Guayana, Appleyard (1969) found several instances of how important they may be. Initially the planners fell back on their own perceptions, supported by their professional rules, equipment, and 'objective' information. But their conception of the city was quite distinct from those held by the population.

Appleyard interviewed seventy-five people randomly selected from each of four districts of the city as it stood. In addition two élite groups were interviewed — twenty in the Country Club and twenty engineers responsible for the city's development. They were asked a range of questions to assess the extent and nature of their knowledge of the city: drawing a city map and recalling important features, describing a journey through the city, particular buildings and districts, and so on.

The planners' knowledge of the city was more extensive and complex, both because they had carried out field and desk surveys and because they had access to more places in the city than the inhabitants. The latter's knowledge was "home-based, with occasional islands around shopping centres, work places or previous places of residence. It was shaped either like a star or like a constellation of stars with tentacles of knowledge along the transportation system . . . Their view was closely correlated with the use of the city . . . [their] world was a familiar territory unclear at the fringes of knowledge; the designer's world was thin in the center but bounded by the distinct outlines of rivers and urban development . . . In psychological language, the inhabitants saw the 'figure', the designers saw the 'ground' ". (pp. 429-430). The inhabitants' knowledge varied with the level of their education, where they lived, and the length of their residence in the city.

"This information can have several implications for policy. Besides improving the knowledge of city designers, we could consider extending and coordinating knowledge among different population groups in order to reduce conflicts, misperceptions and errors . . . Diversity, clearer structuring, and the location of facilities to draw groups across the city are some variables that could be manipulated." (p. 430).

The components of knowledge of the city were examined, particularly landmarks. These were usually buildings, and were known for a combination of their distinctness of form, their visibility, and their functional or symbolic significance.

"The role of imageability is confirmed. The role of personal action in the perception of buildings, either through their direct use or through their visible position on the paths of movements, becomes very clear. The importance of visibility, in fact, emphasizes the roles of both action and location in the recall of

245

urban elements. Finally the part played by significance suggests the importance of prior experience to urban perception." (pp. 433-4)

Again there were differences in attention to these characteristics between different groups, depending on location, length of residence and education.

"The educated, for instance, concentrated more on the skeletal size, shape, and contour — rather than the surface characteristics of form, and more on significance, using a narrower range of attributes in their selection of elements than the less educated." (p. 435).

In line with this higher degree of abstraction and conceptual economy, the educated also drew simpler maps of the city.

This type of information would enable one to predict and adjust the impact of a building in relation to people's attention and use needs. For example, stricter controls could be put on the form and use (significance) of buildings in areas of high visibility along a city's main road system and near to major intersections. The way in which buildings are known through action and experience suggests the inadequacy of the planner's traditional design tools — the land-use map and site plan, neither of which record the critical variables of inhabitants' movements, the visible form of the environment, or significant patterns of use.

The maps which inhabitants drew bore little relation to the structure which the planners had attempted to impose on Ciudad Guayana to give it compactness and coherence. Neither the large-scale geometrical order of the circulation system nor the infilling of spaces between settlements were represented in the maps. Most of them were sequential using as elements roads and river barriers. The rest were spatial, using buildings and districts. Appleyard (1970) has produced an intriguing typology of these maps showing how they range from the primitive and topological to the more elaborated and 'positional'. The kind of map an individual produced depended crucially on his level of education. But at the same time all the inhabitants structured the city in the same way as they recalled its landmarks (above): through relationships created by action, form, visibility and significance.

246

"Given this array of structuring methods and the variety of structuring styles, the designer must face the task of structuring the city to be minimally comprehensible and coherent for all population groups, particularly those who find it more difficult: those with less education, bus travellers, new immigrants, housewives and others. At the same time there are powerful reasons for developing a rich and complex structure for those who can cope with it. If the city is not organized for each population group, then it stands the danger of being either overstructured or understructured for certain groups. It might be monotonous, repetitious, and authoritarian for some or confused and disintegrated for others.

". . . The pattern of physical character should be designed around the settings and patterns of habitual journeys in different travel modes. Prominent and visible sites, skylines, hilltops and spurs should be selected now to give future landmarks a high range of visibility. The pattern of social significance and the naming of related elements should be part of the design." (pp. 442-3)

The planning of a city can be viewed as the task of communicating its significant aspects to different sectors of the population. In Ciudad Guayana many important places were *perceptually* invisible and insignificant because of their location; while insignificant elements such as garages and hoardings were overemphasized. In parts of the city the superimposition of major traffic systems on a pedestrian settlement led to confusion as to where facilities could be expected to be located. The communicability of different facilities will vary according to whether their users are regular or irregular. Some, such as employment agencies or cinemas, may not be made visible enough in the city's structure, despite people's needs, because they are not on the planner's list of key facilities; their precise location is left to the developer.

In a new city change and uncertainty will figure prominently. One of the most potent influences in the Venezuelan city on people's changing representation of their environment was development in the circulation system, and particularly the opening of a new riverbridge. New buildings were less often commented on in interviews. People's anticipations of future changes depended on projections of current trends, since the official plans were not well known. They were guided by building operations currently in train rather than by any ideas of the city's growth pattern or cause and effect.

"The programming of information about change is as important as change itself. The physical construction of a new city proceeds in a manner that creates a jerky sequence in the mind of the inhabitant. New areas are opened up, or links are suddenly made that shift flow patterns and emphasis very rapidly. Ignorance or uncertainty creates surprise, anxiety, and sometimes resentment. Expectations delayed can be equally frustrating. Although ambiguity about future plans may give the planner flexibility of action, it will not help to get public support." (p. 449).

Two critical practical points remain to be added to Appleyard's thorough and penetrating study of environmental representations in Ciudad Guayana. Does knowledge of the city have a significant effect on people's behaviour and other responses? And can planners use this type of survey information in the design process?

"Knowledge in fact exerts a powerful influence over behaviour patterns, attitudes, locational decisions, and ultimately the physical form of the city. The choice of routes to take, establishments to use, jobs to apply for, all depend on perceptions of the choices. Similarly, locational decisions for new industrial enterprises, community services, or commercial establishments are dependent on knowledge of the urban layout. There were many places in Ciudad Guayana where development took place because the location was visible. On the other hand, the projected Centro Civico never expanded because it was hidden from view. Finally the physical construction of the city is affected by the conceptions of the city's boundaries. Witness the contrast between the professionally designed parts of the city and the indigenous areas, built by non-professionals. The former were precisely oriented and patterned from the air but fitted uneasily on the ground; the latter looked haphazard from the air but, like medieval villages, made a better fit with the local context. Both were clear physical expressions of the mental representations of their creators." (p. 450).

On the second point, Appleyard has little to say. He recognizes the temptation for planners to stay with known methods of work. And he sees that while many of the implications of his research lead to a 'pluralistic' city design, this is not an easy goal to achieve. Part of the answer may be in treating the designer's role as educative, a matter of innovating, leading and exploring rather than looking for normative or multi-normative solutions. It may be better to propose structures which are only partly validated by contact with the clients' perceptions and values than to impose a structure which appears to fit them tightly. It is commonplace that educative procedures have to be pluralistic, to deal with the great variety in the students in any class. Although Appleyard does not succeed in demonstrating empirically the usefulness of information about environmental representations to the decision-maker, he probably comes closer to it than any other investigator to date.

Conclusion

In many ways the material we have discussed in the chapter is more conventionally 'psychological' than the contents of the two chapters which follow and which continue our macroscopic treatment of the environment. The notion of 'images' of the city and of environmental 'representations', the focus on the city as an information source, a complex entity challenging our under-standing, is highly mentalistic.

Image research is also typically psychological in its capacity to find self-generated problems. We have illustrated this in terms of the distance estimation work. The preoccupation with sometimes sophisticated quantification, the absence of representative sampling of subjects and stimuli, and the unwillingness to argue the relevance of the work is characteristic of much academic psychology. The worst fault is probably the failure to exploit the potentially very fruitful link to mainstream psychological work on imagery (*cf.* Reed, 1973). Environmental images have peculiar properties, for example their sequential nature, as well as ecological validity. They promise a new dimension to extending our understanding of classical problems in psychology.

There is also a tendency for image research to spawn increasing numbers of studies of individual differences. We have tried to make the best of this tendency in our selection of the studies discussed here. The danger is that researchers eagerly measure differences between any individuals, or groups, which are conveniently to hand, without the constraint of firmly specified practical or theoretical issues. The studies by Lowenthal and Riel and by Maurer and Baxter may be the best that one can expect without such constraints. When there are practical implications in the results — for example, Lee's study of bussing, the mapping work of Blaut and his colleagues — one can get outside the confines of the research itself. It may be significant that Appleyard's work in Venezuela was not only a more comprehensive approach to imagery than any others; it was also more closely integrated, conceptually and operationally, with a concurrent set of policy and decision making requirements.

At a less empirical level there are intriguing possibilities opened up here by the contributions of Wood, Kaplan and Hart and Moore. The latter are very derivative, but we would argue that if they backed up their theoretical account with a critical programme of empirical research, there is every chance that an environmental approach would be shown to add new information to our understanding of developmental processes. Kaplan's model attempts to be more innovative and is particularly useful in turning our attention away from environmental content toward the processing of environmental information; but this model also is surely in need of empirical test. One wonders how susceptible it is to adequate testing.

The sensitive and enthusiastic exploration of San Christobal las Casas is a lonely beacon in this chapter. It deserves to be more readily available. There are signs that the *experiences* of the researcher and of those whom he is studying are becoming more acceptable as a proper focus for efforts in psychology. It would be encouraging to believe that Wood's expedition had blazed a trail that many environmental psychologists in future would follow.

Chapter Eight

Living in the City

Peter Stringer

The urban environment is studied by many disciplines other than psychology. Economists, geographers, political scientists and sociologists, and of course urban planners, often place it in a more central position than psychologists are ever likely to. Nevertheless, life in the city has a number of features which are of distinct psychological interest. Social psychology in particular can contribute much to our understanding of the processes of urban life. It can also offer suggestions as to how to improve the experience.

There are three main threads which can be drawn out of the empirical studies which have been done to date. The most conspicuous is a viewpoint which treats the city as an 'unnatural habitat' (*cf.* Ittleson *et al*, 1974). It is seen as a source of stress and strain, noisy, polluted and overcrowded. The question of urban noise has been dealt with in Chapter Three, and pollution will be discussed in Chapter Nine. Here we shall focus attention on the city as a container of large numbers of people. We shall see that cognitive and social variables are more useful than physical variables in understanding crowding and its consequences.

The residential areas of cities have been studied primarily in terms of the satisfactions and dissatisfactions which they generate. The objective has usually been to look for ways of improving such places, or to understand why redevelopment schemes have not been as successful as their designers hoped. The dilemma is that physical improvements in housing have in recent years often been associated with a break-up in the social fabric of the community. The network of personal relationships in the neighbourhood may be more crucial to satisfactory urban life than the shape and condition of the bricks and mortar which contain them.

The third main topic discussed in this chapter deals with various attempts to enable the public to have an influence on their environment before final decisions on its form are made. It has been demonstrated, as we also saw in the previous chapter, that the planners and their public can have very different ways of making sense of their environment and different ideas about its future development. The usual technique for tapping the public's ideas is by some kind of sample survey. A number of disadvantages of this method are discussed here, and suggestions are made for improved surveys.

Some of these issues of urban living may be resolved by taking a more participatory approach to environmental decision making. This approach would recognize the unlikelihood of solving urban problems by purely physical or social engineering. The solution will come from an experience of greater awareness and involvement in urban processes and change, on the part of all its residents and users. Mutual education of planners and public will be necessary.

The indifferent city

A frequent criticism of cities as places to live is that they appear to generate in the inhabitants an indifference to others which is not found in towns and villages. This may be manifested in many ways, from rude jostling on crowded streets to the apathy of bystanders when they see another person in distress. American psychologists who have attempted to study the problem like to introduce it with the notorious incident of Catherine Genovese. Coming home from work in the early hours one morning in 1964, she was stabbed by an assailant. Although the stabbing continued for half an hour, during which time she repeatedly called out for help, no help of any kind was offered. None of the thirty-eight residents in the respectable neighbourhood where the incident occurred, who admitted having actually witnessed a part of the attack, even telephoned for the police.

Bystander apathy

Some possible psychological processes which may underlie the apathy of bystanders who witness an emergency or crisis have been put forward by Latané and Darley (1970). In a series of laboratory experiments they showed that bystanders were least likely to intervene in the situation if one or more other bystanders were present. The situations included working in a room into which smoke was introduced through a vent; hearing a woman in an adjoining room apparently fall and injure herself; witnessing someone steal a case of beer from a shop; and hearing a fellow experimental subject apparently suffering an epileptic seizure. Whom the bystander was with seemed to influence whether or not he would report the smoke or the theft, or go to the woman or fellow-student's help. He was least likely to intervene if those with him were experimental 'stooges' who put on a show of deliberate unconcern. A stranger with him provided a moderate amount of inhibition; while a friend provided the least. But with a friend subjects were still significantly less likely to intervene than when they were alone.

Latané and Darley suggest that two processes may lead to the failure to intervene — social influence, and the diffusion of responsibility. The bystander may be influenced not to intervene by his interpretation of the other witnesses' reactions. If a number of bystanders all see indecision or an apparent lack of concern in one another, a 'group ignorance' may develop. Even if the situation is seen as an emergency which should be dealt with, the presence of others makes it less necessary to take action oneself; and the responsibility for not helping does not lie with one person, but is diffused over all the bystanders.

The reason why bystander apathy of the kind that allowed Catherine Genovese to die is reported more often from large cities is perhaps due to their different social environment. There are more likely to be other witnesses to an urban than a rural emergency. Even if they cannot be seen we will suppose that they are nearby, and will give the necessary help. If a crowd collects around a dying man in a city street, they are unlikely to be acquainted with him; nor with one another. There are no bonds between the actors, and no social relationship in which they may have to live with the consequences of their inactivity.

Most of Latané and Darley's experiments were carried out under laboratory conditions. The subjects knew that they were taking part in some kind of psychological investigation. Such studies certainly demonstrate that bystander apathy is a phenomenon to be reckoned with, and suggest some underlying processes. But they cannot begin to give us any information about the 'natural history' of social irresponsibility; nor about its environmental overtones, whether and under what circumstances for example it is more frequent in large cities than in small towns and rural areas.

Helpfulness in the city and in the small town

Two more naturalistic studies, with a distinct environmental focus, have been carried out by graduate students at the City University of New York (Milgram, 1970). They compare the behaviour of city and small-town inhabitants who have been asked to give help to a stranger.

In one case the student investigators rang on 160 doorbells, variously in the centre of New York City (Manhattan) and in six small towns in a nearby county. They asked to be allowed to use the telephone. They explained that they had mislaid the address of a nearby friend, and wished to speak to him. They were given leave to enter people's homes to use the telephone on average more than twice as often in the small towns as in Manhattan. For one male student there was a five-fold difference in the frequency with which he gained entry. The two female students had generally greater success than the men, even in Manhattan; though there they were only helped on 40 per cent of occasions, as opposed to more than 90 per cent in the small towns. The city dwellers rarely even opened the door to the students. If they reacted at all, they called through the door, or eyed the visitor through a peephole. Clearly the inhabitants of Manhattan felt vulnerable to casual callers.

In another experiment the element of physical vulnerability was eliminated by contacting people by telephone to ask them for a favour. The female researchers in this case pretended to be a long-distance caller who had been put through to the wrong number. Nevertheless, they said, the person answering could be of help to them. They asked her a series of increasingly more onerous favours, including asking her to 'hold on' for a full minute. Subjects in the city were less likely to be helpful or informative than those in small towns; and this was the case both for housewives who were called and for shop assistants. However the researchers did find quite a high level of cooperation from the urban women.

A stereotyped notion of aloof and unhelpful urbanites is unlikely to be found to apply in all circumstances. To fully understand the differing nature of social relations in different physical environments one has to examine a wide variety of types of interaction. The lack of concern that people show one another will depend on who they are (for example sex, age, race), for what purpose they are interacting, and by what medium.

In describing these experiments Milgram (1970) has attempted to explain the contrasts that they reveal between city and small town behaviour in socio-psychological terms. He points to differences in *role enactment* (for example, the way in which shop assistants perform their tasks in the two situations), in the evolution of *norms* (impersonality and aloofness may not be universal in cities, but it is accepted), in *cognitive adaptation* (being unresponsive to much of the mass of stimuli that impinge in cities), and in *competitiveness* (for facilities such as taxis, tube train seats, goods in shops). All these differences he sees as being instances of the city dwellers' adaptation to the 'overload' of encounters, information and stimuli by which they would otherwise be overwhelmed.

In the last chapter we described Lowenthal and Riel's (1972a) work, which provided comparative descriptions of several North American cities largely in terms of their connotations for individuals. It is also possible to characterize different environments with reference to the behaviour that occurs in them. Feldman (1968) carried out a comparative study of behaviour towards compatriots and foreigners in Paris, Athens, and Boston.

Although he was interested principally in cultural variations, a similar method could be used within a simple cultural setting. He examined five distinct behavioural situations: (a) asking inhabitants of a city for street directions; (b) asking them to post a letter; (c) asking them if they had just dropped some money (belonging in fact, to the researcher); (d) deliberately paying too much in a shop, to see if the excess would be returned; and (e) finding whether taxi-drivers overcharged strangers, or went by devious routes. The application of a range of such objective behavioural measures in a naturalistic setting will tell us more about urban life than could be learned through laboratory experiments.

The ecological approach

In the context of Barker's (1968) ecological approach to psychology, Bechtel (1971) carried out an equally objective comparison of urban and small town environments. He compared the residential areas of a small town with those of two city blocks, using Barker's 'behaviour setting' survey technique.

"The behavior setting is a natural unit. If one looks out on the wide ocean of human behavior with its currents and eddies he notices behavior settings as natural occurring 'nodes' which are as easily recognized by the persons who take part in them as by the behavioral scientist. In a community, the people who inhabit the buildings of the community sort themselves out into behavior settings in order to get the business of living done. The behavior settings are the office meetings, the school classes, the stores, the streets and sidewalks, the athletic games, the church services, . . . the swimming pool party, and all the myriad of human activities that are tied to a particular place and time.

"A behavior setting has a specific geographical location that it is tied to, a specific and regular time for which it begins and ends and a standing pattern of behavior which is understood by its participants. There are particular physical parts of the setting that are necessary to it, merchandise, bottles, chairs, tables, whatever objects are necessary for setting performance.

258

And the geography, the physical objects, the time limits and the pattern of behavior are all tied together and inseparable. They form a behavior setting unit.

"Once one knows the behavior settings of the community it is possible to predict in very extensive and intricate detail the global behavior of any individual or group in that community. No other known technique of behavioral science can make this claim." (Bechtel, 1971, p.348)

Bechtel's main finding was that there were nearly three times as many behaviour settings available to the city residents as to those in the small town. Yet it is the latter who have control over their activities in the available settings. In cities people tend very often to be onlookers or followers. There are too many people in each setting. In the terminology of ecological psychology the settings are 'over-manned', with the result that people are much less involved.

'Over-manning'

The importance of 'under-manning' and of involvement for environmental satisfaction has been emphasized by other ecological studies. Barker and Gump (1964), for example, suggested the superiority of small over large schools could be explained in this way. Under-manned settings "require more of each person in the way of performance to get the job done. The result is that in the under-manned setting the average person has a greater amount of participation in the setting and, consequently, a greater degree of satisfaction and a sense of greater obligation to the setting." Wicker (1969) arrived at similar conclusions about churches. It was not the actual size of the setting that produced satisfaction and a sense of obligation to it, but the level of participation.

These results might be used to suggest that the problems of apathy in the city which we have been discussing are the result of the over-manning of its settings. It may force people to be uninvolved and 'marginal'. Such an account is different from the socio-pathological one suggested by Latané and Darley. There is no reference now to social interaction, nor to individual variations

259

in personality or cognitive processes. Ecological psychology attempts to explain behaviour without making inferences about individual differences or mediating psychological events. There are attractions in this approach to the environmental psychologist. It is always practised in naturalistic contexts, and many of the studies to date have focussed on comparisons between behaviour settings defined by those features of the physical environment, such as schools, hospitals, streets, towns, cities, in which the environmental psychologist is interested. But it is important to recognize that in its assumptions ecological psychology represents a marked break with most existing psychological methods. The view of man which it implies may not be acceptable to all.

Bechtel goes further than Milgram or Latané and Darley, in making some suggestion as to how the problems of large cities might be tackled; even if the practical details are missing.

"The solution, once this problem is understood, is to create many more under-manned settings, settings that will be deliberately constructed so that not enough people will be available to get all the daily task of living done without effort. The solution is to change the city from a low demand, over-manned environment to a high demand, under-manned environment. The solution is simple to propose but not simple to enact. It means decentralization, fragmentation of many efforts, and a new value system that replaces mechanical efficiency of social structure as the highest goal with the necessity of participation of members as the highest good." (p.352).

Crowding

The more usual way in which we talk about what Bechtel calls 'under-manned settings' is in terms of crowding. In the popular mind this has often been identified as the principal evil of urban living. When Zlutnick and Altman (1972) carried out a review of ten years of popular periodical literature, they found as many as seventeen different effects being attributed to crowding and overpopulation. Ecologists and politicians, as well as journalists, were making wide claims for physical, social, and psychological effects. They cited starvation, pollution, slums, disease and physical malfunctions; poor education; poor physical and mental health facilities, crime, riots and war; drug addiction, alcoholism, family disorganization, withdrawal, aggression, and decreased quality of life. It is a formidable list.

Correlational and experimental 'effects'

The formal evidence for effects of this kind is very slender indeed. Correlations between population density (people per acre or people per dwelling) and indicators such as rates of crime, mental illness, and disease frequently do turn out to be marked and positive. However, in nearly all studies which have been made it is impossible to conclude that there is a causal relationship between density and social disorganization. High living density is usually associated with many other factors which might equally lead to breakdown: for example, low economic status, poor educational and other social service facilities, racial discrimination. Complex multivariate statistical methods might be able to detect associations of one variable with density independently of other variables, provided very large sets of reliable data were available. Unfortunately, however, a simple picture of statistical relations would carry few implications for action. If one is dealing with a *system* of interconnecting phenomena, they will need to be treated as a system. Reducing density is unlikely, by itself, to produce any of the desired results.

The very sparse experimental work on the effects of density is equally inconclusive. For example, Freedman, Klevansky and Ehrlich (1971) examined the effects of density on performance of intellectual tasks. Subjects carried out both simple and complex tasks under varying conditions. They worked by themselves, with five to nine persons to the room, in spaces ranging between 35 and 160 square feet in floor area. No differences were found in their performance on any task as a function of the density under which they worked.

Density has been observed to have effects on the behaviour of young children, however. Hutt and Vaizey (1966) examined their aggressive behaviour and social interaction under different 'social densities' — that is with between six and twelve children in the same spatial area. Social interaction decreased and aggression increased in the larger groups. However, in a later study Hutt and McGrew (1967) found that both social interaction and aggression increased with density. In this case density was manipulated by having the same-sized groups in spaces of different areas.

Density is not crowding

Density is not a simple variable. Any effects it may have on an individual's behaviour are likely to be mediated by the absolute number of other people present and the size of the space in which he is as well as by the proportional number of people per unit of area.

More recently, Stokols (1972) has suggested that the physical variable of density is far from equivalent in its effects to the psychological construct 'crowding' which is more properly the focus of one's interest. The most obvious difference between the two is that the experience of 'being crowded' involves an individual's cognitive interpretation of density in a particular context. Hence one might feel crowded in any two situations where the density of other people was very different; or one might be able to accept a high density of others at a party which would be very uncomfortable in, say, a supermarket or railway station. As with many other pyschological questions, the nature of crowding and its effects is unlikely to be understood and explained unless the external variable (density) is examined through the processes of cognitive mediation.

Environmental, social and individual aspects of crowding

Zlutnick and Altman (1972) have described some of the complexities of the psychological phenomenon of crowding. They distinguish environmental, social and personal characteristics of crowding. Within the environment they make the important distinction between 'inside' and 'outside' densities. They suggest that the psychological effect of environmental density may depend on the relation between the two facets. Thus, suburbia is characterized by low densities both inside and outside the home, while at the other extreme a city ghetto or slum usually has high densities both in the home and in the neighbourhood. In between,

262

a rural area may combine high domestic with low community densities; and a wealthy residential area in a city will have the relations reversed. Two other features which may determine the effects of crowding in the environment are its temporal duration, how long one is subjected to it; and the richness of resources that are available to alleviate the influence of crowding. It is certainly typical of the ghetto or slum that its inhabitants are able to see little chance of ever moving to a less crowded environment. They live in houses which may be equivalent in space and density to many outside the ghetto or slum, but which almost invariably are low in the quality of decor, spatial layout and general facilities.

At a social level the most important characteristic of crowding may be that it affects one's ability to control interactions with others. Social interaction is fundamental to the human way of life, but it is essential that it be susceptible to control. We influence our relations with others by environmental manipulations, such as the way in which we arrange furniture. We use both verbal and non-verbal communications. In addition to the content of our utterances, their inflection, silences, interruptions, and so on control the tempo and style of interaction. Non-verbal cues such as eye contact and bodily posture perform the same function. And we have 'autistic' mechanisms for cutting off from others or for heightening the level of contact with them. Zlutnick and Altman suggest that one of the effects of crowding is to break down these control mechanisms. In extreme conditions one might expect various forms of social pathology to result. (Analogous findings certainly have been reported in animal research by Calhoun (1966) and others, even if one should be slow to draw too much from the comparison). In these terms the advantage of rural or luxury urban living in the scheme above would be that one can exchange a high density in one situation for a low density in another. There would always be some context in which one could control interaction with others.

In addition to environmental and social aspects of crowding there are those which might be termed 'individual'. A person's present interpretation of a situation as crowded may depend on his personal past experience. A rural child may later be able to tolerate high inside densities, but find relatively less dense outside environments intolerable because he is used to very sparse outside environments. Individuals will vary in their perceived or actual ability to control interaction. Those of high status may have the power, and extroverts may have the social skill, to adapt to high density situations and find them enjoyable, but this may be beyond many others. Finally, confounded expectations or predictions about the density that will obtain in a particular situation may lead one to feel crowded in circumstances that in every other way might be quite acceptable.

If crowding is analysed into separate components at the physical, social and psychological levels, it is not intended to suggest that these levels are unconnected. Crowding is not only multidimensional; its dimensions interact. These features must be reflected both in the research strategies by which one investigates crowding and in the policy decisions and solutions one adopts to counteract any of its ill-effects.

Residential areas

The argument in this chapter so far has been that if the contemporary city is a source of stress to people it is because of the way it disrupts social relationships. It is not so much that cities can be noisy, dirty, smelly, unaesthetic; but that their physical arrangements encourage patterns of activity in which proximity between two persons is accidental and without any particular significance to either of them.

Slum clearance or community break-up?

The unsatisfactory nature of many urban housing developments, especially those built in city centres for working class occupants, may be explained in similar terms. Several studies have suggested that the working class have been able to adapt to poor physical conditions in the older urban areas, to poverty and run-down housing, and to compensate through an informal but very rich set of social relationships. The East London study of Young and Willmott (1957) pointed to this conclusion. Redevelopment uprooted East Enders from an environment in which the family, friends, work, and the pub or shop on the corner were close to home and underlain by a close set of social ties. The subsequent move to suburbia introduced a new style of life that emphasized the nuclear rather than the extended family or sex-segregated peer groups.

In the case of Londoners relocated from the East End there is little evidence of long-term distress, perhaps because surburbia does offer an alternative, if restricted, social setting. In other cases, however, where the physical provision does not offer this, serious problems may arise. The notorious, and now demolished, Pruitt-Igoe Housing Project in St. Louis has been the subject of a number of studies which suggest that it was its architectural design which was at the root of the social pathology observed there. More specifically, it was the absence of semi-public spaces and facilities which prevented informal social relations from developing. The absence of these relations resulted, in turn, in a failure of any form of social control over behaviour outside the privacy of each dwelling. Every part of the project was vandalized, windows were smashed, rubbish was littered in the streets and stairways. Fences and play facilities were destroyed. Lifts and service areas were used as urinals. Residents went in danger of assault and theft.

Interestingly, those who lived in Pruitt-Igoe did not find the project entirely unsatisfactory (Yancey, 1972). There was a distinction in the residents' attitudes to their own accommodation and to the project as a whole. A marked dislike for the project was often accompanied by a liking for many features of the space where the family lived. For example, separate bedrooms for parents and children, constant hot water and modern plumbing were new experiences to many residents and were fully appreciated. By contrast, slum dwellers are prone to criticize their dwelling for its poor physical condition, while expressing satisfaction with the neighbouring areas.

The relative provision of places where children may play is a striking point of difference between older urban residential areas and the redevelopment zones. In many instances the actual physical provision and the facilities offered are better on the new developments. But the complaint is always that the children have to play too far from the dwelling for adequate supervision. More important than this in the long run, however, is the fact that the children's play does not encourage the growth of wider social links between adults. In the older areas a young child or a child newly arrived plays close to the home. In this way "small, continuous face-to-face associations develop around the immediate proximity of the home" (Yancey, 1972, p.132). Neighbours know where different children and their mothers belong as a result of continuous casual contact in an environment where high visibility outside the dwelling is the rule. Everybody can be instantly identified and categorized. A stranger is quickly noticed. In the newer developments this is not the case. Physical proximity of dwellings does not ensure contact between neighbours. Where the majority are strangers, an intruder is not noticed.

Satisfaction and dissatisfaction

The different satisfaction with public and private parts of residential areas in older urban and redevelopment sites is an important observation. It is a common tactic of planners and other urban decision makers to identify priorities on the basis of problems or shortcomings noted by themselves or reported to them. At present random sample surveys are increasingly being carried out by planning authorities as a part of 'public participation' exercises. The public is believed to participate in planning decisions, to the extent that a representative cross-section of them are asked to identify the objects of their satisfaction and dissatisfaction in the physical environment. We shall consider the value of these surveys again later in the chapter. But for the moment it is worth pointing out that there is a frequent emphasis in the questions asked on *dis*satisfaction. Planners appear to see their role as being one primarily of righting wrongs, filling in gaps, and relieving tensions. They may or may not believe that the people for whom they plan also see their world defined by negatives.

The consequences of this emphasis in slum clearance programmes have been serious. The over-riding goal has been to remove objectionable physical living conditions, and to replace them as economically as possible, with regard where possible to aesthetic and technological fashions, by dwellings whose characteristics are again defined in entirely physical terms. The satisfactions that slum dwellers derived from their social environment, which was itself dependent on aspects of the physical environment, were

266

uncharted or ignored. It is not surprising, then, that after redevelopment the sources of satisfaction and dissatisfaction were reversed. A concentration on making good environmental deficiencies, independently of preserving or enhancing environmental qualities, will always be an incomplete strategy, and may often lead to results opposite to those looked for.

There are many studies, particularly by academics, which fall into the opposite error. They attempt to predict residential satisfaction on the basis of what people like about their area. It is assumed that dissatisfaction results from the absence of those characteristics, or the presence of opposite ones. The flaw in this approach is that no empirical optimization of environmental quality is likely without associated disadvantages. The problem for planners is to balance the two.

Social class differences

Most psychologists would tend to assume that there were wide individual differences among people in the kinds of satisfaction and dissatisfaction that they felt with their environments. Another set of problems which planners have to face is to identify these differences, decide which ones to try to cater for, and work out methods of doing so. Most attention has probably been given to differences that in some way parallel land-use dispositions. For example, working class and middle class citizens usually live in distinct areas. There is thus an opportunity to provide separately for their different desires. Fried and Gleicher (1961) have pointed out some of the differences in space organization between the classes in North American society.

> ". . . in the urban middle class space is characteristically used in a highly *selective* way. The boundary between the dwelling unit and the immediate environs is quite sharp and minimally permeable." There is a sharp distinction between the privacy of the home and the outside. "The dwelling unit may extend into a zone of lawn or garden which we tend and for which we pay taxes. But apart from this, the space outside the dwelling unit is barely 'ours'.

267

"As soon as we are in the apartment hallway or on the street, we are on a wholly *public* way, a path to or from some place rather than on a bounded space defined by a subjective sense of belonging. Beyond this is a highly individualized world, with many common properties, but great variability in usage and subjective meaning . . . and contiguity between the dwelling unit and other significant spaces is relatively unimportant. It is primarily the channels and pathways between individualized significant spaces which are important, familiar, and common to many people. This orientation to the use of space is the very antithesis of that localism so widely found in the working class.

". . . most middle-class observers are overwhelmed at the degree to which the residents of any working class district and, most particularly, the residents of slums are 'at home' in the street. But it is not only the frequency of using the street and treating the street outside the house as a place, and not simply as a path, which points up the high degree of permeability of the boundary between the dwelling unit and the immediate environing area. It is also the use of all channels between dwelling unit and environment as a bridge between inside and outside: open windows, closed windows, hallways, even walls and floors serve this purpose. Frequently, even the sense of adjacent human beings carried by noises and smells provides a sense of comfort . . .

"We would like to call this way of structuring the physical space around the actual residential unit a *territorial* space, in contrast to the selective space of the middle class. It is territorial in the sense that physical space is largely defined in terms of relatively bounded regions to which one has freedom or restriction of access, and it does not emphasize the path function of physical space in allowing or encouraging movements to or from other places . . .

"In conjunction with the emphasis upon local social relationships, this conception and use of local physical space gives particular force to the feeling of commitment to, and the sense of belonging in, the residential area. It is clearly not just the dwelling unit that is significant but a larger local region that partakes of these powerful feelings of involvement and identity. It is not surprising, therefore, that 'home' is not merely an apartment or a house but a local area in which some of the most meaningful aspects of life are experienced." (pp. 311–314).

Neighbourhood

In other contexts, the 'local area' to which Fried and Gleicher refer is often discussed in terms of 'neighbourhood'. The concept is very much a part of planning vocabulary. In the design of residential areas it has been one of the major goals. Most academic studies on the concept have been carried out by sociologists. The main psychological contribution has been by Lee (1968). He outlines the functional significance of neighbourhood for planners in this way:

". . . it has been suggested that the neighbourhood unit should comprise a physically distinct area containing 10 000 to 15 000 people, be flanked by main roads and open spaces and given a radial system of residential roads leading to a central 'focus' where a shopping precinct, primary school and community centre are sited. Many houses should have path access. The population should be 'balanced' in socio-economic terms and industry sited as near as possible to the edge of the unit. The aims are aesthetic and economic, but most important *social* to create a feeling of identity and a sense of community.

"There has been considerable criticism of the neighbourhood as a way of planning cities, of which the most general expression is that the modern city dweller is mobile, rootless, prefers to be anonymous and is no longer dependent upon his immediate environment and intimate relationships with helpful neighbours, leaning instead on the matriarchal welfare state and on special interest groups which he locates in all parts of the city." (Lee, 1971, p.475).

A study in Cambridge

Lee's first task was to find out whether neighbourhood was a concept people could apply, or whether it was an item of specialist jargon. The Cambridge housewives whom he interviewed showed no hesitation. They knew that they had a neighbourhood, and could describe it in considerable physical detail. Neighbourhood maps drawn by residents of a single street showed very few coincidences of boundary, however. Lee concluded that the traditional neighbourhood concepts of a common piece of territory or an identifiable social group were insufficient. He replaced them by the term 'socio-spatial scheme'.

". . . perceptions occur during interactions with the physical and social environment, but in the continuing circle of behaviour and sensory feedback the relatively endless images . . . must influence future perceptions and, in some way not yet understood, control future actions." (1971, p.476).

The area of the neighbourhood maps was found to be meaningful. Size was related positively to the number of local friends a woman had, the number of local social organizations to which she belonged, and the likelihood of her using the local shopping centre. The extent of her neighbourhood appeared to indicate the degree of her social involvement in the local environment.

Practical implications

One of the attractions of Lee's study is that he has been able to draw from it a number of practical implications. For example, he notes that neighbourhood area remains approximately constant irrespective of population density. He suggests that newly planned neighbourhoods should be 30 to 40 hectares in size; and that deriving size in terms of absolute numbers of people and recommended densities would give a figure far in excess of this. In a rather more speculative way he goes on to propose a planned structural subdivision for the environment; a kind of mosaic of units, which would allow people individual variations in their perceived neighbourhoods.

Advice on the distribution and level of provision of leisure facilities was derived in a similar way. It was found that the probability of women joining clubs and centres of organized leisure was a direct function of the level of local provision. A saturation point of joining did not appear even at the level of 65 amenity buildings per half mile radius from the home. However, there is a point at which the proportion of 'joiners' levels off. That is, at about ten amenity buildings per 1000 dwelling units, when about 40 per cent of the sample studied were members of at least one club. It is suggested that this may be the appropriate ratio of amenity buildings to dwelling units to recommend to planners.

What do people want?

Work like Lee's illustrates the necessity for, as well as the practical significance of, empirical research which attempts to unravel what a semi-technical term, or area of specialized concern, can mean to non-experts. Fried and Gleicher (1961) point out the surprise that middle-class people may experience at the very different significances that are attached to the environment by working class people. Because planners usually come from, or have adopted, a middle-class ethos they may be quite unaware of these differences. This issue was confronted by Lansing and Marans (1969) when they compared the evaluations of neighbourhood quality of citizens and of planners.

Experts and non-experts

One hundred clusters of three or four homes were randomly sampled from the whole metropolitan region of Detroit. The people who lived there and an architect/planner made overall evaluations of the neighbourhood and of its attractiveness. The planner also made a number of more detailed assessments. Only a small measure of agreement (a correlation of 0.35) was found between the planner's rating of pleasantness and the inhabitants' overall evaluation of their neighbourhood. When evaluations of its 'openness' and 'interest' were compared there was virtually no agreement at all. The only exceptions to these discrepancies of judgement were in the case of the more highly educated residents, who did tend to rate their neighbourhoods more in line with the planners.

Lansing and Marans point out that these discrepancies are understandable.

271

"The planner tends to judge the neighborhood on the basis of physical characteristics. His ability to evaluate its other dimensions is limited by his training and what he can observe on a visit to the area, while residents tend to consider social factors such as neighborliness in addition to physical environment." (p.197)

The argument of the section on residential areas is reinforced. Detailed ratings were made by the planners of specific features related to land use, dwelling size, age, condition, and landscape characteristics. The relation between each of these features and the residents' overall evaluation of the neighbourhood was examined in order to determine the components of perceived environmental quality. The planners were surprised to find their rating of the physical condition of neighbourhood structures was by far the most important predictor of how much people liked their neighbourhood. The list of features that appeared less relevant was equally remarkable: land use character; land coverage; age of structures; general maintenance level of the area; proximity of adjacent structures; set back; offstreet parking; tree coverage; noise intensity; pollution-smoke level; and so on.

Pro's and con's of surveys

Surveys of this kind are recommended by Lansing and Marans on several counts. They involve citizens in the planning process on a more representative and participatory basis; they offer scope for developing predictive models of neighbourhood satisfaction for any particular group; and they chart the relations between the attitudes of planners and citizens.

But how useful are surveys for such purposes? Unless the total population affected by planning proposals is interviewed, they can hardly be taken seriously as tools for public participation in planning. The representative answers of a large random sample may be a counterbalance to the vocal élite who are more usually heard. But the sample is approached as a passive body, without any stimulus to actual involvement.

The goal of developing predictive models of satisfaction from attitudinal questionnaire data will almost certainly be frustrated.

Social psychology has shown that there are great technical (and theoretical) difficulties in predicting anything from verbally expressed attitudes. It could be questioned whether satisfaction is the appropriate criterion anyway, rather than more tangible components of satisfaction the extent and intensity of social relationships, for example. The static and deterministic bias is unfortunate. Buttimer's (1972) arguments, which we shall come to later, are relevant. Neighbourhood satisfaction is more likely to be a dynamic and evolving process, compounded of interactions between environment, behaviour and experience. Before this interaction occurs, and before the new planned environment is actually on the ground, the highly indeterminate mix is unlikely to be predictable.

The most valuable contribution which surveys may make is probably to attune planners to behaviour, attitudes, and opinions of which they are unaware; to give them the 'feel' of those for whom they are planning. This can only be done validly however if people are allowed to respond in their own terms as well as those of the experts. They must be allowed to frame questions which represent issues of importance to themselves, but which the planner may not anticipate or think irrelevant to his way of conceptualizing the planning process. At the same time people need to know the implications of any questionnaire answers they may give if they are to be politically valid within a context of public participation. For this to be possible they will need an appreciable amount of background information before they can answer questions. The state of ignorance about planning matters which is usually all that is tapped by surveys is avoidable. Mutual education between planners and citizens is required to meet these objectives (again, see Buttimer, below). But the random sample survey is unlikely to be the best tool. A variety of alternative techniques, such as group and depth interviews, are available.

Another weakness of many attitudinal surveys from the planner's viewpoint is that the data do not translate readily into planning decisions. There is a discontinuity between the highly quantified and 'objective' information which he has on population, employment and transportation requirements, landscape resources, and so on, and the more qualitative and value-laden

273

statements of attitude and preference. The former are translated directly into planning terms, because that is what planning techniques have been evolved to achieve. The latter newcomers sit very uneasily in planning models.

The Priority Evaluator

One suggestion for overcoming this difficulty has been by Hoinville (1971) in developing his 'priority evaluator'. This is a technique for measuring a community's environmental preferences in financial terms, and by a procedure which forces people to trade-off various advantages and disadvantages against one another.

Respondents are told to think of themselves as moving to another house. The cheapest house available is described pictorially for them in terms of a number of variables such as the level of environmental noise, pedestrian safety, ease of shopping, the time taken to get to work, to an evening recreational centre, or to the open countryside. Respondents are given an additional sum of money, say £1500, in units of £100 which they can distribute among the variables in order to 'buy' improvements to their new home's situation. For example, they can buy freedom from traffic fumes for two units, whereas off-street parking in the neighbourhood will cost eight units. Having an evening out twenty minutes away instead of forty minutes, as in the cheapest house, costs two units as well; to have it only ten minutes away means spending four. In this way respondents can buy varying levels of improvement to some aspects of their environment, and at varying costs, at the expense of poorer quality in other aspects.

"Perhaps the main value and advantage . . . of the Priority Evaluation approach is its flexibility. It can examine the preference structure at a micro level in order to establish differences between different types of person, different types of situation, large and small changes in individual variables, and so on. It is a method which can be used to yield aggregate community values but, more important, it can be used to examine how these aggregates are formed. This makes it

274

possible, for example, to see the variation in preferences between a slight reduction in traffic in the shopping centre and a full reduction; or again between a moderately quiet environment and a very quiet environment. We can see how the new generations have values different from their fathers; or establish the relationship between income and preferences. We can also find out how much people who possess a particular amenity value it in relation to those who do not have it". (Hoinville, 1971, p.49).

Other advantages of the Priority Evaluator are that the use of illustrations of environmental variations reminds people of similar experiences; it confronts them with the complex choice and trade-off situations which are an inevitable part of planning; and it asks them to express their choices in terms that reflect the resource allocation and investment decisions which have to be made. Among the disadvantages is the lack of interdependence between environmental variables and the fact that people's choices are discrete and minimally constrained. We understand little about what people might be doing when they respond in terms of cost; or how these responses might relate to behaviour and to experience. And although some kind of 'cost/benefit' output appears suited to the planning process, it may in effect be less valid than a less formal and political accumulation of impressions by the decision makers.

Towards participation

Much of the discussion in the section on residential areas might be taken to suggest that slums ought not to be redeveloped. Obviously this would be an incomplete conclusion. There are many cases in which slums harbour not only vile physical conditions, but also a social pathology which is the enemy of the rich social framework which is often found and which should be valued. But what general guidelines *can* be drawn for the planning of residential areas? A straightforward adherence to physical or social standards has been discounted. Similarly there are many problems associated with the use of attitude surveys and related instruments for deciding the issue.

275

This was also the conclusion arrived at by Buttimer (1972). She argued that a 'managerial perspective' would not provide solutions to the design of residential areas:

". . . life in residential areas involves a dialogue of behavior and setting, of demand and supply; it is thus essentially a condition of *becoming*. Such a condition is seen to arise when resident communities engage in creative dialogue with their environments, moulding, re-creating and eventually appropriating them as home . . . the planner can no longer be seen solely as the manipulator of supply; neither can the academician be seen merely as the investigator of resident aspiration and satisfaction. Least of all can the citizen be considered a passive pawn of external social or technological processes." (p.281)

Buttimer also has something pointed to say bearing on the environmental perception approach. ". . . the success of a residential development is contingent on the existential meaning it acquires for its residents. Who better than they can derive and infuse meaning into an environment?" (p.311). In other words, it is not adequate for planners and academics to study how people perceive their present environment, and then to attempt to encapsulate that structure in a new environment. Perceptions and meaning are not something that exist independently of perceivers. Nor are they static. They are the outcome of *process*. Meaning cannot be manipulated in the same way as built form or land-use dispositions. As Buttimer suggests it arises from the dialogue between behaviour and experience and the environment. For successful planning it is essential that people become conscious of the dialogue and learn to control it.

Education for city-living

"The problem ultimately becomes one of education both for suppliers (politicians, planners, architects) and demanders (residents). The supply structure should not be regarded as a prefabricated network of physical provisioning rationally allocated according to the constraints of technological efficiency, scale economics, and market-area potentials. It should be

276

regarded as a potential supply system, a potential to be tapped and molded by the consciously articulated demands of resident communities.

"How to enable communities to grow and develop to the point of appreciating and claiming their rights and responsibilities within the framework of the urban system as a whole is, of course, the critical problem. . . . Is it not conceivable, then, that the collective challenge of designing and provisioning their environments could become a learning experience, generating a sense of community responsibility and contributing to identification with place?

"Why not, for example, in some areas subject to renewal, present the range of available choices a year or so beforehand to all those who are about to be moved? Ideas could be exchanged and action initiated upon consultation and collective decision. . . .

"Through preparatory dialogue and interaction, a sense of collective community consciousness might emerge. After relocation, families would still be able to count on the support and challenge of pre-existing social order, and the business of finishing the estate design could be confronted collectively. . . .

"Such experimentation would counteract the conventional model of fitting a population into an environment prefabricated on the basis of technological, political and economic constraints. But it would also check the utopian . . . model of having everyone choose his own house style and location. It calls for education toward responsible community appropriation of the rights and responsibilities for the design of environments within the context of the urban system as a whole." (pp.311–313).

The answer to the problems posed in the second half of this chapter, of how to maximize people's satisfactions with life in their residential neighbourhoods, can be seen to lie in giving everyone a greater measure of participation in the planning process itself. Satisfaction will then come from the process of 'travelling' towards a better neighbourhood, and from a growing collective consciousness as experts and non-experts collaborate in their joint venture.

Conclusion

We have moved a long way in this chapter, from the murder of Catherine Genovese and the apathetic bystander, to calls for citizen participation which evoke the spirits of Rousseau and John Stuart Mill. But at all points of the journey we have found researchers who were trying to obtain a better view of the city and its problems. Urbanization involves a high density of population and use, and complex managerial institutions. We need to know in more precise detail what they entail and how their disadvantages can be overcome.

The central point in the first two sections is that the effects of high density and crowding are not physical but psychological. More properly, they are cognitive, and in particular manifest themselves in a social form, in how we view and manage our relations with others. The programme of research by Latané and Darley is an excellent example of how light can be thrown on the peculiar social relationships, or perhaps lack of relationship, which other workers' field studies and everyday observation have demonstrated to be a feature of urban living. But if these psychological explanations open up the inside of the problem, do they also reveal a solution?

One might criticize them because the solutions they offer are predominantly reactionary. They advocate, directly or by implication, a return to less urbanized settlements and to smaller settings for our activities. There is nothing in the shape of the research results which indicates a progressive solution: how we might restructure our cognition of urban phenomena, or how we might encourage the urban setting to evolve into newer, more adaptive forms.

A not dissimilar conclusion emerges from the second two sections of the chapter. Housing problems in our cities have often been treated as capable of solution by physical measures. Comprehensive redevelopment, however, has been found in some cases to produce more problems than are dispelled. Slum clearance achieves better physical living conditions at the cost of community disintegration. But again the research implies little beyond a return to a neighbourhood of a size that has become obsolete. We may ask if indeed we have gained in our understanding of how people live in cities, if our knowledge does not tell us how to act in a progressive way.

Asking people what they want, allowing them to participate in the development of their environment, is an attempt at a more progressive solution. The shift is from allowing professionals to assume the responsibility for managing our environment to encouraging the non-expert to become active in the process himself. Many people choose how to fit out the interior of their dwellings and take great pains with their gardens. Their interest and energy could be exercised on the more macroscopic levels. A genuine participation will involve more than asking people what they want. Surveys are anyway imbued with many drawbacks. Participation can be treated as an existential matter, a developing civic and urban awareness. Cities will become satisfactory places in which to live when people generally become more aware of the total process of urban living.

We shall meet elements of this theme again in Chapter Nine in the section on pollution; but again it is at a suggestive level only. We wait eagerly for empirical research devoted to this theme.

K

Chapter Nine

The Natural Environment

Peter Stringer

Behavioural science research on the natural environment has been dominated by geographers, and by North American geographers in particular. This has led to a concentration on two aspects of the natural environment. Firstly, natural hazards (earthquakes, hurricanes, etc.) are interesting as critical geophysical events to which man is still learning to adjust by both technological and psychological means. Secondly, the state and role of 'wilderness' in some parts of the world raises important questions about the balance between conservation and environmental enjoyment. Both aspects show promise of illuminating our understanding of the relationship between man and nature.

Man's attitude to nature is also becoming more apparent as we study some of his grosser interferences with it. On the one hand grave problems are unwittingly introduced by pollution of the atmosphere and of the land and waters. In other circumstances, such as weather modification, the interference is more deliberate. In both cases environmental psychology has something to say about people's threshold of awareness of the problems, their perception of who is responsible for them, and the communication processes through which they receive information and pass their comments on the problems on to higher agencies.

Research into wilderness and landscape is interpreted in this chapter in terms of the three main themes of Chapters Seven, Eight and Nine. We shall deal at some length with the methodological weaknesses of studies of attitude and preference. Similar criticisms could be applied to much of the work that has been done on the urban environment. The value of a strong basis in psychological theory is illustrated well by applications of adaptation level theory and role theory; and negatively by a rather spurious 'commonsense' cataloguing of psychological needs. The intended practical implications of the research are nearly always apparent; though their realization tends to be in proportion to the methodological and theoretical sophistication of the investigator.

Hazards

One of the most energetic areas of research on man's relations with the natural environment has dealt with hazards. The early work started in Chicago under Gilbert White (1952) looking at human responses to floods. Since then a wide variety of natural hazards have served as the context for the study of man-environment relations. Although there has been a concentration on drought and floods, studies have also been carried out which deal with hurricanes, tsunami, earthquakes, tornadoes, gales, thunderstorms, snowstorms, volcanic eruptions, landslides, avalanches, and frost. The main centre for this research in recent years has been the University of Toronto (Burton *et al* 1968). The initiative for the work at all stages has lain with geographers.

Research on the human ecology of extreme geophysical events, as Burton *et al* (1968) term it, has both practical and academic importance. Practically, these events involve considerable loss of life as well as property damage. For example, it has been estimated (Sheehan and Hewitt, 1969) that over 173 000 lives were lost in 209 floods world-wide in the years 1947—67; while even in the 32 gales and thunderstorms studied in this period nearly 21 000 people died. Property damage from flooding in the United States in a single year may have been as high as 1000m dollars (Burton and Kates, 1964), or from hail, wind and thunderstorms as much as 300m dollars. Losses of this order establish a clear priority for

282

further understanding of how we deal with hazards, particularly at a time when one might assume that man was gaining an increasing technological control over the environment.

The dilemma of these losses is in fact that they appear to be the *result* of technological progress, rather than being prevented by it. Despite the recurrence of disaster in hazard zones, populations not only settle there in large numbers, but return very shortly after a disaster may have driven them out. The massive engineering works undertaken to control floods, for example, keep all but the highest water levels at bay. They give inhabitants of flood areas such confidence that they invest considerable amounts in building and other ventures. When a disaster does eventually occur it tends to be of catastrophic proportions. The number of natural events with disastrous consequences will double at least in the next twenty-five years.

The impact of scientific and technological advance in this way on nature and consequently on society is one of the issues which give hazard research its academic interest. Other issues have been summarized by Burton *et al* (1968):

"Extreme variations in nature provide a handle by which to grapple with the role of risk and uncertainty in the affairs of men. Crucial tests of our knowledge of the psychology of perception may be formulated in terms of environmental hazards. We share with students of international relations a concern about the role and significance of crisis. . . . (We) pursue our studies of extreme geophysical events in the intuitive belief that this will lead to new insights into man and nature and the nature of man."

These are obviously issues of superordinate psychological interest.

A research programme

The natural hazard research programme was planned along five main lines.

(1) The first goal is to assess the *extent* to which hazard zones

283

were occupied by man and his property. For example, there are 2000 cities in the United States lying in flood-plains. Of particular significance are the questions of definition of what constitutes a hazard, and of the increasing trends in occupation of hazard zones.

(2) There is a wide range of theoretically *possible adjustments* that may be made to any natural hazard. It is of interest to establish what the theoretical range is, as well as what actual adjustments are chosen. A distinction is made between technological and behavioural adjustments. The former involve the manipulation of nature, and variously seek to affect the cause of hazards (for example by cloud-seeding), modify the hazard (levees against floods), or modify loss potential (warning systems). They are usually carried out at public expense. Behavioural or social adjustments are commonly left to private citizens. The major social adjustment occurs after a disaster in the form of bearing or spreading the losses. Technological adjustments tend to be preferred to behavioural ones because their cost can be spread evenly over society. However, as suggested above, this techno-logical 'fix', when unrelated to behavioural considerations, can lead to even greater losses in the long run.

(3) Another reason for the failure of social adjustments is the great difference among individuals in the *perception* of hazards, and in particular in their estimates of uncertainty. (For a treatment of this topic in mainstream psychology *cf.* Kahneman and Tversky, 1973). For example, the layman may often assume that a flood estimated by a hydrologist as occurring with a hundred-year frequency actually occurs at intervals of one hundred years. The element of uncertainty in natural hazards leads to a variety of common responses. Either the hazard is eliminated cognitively by denying or denigrating its existence or re-occurrence, or the uncertainty is eliminated, by making it determinate or by shifting the responsibility to a superior power.

(4) The *actual adjustments* which are adopted depend to a considerable extent on these sorts of perceptual (though we would prefer to call them *cognitive*) processes. They may depend also on people's perception of the available technology, on judgments of

284

the economic implications of alternative adjustments, and on social and administrative roles and relations. An individual differences approach is used in the research at this point.

"Empirical evidence from personal interviews suggests that adoption of damage-reducing adjustments bears little or no relation to age or education. There is a weak relationship with previous experience (of disasters) that becomes most evident in areas where very heavy damage has been sustained. Adoptions do not appear to be related to socio-economic status except where the cost is high. . . . There is a strong relationship, however, between adoptions and frequency of hazard and especially the perceived frequency of hazard." (p.19 *op. cit.*)

This relationship is strong at the extremes of the distribution of frequency. At intermediate points there is a wide variation between individuals in the type and extent of adjustment to hazard which they make. Interestingly there appear to be discrete shift points in people's responses at frequency points of one to two and four to five years. Laymen only appear to consider the full range of adjustments under conditions of 'positive certainty'. Professionals are characterized by their technological fix, and a distrust of 'social engineering' or behavioural adjustments.

(5) Finally, one may attempt to estimate the *optimal* set of adjustments in terms of anticipated social consequences. This line of research tends to follow econometric models, though relatively little has been achieved to date (perhaps because of the un-certainty and complexity of the relevant man-environment system). From a psychological viewpoint one of the most interesting issues is whether and how such optimal adjustments would be made if they were identified. Perhaps man might adapt to the costs of natural disaster, by perceiving it as "a natural rent imposed upon mankind for the use of the earth".

Hazard perception

Generally there are two different sets of questions underlying this research. The first has to do with broad societal responses to

285

hazards. As this is more properly the province of sociology, we shall not deal with it here. The second set which deals with individual differences in human response is readily suited to investigation by psychological methods. As we have seen, early attempts to account for variations in adjustment to hazard in terms of standard socio-economic variables has been a failure. More recently explanations have been sought in terms of hazard perception, and in this phase of the research geographers have begun to enlist the aid of psychologists or of their techniques. There has been an attempt to mix the pragmatic, empirical and field work orientations of the former group, with the latter's theoretical frameworks and particular instrumentation.

Hazard perception may usefully be approached in terms of cognitive consistency, for example, risk-taking behaviour, or response to stress or frustration. Studies have been made which use projective tests of various kinds, and rating scales akin to the semantic differential. The former seem to be particularly popular. Hazard research has tended to use techniques relying on the 'construction' and 'completion' forms of response (*cf*. Lindzey and Thorpe, 1968).

A thematic apperception test

Saarinen has used a modified version of Murray's (1943) Thematic Apperception Test to investigate the perception of drought hazard by wheat farmers on the Central Great Plains of the United States (Saarinen, 1966; Sims and Saarinen, 1969; Saarinen, 1973). He was interested in particular in the way in which the farmers coped with an environment full of threat and conflict. The farmers' basic problems are summarized in the following response to one of the few additional, special hazard TAT cards used by Saarinen:

"Well I'd say this was a scene in Western Kansas in the dirty 30s. Because of the great opportunities in the late 20s and early 30s this farmer moved to the drylands of the High Plains. His first few years were very successful in harvesting good crops and increasing his bank account. Each year more land was plowed up, vegetation destroyed and lack of moisture made a situation perfect for wind erosion. And for the next four of five years the wind blew and the soil drifted and the farmer's bank account and assets were liquidated. And in despair with his hands in his pockets, and his head bent low he started his return to the big city."

One way in which the TAT stories were interpreted was in terms of their apparent attitude to man's relation with nature: variously 'man in control of nature', 'man in harmony with nature', and 'man as the victim of nature'. Brief examples of each of these attitudes would be: ". . . that man is probably inspecting his ground to see what he should do to it. Probably ended up tilling it to stop the dust from blowing"; "You have to try to keep this from blowing even if you're almost sure you can't when you begin. . . . Nature will take care of it if he gives a little help"; and ". . . Well there's been a big wind . . . He went out to his wheat field to see if there's any chance that there'd be wheat left. 'Bout the most hopeless feeling there is in the world." The last of these attitudes was by far the most common response from the 96 farmers interviewed. Two-thirds of them saw nature as dominant, and only one in six took each of the other viewpoints. Although the farmers came from six different regions varying considerably in aridity, the distribution of their attitudes was very similar. The only exception was one area in which cultivation had only been started 20 years previously and in which farming had since considerably thinned out. The combination of original settlers and tough persisters perhaps led to less than half of the farmers in this area taking the more passive viewpoint.

More detailed analyses of elements of conflict in responses to individual TAT cards were made — for example, Murray's Card 1 (a picture of a young boy contemplating a violin which rests on a table before him). This card usually taps the way in which people handle questions of achievement. 88 per cent of the farmers' responses to this card contained elements of conflict. Thus, they see achievement as a conflicting issue, either being pressed to achieve and not wanting to, or wanting to achieve but meeting obstacles. This proportion is much greater than has been found in government officials or business executives, for example.

The outcome of the projected conflicts might be resolved in several ways. Where there was a press for achievement, the boy could either be seen to give in to it and achieve, or not to and

287

maintain his autonomy. Where there was an impeded desire for achievement, the boy could either overcome the obstacle, or fail to do so. In half the farmers' stories a possible resolution was quite absent; and in a further quarter the resolution was unsatisfactory, being accompanied by concealed rebellion. Conflicts over achievement, and even unconflicted achievement motivation, is an unresolved issue for the wheat farmers. Furthermore, whether or not there is conflict in the stories, there is rarely an outcome. Achievement for the farmers is an ongoing problem without ready solutions.

Saarinen interprets the intellectual confusion and emotional disturbance he finds in the stories as a function of the risk and uncertainty in the natural environment. He points out two policy implications that may be derived from his analysis. Firstly any attempt at resettlement would not be enthusiastically received, since the farmers take great pride in 'sticking it out'. Secondly, new farming methods may not be accepted by them, because they see success more as the ability to hold on until the rains return. To be able to find practical implications in material of this kind is extremely promising. From other questionnaire data, Saarinen was able to suggest that although farmers were responsive to the occurrence of drought, they needed help in appreciating its frequency and probability. Their short memory for drought meant that campaigns of instruction designed to combat drought effects should be given in dry periods when they were suffering from it. It would be more profitable to concentrate such campaigns on farmers who could be identified as more innovative. Willingness to adopt new methods of farming also depended very much on the farmer's perception of what constituted a drought, which varied with the degree of aridity of their region.

Other techniques

Other uses of projective techniques for studying hazard perception have not yet progressed beyond the development stage. Barker and Burton (1969) describe a modification of the Rosenzweig Picture-Frustration Test. This test was originally (Rosenzweig, 1945) designed for use in clinical contexts. Items depict cartoon drawings of two people, one of whom is frustrated by the situation shown. Subjects respond by identifying themselves with the frustrated person and indicating what statement they imagine the person to be making. Responses can be classified according to type of response (obstacle dominance, ego defense, needs persistence) and direction of 'aggression' (intropunitive, extrapunitive, impunitive).

Nine new pictures were introduced into the test, in which the source of stress was derived from or somehow associated with the natural environment. For example, a farmer is shown accusing his neighbour of taking more of his share of the irrigation water and then damaging the first farmer's crop. Or two men are stranded at the airport where all flights have been cancelled because of snow. The first man is apologizing for having asked the other to drive him all the way to the airport to no avail.

The test was given to 71 geography summer-school students. Their responses were analysed in various ways, including a comparison between the original 'social' situations and the newly introduced 'environmental' situations. The comparison is a difficult one, because the environmental situations necessarily contain strong social elements — the situations always involve interaction between two people. In addition, the range of physical stresses (from a shower of rain to an earthquake) was much wider than of social stresses. Nevertheless it was found that 'needs persistence' played a more important role in social than in environmental frustration. Barker and Burton conclude that:

"people see themselves to be more capable of improving the situations of social stress . . . rather than changing the stressful circumstances shown as arising from the natural environment. There is in our society a strong belief in the efficacy of powerful technology in controlling the natural environment; however when individuals are experiencing stress arising from the physical environment they may tend to emphasize the obstacle or origin of stress rather than offer an immediate solution to the frustrating circumstances. Reliance on the 'technological fix' probably occurs when the immediate stress from natural hazards is remote, but an entirely different kind of response occurs when individuals are experiencing an earthquake or tornado." (*op. cit.* pp. 7, 11).

Each subject's responses were compared with the mean sample responses, in order to derive a 'conformity' rating. In general, greater conformity was found in the social situations — perhaps because of the narrower range they depicted.

An alternative approach to understanding people's ideas or expectations about natural hazard is by way of a semantic differential. A study by Golant and Burton (1969) has the unusual merit of using a proper differential, that is as devised by Osgood *et al* (1957). Their 58 subjects (again from summer-school) rated 12 hazard concepts on 21 bipolar adjectival scales. One way in which the results were analysed was to infer the average 'meaning' for each of the hazards. For example, earthquake was seen as active, chaotic, moderately natural, unstable, moderately localized, ferocious, moderately unfair, dissonant, fast, strong, public, important, tense, moderately tenacious, natural, uncontrollable, unpleasant, moderately heavy, and free; the average response was neutral as to erratic versus periodic and determinate versus fortuitous. The 'intensity' of meaning of each concept was examined in terms of the polarity or neutrality of ratings. Sixteen of the 21 ratings for tornado, for example, were polar; while for snowstorm six were polar, eight moderately polar, and seven neutral; and for water pollution four were polar, 14 moderately polar, and three neutral. Factor analysis of the scales produced four factors, accounting however, for only 46 per cent of the variance. These were labelled 'stability', 'controllability', 'magnitude', and 'expectancy'. Three concept factors were extracted, accounting for 77 per cent of variance. The first two — 'man-made hazards' and 'natural hazards' — are illustrated in Figure 9.1. The third was labelled 'quasi-natural hazards' (that is, pollution).

Both of these studies have the disadvantage that subjects' responses are unrelated to any characteristics or behaviour outside the test used. This relationship is an essential step if judgments about people's perception of hazards are to be derived from the tests and used to predict their response to threatening or actually occurring hazards.

In more recent work, which has a strong cross-cultural emphasis, it has been found more convenient to use a simple sentence completion test than any of the techniques above. Stems have been devised and pretested of the following kind: If a

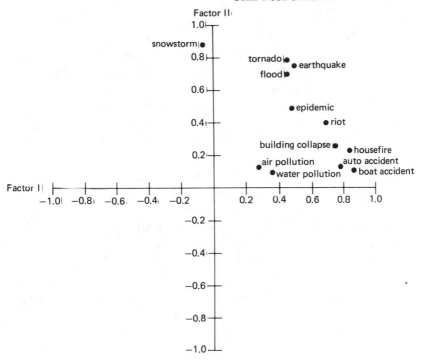

Figure 9.1 Loading values of concepts on two principal factors

drought (or hurricane, etc.) is predicted, I . . . ; The emotions I feel while I am going through a drought are . . . ; When a community experiences a drought, the feelings among its people . . .

Man-made hazards

A source of confusion in these studies has been the weak distinction between natural hazards and man-made or social hazards. Their differences have been discussed in more detail by Kirkby (1973):

"Generally speaking, natural hazards tend to operate from the physical environment on to man; man-made hazards are the effect of man's activities on man through the medium of the physical environment; and social hazards tend to be the direct effect of man's actions on man".

291

Examples of the latter two categories are air and water pollution, soil erosion and exhaustion; and racial conflict, resource depletion, economic deprivation (poverty, unemployment, etc.). These three hazard categories exhibit an increasing ambiguity of cause and effect, increased uncertainty in their size, nature, and probability of occurrence, and more complex relations with a variety of social, economic, and political factors.

Kirkby highlights three particular aspects of the adjustment process to man-made hazards, which are of considerable psychological interest. (1) In the case of natural hazards we saw that one of the central problems was increasing the perceived range of possible adjustments, and moving people from a technological fix to consider social solutions. For man-made hazards the key perceptual problem is the very recognition of the hazard or of the contributing physical events. This is a question of *thresholds of awareness.* For example, the effect of contaminated water supplies or of lead or mercury emissions on the general health level may go undetected for a long time. (2) People typically see a hazard such as air pollution as quite outside their influence − they neither cause it nor can they control it. The *attribution* of the hazard to external agents is heavily dependent on sociological factors. Attribution theory (*cf.* Jones *et al,* 1971, 1972) has recently become an area of growing interest within psychology. (3) *Communication* processes influence the recognition of a hazard and any action to end it. Intergroup relations, for example, between scientists, politicians, industrial interests, mass media, action groups and laymen, may in turn influence the movement of information about the hazard. The nature of information transmitted, delays or changes in its content, and the way in which it is interpreted may each be affected by the dynamics of relations between sender, channel, and receiver. Processes such as conflict, cooperation, negotiation, group identity, categorization and social comparison will be important.

A model of adjustment to hazards

An important characteristic of the theoretical work under-lying recent hazard research is the systemic nature of the models proposed. These contrast with the deterministic, cause-and-effect

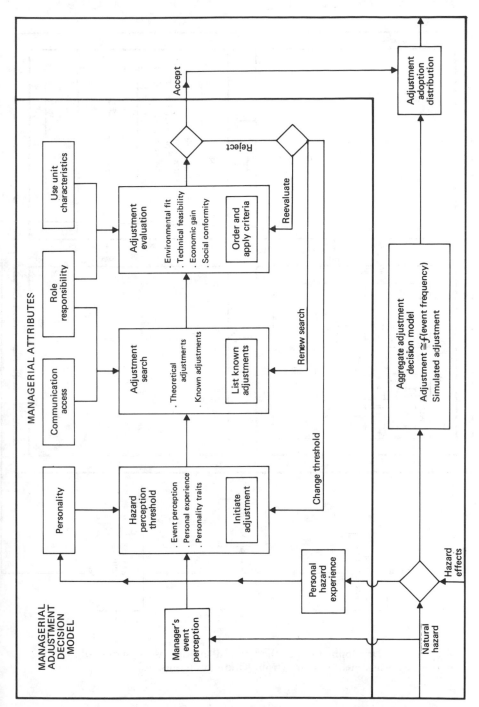

Figure 9.2 Adjustment Process Control (from Kates, 1970)

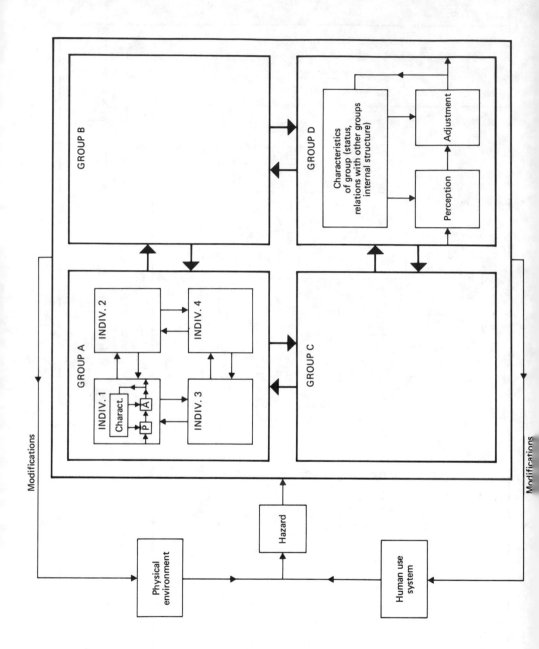

Figure 9.3 Development of the hazard model as a series of nested perception-adjustment systems (from Kirkby, unpublished)

models which are more familiar in classical psychology. An example of such a model is that by Kates (1970) in Figure 9.2. This has been extended by Kirkby, in particular to take account of intra- and inter-group processes (Figure 9.3). A model such as this, if fully elaborated, permits distinctions to be made between degrees of perception and adjustment for individuals and different levels of social grouping. It emphasizes the role of networks in perception and decision-making. These group networks may be thought of as defined by information flow — by the type, amount, speed, quality and accuracy of information transmitted. A definition of this kind has the advantage of accounting for changes in a group network over time.

Some of the features in this model may be tested by a study, for example, of adjustment to industrial air pollution of heavy metals from a large smelter.

"The aim is to analyse the inter-group network that developed during threat of the hazard and to measure the flow of information between the links. . . . Information about the hazard is channelled along three routes in addition to direct perception and observation. This direct route is probably the weakest since heavy metal contamination is not visible and cannot be observed externally to kill animals or man.

"The three information routes are through measuring the effect on air quality; measuring the effects on soil, plants and animals; and measuring the effects on man directly. Each of the sets of effects are measured by several different groups of local and national government, the industry causing the hazard, university scientists and the trades unions. Often communication between the groups monitoring the hazard is poor or non-existent. Almost all the information is classified as highly confidential and is passed along restricted official channels only. Detailed information on the effects and their probabilities is concentrated in the hands of two groups. One is the industry causing the hazard and the other is the local authority. The central government also have access to much information if it is successfully collated between ministries and semi-independent departments. The danger of this information hierarchy is that those groups who have the most to lose by controlling the pollution are the only ones with adequate information to evaluate its severity.

". . . the information and decision-making network is largely separated from the information network surrounding the people who are actually threatened by the hazard. Their information is not only fragmentary and therefore of a much poorer quality; that they have any at all depends mainly on chance. In this case, some university scientists and trades union officials independently informed the public through the press about the existence of the hazard on the basis of their own evidence.

"An important aspect of the research design is that information flows are related to attribution of causality for the hazard situation and the perceived motivations and responsibilities of each of the groups involved. It is hoped to obtain each group's 'mental map' of the inter-group network and their group constructs. In this case, the various adjustments appear to have resulted from an interaction of information filtering down and pressure building up."

Finally, Kirkby makes two further suggestions about possible advances in hazard research, both of which could have considerable implications for environmental psychology. She suggests turning our attention from hazard to the wider question of behaviour in uncertainty. The centrality of the latter concept for psychology as a whole should be self evident. It can be related either to mechanistic approaches to psychology (*cf.* Garner, 1962), or to the phenomenological. It fits neatly into a view of 'man as scientist' (Kelly's (1955) personal construct theory), manipulating uncertainty in construing, in his search for ever more progressive and interesting theories about the nature of the physical, social and individual world.

More specifically the view of 'man — the environmental-scientist' might be examined through Rotter's (1966) trait of 'internal-external locus of control'. This concept expresses the way in which people perceive events in their lives as being self-determined or controlled by outside forces. It is probably a multi-dimensional trait, with such components as: (a) the separation of external forces into factors such as systematic versus random forces; chance, fate, and other people's actions; benevolent versus malevolent forces; or (b) acceptance of responsibility for success as opposed to failure. The concept has already been profitably used in studying the social hazards of racial conflict and poverty.

Pollution

There has not yet been the opportunity for most of Kirkby's suggestions to be followed through in research programmes. Most of the work that has been done on human aspects of environmental pollution has been in the form of public opinion surveys, and has tended not to incorporate much in the way of psychological interest. One finding replicated in several studies is that few people say spontaneously that they are concerned about air pollution, even if they live in an area where it is known to be high, and even though they may acknowledge the fact when specifically questioned about it. At the same time people may say they are bothered by air pollution without acknowledging its presence where they live. In this case it is possible that their attitudes are derived from the mass media rather than through actual sensitivity to the problem. And a general methodological difficulty in surveys of this kind is indeed in disentangling direct and indirect awareness of pollution. We have already referred to the problem of thresholds of awareness in relation to man-made hazards. Swan (1970) found that youths of lower socio-economic level in Detroit were significantly less perceptive of air pollution in a specially prepared series of slides. He suggested that they may have had less opportunity to leave the city and have come to accept brownish-blue as an acceptable sky-colour.

The apparent contradictions revealed by these surveys go further. People may be intensely concerned about pollution, and recognize its existence, and yet do nothing about it even in terms of complaining. This may be because they see pollution as an aesthetic rather than health issue. Or because of their attribution of its cause or their perception of those who could be responsible for preventing it, as in Kirkby's model above. The individual's view of his own role is important here. In another area of environmental decision-making, White (1966) found that people were

297

only likely to become involved in water resource management if they felt that they could play a meaningful role in the decision-making process. Making a complaint often seems quite meaningless, when one knows nothing about the structure and operation of the institution that receives the complaint. People of higher socio-economic level are more likely to have such knowledge, and not surprisingly most of the complaints come from them. In urban areas where the decaying centres and polluted industrial zones will be occupied by those of lower socio-economic level this becomes a very serious matter.

Social differences in response

Swan (1970) has pursued this latter point in more detail. By means of a gaming simulation he studied the responses of a number of black and white youths, who were highly concerned about air pollution, to the task of convincing the authorities to take some action over a specific instance of pollution. He was particularly interested in their response when confronted with rejection by the authorities, hypothesizing that more persistence would be shown by the youths who in another context showed themselves more open to change, preferring a diversity of social relationships, and willing to participate in activities involving a change in existing conditions. (This sort of coping behaviour has been called 'exploration', and can be measured by questionnaire.) Swan found that his hypothesis was disconfirmed in the case of black, though not white, youths. The blacks were uninterested in the task. For them, but not for the whites, exploration was related to interest and participation in local community problems. It seems that the blacks, faced with issues of race relations and police-community relations, could not afford to be concerned about pollution. The whites' level of 'exploration' may have been unrelated to community interest because of the lack of organizations to foster such interests.

Swan's conclusions as to the role of psychologists over a problem like pollution tend to be activist. Behavioural scientists could help to improve the quality of information about the problem that is given to the public. They could also help the public to use that information once they have it, by devising

298

educational programmes to equip them to act effectively within existing political institutions. Finally psychologists could also work from within governmental bodies to advise on ways by which the public could be meaningfully integrated into planning processes at all stages.

An even more energetic approach is advocated by Buckhout (1972). He points to the need for longitudinal studies of life-styles which are constrained by pollution, depleted resources, and other ecological factors. (Longitudinal, like activist, studies are too rarely conducted by psychologists. They pose too many problems for the determined careerist!) Pollution should be studied in the context of related problems such as population control. Techniques of psychological warfare might be used to make people more aware of pollution, and to achieve a little political 'hell raising'. Community encounter groups should be established to deal with areas of potential community conflict. Games and scenarios could be used to persuade people to expand their horizons and think of the unthinkable. Teams of psychologists and other professionals could emulate Ralph Nader, and begin to prosecute the class-action suit. Forms of psychic guerilla warfare might even be adopted to suppress one's local polluter.

Climate and weather

"Everybody talks about the weather, but nobody does anything about it" — Mark Twain. This is certainly as applicable to psychologists as to anyone else. The more benign aspects of the climate — that is, excluding violent storms and prolonged drought — have been neglected by researchers both in environmental psychology and in human geography. And yet climate and weather are unavoidable features of all bar a very few environments. From everyday experience they would appear to affect a wide range of our activities. We dress for them, build for them, and go on holidays for them. But what other effects do they have?

There are three approaches that might be taken to weather change. (1) How sensitive are human activities of different kinds to weather changes? For example, they presumably affect transportation, construction, tourism and many other industries. What

299

is their economic significance? What is their effect on productivity and sales, by psychological mediating variables? (2) How sensitive are we to information about weather changes? How are weather forecasts perceived and used? What adjustments are made to what kinds of impending changes in weather? This is an area of everyday decision-making and indirect environmental manipulation that should richly repay study. (3) What initiatives are taken to bring about changes in the weather other than by relocation? What are our perceptions and attitudes towards weather as a modifiable natural resource? Do we appreciate the weather changes brought about by human activities such as deforestation, urbanization, or atmospheric pollution?

Weather modification

It is the last of these approaches which has received most attention. Weather modification has been a major programme of scientific and technological activity for well over a decade. Experiments have been carried out on artificially increasing rainfall, dispersing fog, and reducing hurricane winds. 'Cloud seeding' has begun to be a regular part of life in several areas of the world. From a behavioural science viewpoint a number of questions immediately arise. For example, one wants to know how such direct modifications of 'natural' events are perceived by people; and how their perceptions are related to their views on technology and nature generally. Do socio-economic characteristics affect acceptance of weather modification? The mass media, and a variety of reference groups may be important influences here. The implications of weather modification for an individual's own behaviour may be crucial. Methodologically these are difficult questions to answer. Weather modification is still an unfamiliar phenomenon, and in many cases only at a trial stage. Its effectiveness can only be adequately tested in the long-term. Perceptions and attitudes might change significantly as the technology becomes cumulative and widespread; and the ambiguity of its effects resolved.

A survey done at the trial stage in the United States has begun to answer some of these questions (Haas *et al*, 1971). Communities in areas directly affected by weather modification

300

trials were compared with controls outside these areas. It was found that there was a difference in the level of acceptance between people living in the two areas. Acceptance for the actual trials gradually increased during the experimental period, but decreased slightly for the general concept of weather modification. People in professional and managerial occupations were more likely to accept than others. As were those of a higher level of education, younger adults, and people who were active in local political affairs. Only one per cent of the total sample felt that they had been inconvenienced by the cloud-seeding experiment, and only three per cent had thought of making a complaint. Two-thirds (65 per cent) said that they would vote for continuation in a referendum, while 12 per cent were against it. Those who saw the programme as an attempt actually to change the weather, that is as operational rather than experimental, were less likely to be accepting of it.

Several additional and interesting observations were made on the decision-process underlying weather modification policy. At the initial experimental stage 85 per cent of respondents thought that the decision to undertake it should be made at the local as opposed to state or federal level. At mid-stage a majority was still for continuation being decided by local people; but now only 38 per cent took this view. Nineteen per cent thought that those directly affected should decide; and 31 per cent scientists or higher governmental authorities. Most significantly, respondents also recognized that the decision was unlikely to be made in this way; 53 per cent thought that scientists and central government would decide, and only 21 per cent thought that local people or those affected would do so.

Wilderness

The main area of research into the natural environment, other than hazard research, which has some direct or indirect psychological interest concerns landscape, and more particularly wilderness. 'Wilderness' tends to be a non-European construct. In Europe it is generally recognized now that it is some considerable time since any of the natural environment has been unmarked by human interventions. In the United States, however, something between one and two per cent of the area outside Alaska is wilderness. In both the United States and Canada there has been a growing concern during the twentieth century to conserve the wilderness.

Wilderness is treated both as an amenity and an ecological sanctuary. Much of the research exhibits an understandable confusion of the two viewpoints. The basic policy questions are ones of how to conserve the wilderness in its pristine, or at least as near to its present, condition while permitting it to serve as an aesthetic and recreational resource. Although the research attempts to provide information which will help decision-makers answer such questions, the fundamental dilemma underlying conservation and use is rarely met head on.

The value of wilderness

What is it that might be of value to people in areas of wilderness? McKenry (1971) lists fourteen types of resource that wilderness areas can supply: water; oxygen; animals; vegetables; minerals; energy; land; aboriginal habitats; opportunities for scientific research and education; tourist income; recreational locations; psychological benefits; and societal benefits. Obviously these categories are not all on the same level; some include others. And some resources if actualized would inevitably involve the destruction of the wilderness as such; but the list is valuable, if only as an indication of the range of discriminable values that might underlay differing exploitations of wilderness or pressure for its conservation.

The ramifications of each category of value are considerable. For example, an argument about conserving wilderness for animals might entail a variety of explicit or, more likely, implicit assumptions. Animals might be construed as suppliers of food; as sources of recreation and tourist revenue; or of interest and beauty; as useful in pest control; or as a supply of pests and predatory animals; to supply zoos and circuses; or domestic pets; to restock depleted areas; for introduction as exotic species to other areas; or as stock for the breeding of new species; as a supply of animals for scientific study and research. In any particular instance several of these assumptions may be made, but not all of them would necessarily be satisfied by any one course of action.

The psychological benefits of wilderness?

An equally elaborate list is given by McKenry for the so-called psychological benefits of wilderness. He first distinguishes specific from diffuse benefits. The former are distinct, well-defined, and clearly perceived by the beneficiary. But diffuse benefits may not be so clearly perceived nor defined. The nature of these benefits is sub-divided under ten headings.

(a) Improvement or maintenance of mental health

". . . it is questionable that man can retain his physical and mental health if he loses contact with the natural forces that have shaped his biological and mental nature. Man is still of the earth, earthly, and like Anteus of the Greek legend, he loses his strength when both his feet are off the ground." (Dubos, 1968).

"Human nature is a reciprocity between organism and environment. It can be expected that it is possible for an environment to have therapeutic effect on people who are disturbed, frustrated and hostile." (Rosenberg, 1967).

"We should expect as much genetic variability in the capacity of individuals to adjust to artificial environments as we find in the physical characteristics of man. Some portions of the population should be expected to have a greater commitment to the natural environment, and will react strongly if deprived of it." (Iltis *et al*, 1970).

(b) Realization of human potential

"Human beings perceive the world, and respond to it, not through the whole spectrum of their potentialities, but only through the areas of this spectrum that have been made functional by environmental stimulation. In other words, life experiences determine what parts of the genetic endowment are converted into functional attributes." (Dubos, 1968).

303

(c) Attainment of spiritual benefits
'Communing with nature', 'being closer to one's Creator', 'finding peace with oneself'.

(d) Escape from the 'rat-race'
'Thoughts of the world outside can be expelled from mind and a body can relax in peace.'

(e) Beauty of nature
An aesthetic, and partly spiritual, motive.

(f) Sociability
Wilderness gives an opportunity to enjoy and make friendships.

(g) Pioneer spirit
Some visitors to the wilderness, with caravans, gas cookers, and refrigerators, still consider that they are conquering the wilderness in the true pioneer spirit of old.

(h) Heritage
Getting closer to life as one's forefathers lived it, and sharing their heritage.

(i) Achievement of personal gratification
The experience of self-sufficiency, or being depended on, helps people realize their full personal capabilities and enables them to meet the world more confidently.

(j) Inspiration
Artists and religious leaders have drawn inspiration from the wilderness. It encourages individuals to discover something extra within themselves.

This list has been reproduced at length as an example of the vague and careless thinking that so often emerges in any discussion concerned with values; and, more particularly, many discussions of landscape as amenity. The first type of benefit (mental health) presumably owes its priority to the number of supporting (sic) quotations McKenry could adduce. These quotations are almost entirely rhetorical suppositions, derived from a widespread but unsupported idea that mental ill-health is principally caused by the products of civilization and urbanization. It may be associated with poverty and high density living, for example, in the developed countries; but these conditions can as easily obtain in agrarian societies. It is unlikely to be the environment as such which causes mental ill-health, so much as the societal factors that lead to the environment being the way it is. If this is so, the flight to nature might have therapeutic or prophylactic value, not because of the influence of the flora and fauna, rivers and rocks; but because the disturbing elements of an urban society and its institutions are left behind.

The list of psychological benefits is noteworthy for its lack of empirical evidence to support it. However intuitively reasonable it may be, it still needs to be shown that they are indeed benefits (and by what criteria). It would be quite possible, also, to establish the extent to which each of them was a primary value-orientation in relation to wilderness. Sociability, for example, appears to be a curious value in this context. If it is a relevant value, its operation is likely to be very different here than in non-wilderness settings. Its interest would lie in this difference, rather than in sociability itself. In fact many of the benefits listed are ones that might be enjoyed in almost any setting. Wilderness then becomes reduced to one of a number of settings in which human values may be exercised. There is nothing 'sui generis' that gives the wilderness a priority for conservation.

The disadvantage of an atheoretical approach like this to the psychology of environmental response is that it has nothing to do with psychology, except in the sense of the naïvest, 'common-sense' psychology evident in so much received opinion and special pleading. A preferable approach would have been to base an analysis upon a scheme of values or of motives that had been formally established and scientifically validated in a variety of other contexts and by various methods. The role of landscape and wilderness value and use could then be fully appreciated in relation to other values and other behaviours.

Techniques of measuring responses to the natural environment

There are similar drawbacks, however, to much of the empirical work that has been done in this area. The purpose has generally been either to explore how people learn about their environments and how they view the world about them, or to derive criteria for planning policies; often both objectives are implied. The general cognitive goal is vaguely formulated and scarcely ever firmly related to a theory of cognition. Landscape is examined in isolation, because the researcher happens to be interested in it; rather than in parallel with other comparable environmental categories. Often it is assumed that the results of any enquiry that happens to throw up empirical findings will generate information that is of use to decision-makers. But no attention is paid to the need to define research objectives in terms that are consonant with the ways in which the decision-makers operate. Unless the questions the research is trying to answer, and the methodology being used, bear such a relation, there is little hope that it can influence practical matters.

Typical of these studies are a number that have elicited responses to the natural environment by means of rating scales, attitudinal statements, or even eye-pupil measurements.

Photographs

For example, Calvin *et al* (1972) had two groups of students rate fifteen photographed views of 'natural scenery' on twenty-one bipolar rating scales. Numerical analysis revealed that two main dimensions lay under the judgments made: (1) natural scenic beauty, which was associated with the area of the photograph filled by distant non-vegetation; and (2) a dimension contrasting natural force with natural tranquillity — the degree of tranquillity being associated with area of any kind of water in the photograph. Comparisons of these dimensions are made with ones identified in studies of house plans and elevations (Canter, 1969), row houses and apartments (Sanoff, 1969), and house interiors (Vielhauer, 1966), and it is concluded that general aesthetic quality is an important factor in describing differences among a variety of environmental displays.

Although it is important to look for such concurrence, it is scarcely surprising in view of the situation in which the experimental subjects found themselves that it emerged. What can people make of being gathered together by a psychologist or other academic specialist and asked to rate a number of photographs, drawings or other representations of the environment? The demand characteristics (*cf.* Orne, 1962) of such a situation are not appreciated by the researcher. It is surely very likely that aesthetic judgments will be made. The kind of response is also influenced, indeed limited, by the range of stimuli presented and by the response-terms provided — in the present case the particular photographs and rating scales supplied by the investigator. One should also note that it is photographs and not the actual scenery which is being put before people; and that these people are a particular élitist group (students), are not randomly selected, and bear a special relationship to the investigator. Even if all these shortcomings were corrected it is not clear what the value of this study could be. If it were conclusively established that the majority of people's responses to landscape features were aesthetically based, and that this was related to the extent of elements other than vegetation visible in the distance, what could a decision-maker conclude from that as advice to his actions? What more could it tell us of the fundamental processes by which people make sense of the world, unless the aesthetic mode of response were hypothesized to play a particular role in cognition generally and this hypothesis were tested?

The ambiguity of environmental studies which use rating scales (often quite erroneously called 'semantic differentials'. The semantic differential is a specific set of rating scales and incorporates a theory of meaning which strictly should be adopted when one says one is using a semantic differential) makes it important to criticize one or two examples as negatively as they deserve.

Face to face with wilderness

Shafer and Mietz (1969) in their attitudinal approach to wilderness reactions improved on one of these sources of criticism by interviewing people while they were actually in a wilderness area for recreational purposes. Five types of statement, dealing with physical, emotional, aesthetic, educational and social experiences associated with wilderness use, were presented to hikers in a paired comparison format. They were also asked initially 'what is the most important thing you enjoy about wilderness recreation?' The rank order of importance of the five values emerged as aesthetic, emotional, physical, educational and social in both of the wilderness areas where the survey was conducted. Scale differences were found, but no information was available to make sense of them.

This study is an advance on McKenry's categorization (see above) in that it attempts to order the values empirically. But their derivation is still theoretically weak, having no firm psychological nor axiological basis. The values were expressed in the investigators' terms, rather than the interviewees'.(To the open-ended question, 47 per cent of responses were primarily emotional in reference, 37 per cent aesthetic, ten per cent physical, and six per cent social ['to be alone']. But little can be inferred from a single open-ended question.) Other comments made by the hikers indicated the importance they attached to scenic variety. The researchers concluded that trails should be engineered so as to provide such variety; they should also cater for emotional experiences (but how?), and provide physical challenge. Although educational and social values are low on the list, they should not be ignored, since it was inevitable that something should be ranked lowest. A conclusion of this kind however, only points out the very imprecise advice which preference rankings can offer the decision-maker.

Method of comparisons

A method of comparisons administered to people at the time of use of natural environments (or rather landscaped recreation facilities) was used by Shafer and Burke (1965). They interviewed 1600 people in four parks over a two-week period, and showed some care in their sample selection. Campers and non-campers were asked for their preference among three photographs showing differing types of provision for swimming areas, picnic areas, toilet facilities, fireplaces, camping space, and camping facilities. A cost was given for each of three options, which respondents were asked to consider. Some consensus in preferences was found. For example, beaches were greatly preferred to lower cost areas adjacent to streams; and a beach with trees, at five times the cost of the stream-site, was most preferred. For cooking, a large built-stone fireplace and a metal fireplace were almost equally preferred, despite an eleven-fold differential in cost; while only one in ten people opted for a piled stone fireplace, despite its being more than fifty times cheaper than the larger version. But campers and non-campers differed in their priorities; and interestingly only the latter's preferences were apparently related to characteristics such as their age and the distance they had travelled to the site.

"Results of this study", it is concluded, "suggest that the day-user and camper at state parks on the megalopolitan fringe prefer, and are willing to pay for, modern recreational facilities set in an open, spacious environment surrounded by a tapestry of woodland. The implications for land-acquisition programs are that open farm lands that have scattered woodlots and lakes, or streams that can be dammed for artificial lakes, are probably more desirable for public and private recreational development for this segment of the recreating public than large tracts of heavily wooded areas." (p.518).

However, there are still a number of disadvantages in this procedure. The nature of facilities presented to interviewees for comparison are determined by the investigators. There is no scope for the public to indicate facilities perhaps of a rather different kind. The facilities offered are also ones that could be currently found in camping areas. No scope is afforded for significant innovation, although this is of the essence in progressive planning. The response mode used in this study is also incomplete. Cost-figures for each facility were introduced as a realistic user-fee, based on the cost of construction, maintenance or improvement, but there is no evidence of what they might have meant either to the survey respondents or to the administrators of the camping areas. The people who were interviewed do not appear to have been asked to consider the total potential fee-cost of their preferred facilities. They might have been asked to apportion costs between facilities from a given sum of money. That sum might have been independently determined as a realistic figure that might be spent on camping fees by people of varying age, income, and so on. In addition, if an economic preference model is assumed for the camping user, one would expect to see the financial implications of elicited preferences spelled out as guidance to administrators; rather than the simplistic conclusion quoted above.

Landscape and psychological theory

There are two particularly interesting examples of approaches to the natural environment which escape the criticisms made so far. The first by Sonnenfeld (1966), a geographer, relates empirical results on landscape preferences to Helson's (1964) theory of 'adaptation level', and additionally is able to derive a number of practical conclusions for planning decisions. Craik (1970), who is a psychologist, has analyzed landscape uses with reference to Sarbin and Allen's (1969) 'role theory'.

Preferences

One of the tests which Sonnenfeld (1966) used was concerned with the visual landscape. He showed 50 pairs of photographed slides to a range of samples — Eskimo from coastal and inland villages in arctic Alaska, various non-natives in the same areas, and student groups in Delaware. Subjects indicated their preferred environment. The photographs were selected so as systematically to vary the types of vegetation, topography, water features and apparent temperature portrayed.

There were cultural differences, sex differences, and age differences in the kinds of landscape preferred. The most interesting differences for the discussion that follows were those between native and non-native samples. For example, natives, whether in Alaska or Delaware, preferred landscapes similar to

310

their home environments, or which differed from others in a way that was consistent with their home environments. Among the arctic groups non-natives differed significantly from natives in having more extreme preferences: for landscapes with rugged relief; for more heavily wooded land; and for apparently colder environments. There were differences between non-natives as a function of their occupations and previous environmental experiences. And the influence of this latter variable was also apparent in the preferences of natives: Eskimos who had experience of non-arctic environments had significantly different preferences from those without such experiences, and in a direction which was consistent with the landscape preferences of non-native groups in the Arctic.

Space, landscape, the native and non-native

Sonnenfeld goes further than many researchers before and since who have elicited environmental preferences. He interprets results like those above in terms of man's perceptual variability and adaptibility. He examines

"the ostensibly basic human need for 'open space' and exposure to 'elemental nature'. Granted there are primary environmental needs for unpolluted atmospheres and waters, and for land capable of providing necessary foods, all required for organic well-being: to what extent are there also secondary environmental needs for adequate open space, parkland, or wilderness areas for mental well-being? What constitutes adequate space and landscape?"(p.73).

A distinction is made between space and landscape. Landscape has many possible meanings — concrete, utilitarian, emotional, symbolic. It "involves a complex of real elements which yield a quite specific imagery". Space is conceptually abstract, "is more symbolically manifest and thus is much more variably perceived." At the same time, three of the most obvious possible determinants of spatial and landscape preference — culture, society, economy — are rejected as being problematic bases for analysis. There are, for example, difficulties in establishing base cultures, bias is introduced by the distinctive environmental traditions of different cultures, and culture is often confounded with economic differences. Economic criteria, on the other hand, are primarily non-aesthetic, while Sonnenfeld chooses to treat landscape mainly in aesthetic terms.

As an alternative basis, he prefers the distinction between native and non-native which emerged as important in his empirical study. This is a simple distinction, which is quite appropriate at least in societies which have geographical as well as social mobility. It rests on residence. The non-native is a migrant who has had more variable environmental experiences. Sonnenfeld further suggests that there may be two 'personality types' among transients: those who are seeking richer environments or environmental variation, "the adventurous, hyperactive, and unsatiated"; and those who are unwilling or unable to adapt to a previous environment, the restless, irresponsible, and dispossessed.

"By contrast, the native would include those contented individuals who may dislike their environment but who are unable to accomplish either a move or a change; and the environmental eunuchs who are largely insensitive to environment." (p. 78).

Adjustment and adaptation

Individual or societal changes in environmental values and demands for space or landscape, and changes in the availability of resources or opportunities to satisfy them may lead to two kinds of 'accommodation'. The first is a type of 'homeostatic' mechanism, an *adjustment* that occurs whenever any imbalance occurs in the relation between the individual or society and the environment. The adjustment may be physiological, as when an individual moves from a temperate to a tropical environment. It may be in a sublimated form, when he adjusts to a lack of contact with nature by gardening, reading, or placing landscape paintings on his wall. Society adjusts to imbalances by instituting 'green belts', for example, or improved leisure and recreation policies. However, when *adaptation* takes place, adjustments of this kind are unnecessary. Man appears capable of both reducing and increasing

312

his sensitivities to cope with unsatisfactory stimuli from the environment. One may adapt to the urban environment by becoming less sensitive to its noise, smells and crowding; and more sensitive to the rare elements of nature — birds, trees, flowers — that are present.

"What then represents the ideal accommodation: 'adjustment' or 'adaptation'? To the extent that these really are mutually exclusive, I would submit that while adjustment seems the preferred human (sapient) means for accommodating to deficiencies of space and landscape, that the capacity of the human organism to *adapt* to these deficiencies has been underrated, and necessarily so." (p.75).

Catering for different tastes

These concepts are applied to the question of how one might plan for the differing environmental preferences of the native and non-native.

"The native is generally accommodated for within any setting; if he is not completely contented with his lot, he is at least resigned to it as one form of adjustment. More likely he has adapted to it through extended residence to the point where it at least does not provide him with any motivating force of discontent; and if offered alternative environments for living, he might even prefer that with which he is most familiar. . . . By contrast, there is less reason for the non-native to be as placid about an inadequate space and landscape. . . . He comes with adaptation levels at least partially determined by prior occupations of space and landscape, and these one can assume to have conditioned his environmental attitudes and preferences . . . given his mobility, the availability of space and an acceptable landscape, which for others less mobile may be unimportant or incapable of precipitating a change, may loom sufficiently large to precipitate further change." (p.75).

In these terms there ceases to be a problem in trying to satisfy the diverse environmental preferences that people may have.

"Attempts to improve the amount of space and quality of landscape for the native may result in wasted space, expense, and effort, given the capacity of any population, especially one of limited environmental experience, to adapt over time to practically any spatial and landscape change which can still provide for private living space and movement. Much of the current concern over the adequacy of space and landscape is related to the existence of an important mobile non-native group, but given their varied geographical experience, no specific kind of space or landscape is likely to prove satisfactory to them. Furthermore, the value of any space or landscape is likely not to rest on its specific character, but rather on the symbolisms — social, aesthetic, and material — that it represents. A solution to the problem of diminishing space and depreciating landscape is, first, to assume and thus require adaptability on the part of all populations; and second, to abstract desirable qualities of space and landscape — privacy, diversity, freedom from the coventional — and to provide for these architecturally. . . . The real problems of a future environment are not so much spatial and aesthetic as they are ecologic — in terms of what population densities and alterations in man-environment relations can be accommodated for safely, and these in terms of physiologic health rather than mental well-being." (pp.81–2).

An analysis in terms of role theory

Craik's (1970) analysis of environmental response in terms of role theory is devoted to the tourist rather than the migrant, though the focus of his attention is another class of non-native than that considered by Sonnenfeld. From this viewpoint

"responsiveness to landscape is structured by the particular role of scenic observer which the individual enacts when touring the countryside" (p.96) ". . . Efforts to achieve an empirical analysis of contemporary environmental roles can employ the network of concepts which constitute role theory, including the notions of role expectation, role acquisition, role skill, role location, and role conflict (Sarbin and Allen,

1968). As the structure of the contemporary taxonomy of environmental roles is identified, research can proceed, relating dimensions of environmental role enactment to personal characteristics of individuals, their significant reference groups, their educational and socio-economic status, and so on." (pp.99—100).

Such a taxonomy might include the observer of picturesque landscape, of romantic landscape, or wilderness landscape. We have already noted that a good deal of attention has been paid to the latter for policy reasons. Craik, however, discusses the first of these in some detail, relying, unlike most environmental psychologists, on historical documents. These have perhaps been too much neglected. The picturesque movement in England during the period 1770-1820 produced a wealth of writings from which one might derive the 'role expectations' of the scenic observer. He was to tour the countryside searching for appropriately picturesque scenes as subjects for painting, and to locate the best viewpoint; he was to keep a tour book as a description, in words and sketches of these scenes for himself and others. The 'role enactment' had its own peculiar paraphernalia of 'Claude glasses' and viewing mirrors. The tour-books and other publications assisted in 'role acquisition', inculcating in the reader the proper principles of the picturesque composition and its particular terminology. Often people accompanying this dedicated tourist constituted an 'audience' for his role, in role theoretic terminology. To them he demonstrated his 'role skill', in knowing how to explore the landscape, look at it, and describe it properly.

Yet another element in role theory which Craik sees as important for the tourist is 'role conflict'. The role of this traveller, concerned about his safety, comfort and arrival at a destination may often be quite in conflict with the peaceful, relaxed and contemplative state required of the scenic observer. Role conflict of this kind must be commonplace to most tourists today.

Finally, the relation of 'environmental props' to scenic role enactment is considered.

". . . the three scenic roles described may place different demands

315

upon landscape in ways that have design and management implications. The observer of picturesque scenery limits himself largely to visual configurations. The observer of romantic landscape also notes sights, sounds, and smells, and desires somewhat more dramatic physiognomic landscape forms. The requirements for enacting the role of wilderness landscape observer are especially stringent, demanding intact ecological niches and genuine isolation. Thus some landscape features are environmental props essential to the full enactment of scenic roles. Environmental props also function as cues that locate the person in a scenic role, rather than in one of the many other kinds of roles concurrently available to him. Other environmental props, such as billboards, may locate the observer in competing, non-scenic roles, such as that of consumer, voter, or traveller. As increased understanding of the effects of environmental props upon *role location* is attained, the design and management of regional landscape may eventually include systematic consideration of the sequence and mixture of environmental props that foster and sustain the enactment of specified roles or combinations of roles." (p.99).

Landscape evaluation and policy

Although an analysis of this kind has considerable psychological interest, it is by no means certain that the theoretical assumptions entailed will be acceptable to policy-makers. It is more likely that they will require an apparently more straightforward appraisal of landscape quality. Craik has reviewed (1972) the bases by which inventories of landscape value and surveys of scenic resources have been carried out, and has made some suggestions as to how they should be organized in future.

The advantages of such appraisals, he points out, are various. They draw attention to the appropriate criteria that may be used when making decisions that affect the landscape — the alignment of roads, or the development of recreation facilities. If the appraisal covers a complete planning region, as did Fines' (1968) study of East Sussex, a context is supplied within which planning choices may be made. If the appraisal is cast in quantitative form, it may lend it more authority in cases where planning proceeds by way of quantitative models. Periodic re-appraisals of an area enable one to monitor improvements or deterioration in a landscape's quality.

East Sussex

Fines' evaluation of East Sussex was carried out by making ratings of the overall beauty of the view from two points in every kilometre square of the county. The view-values were converted into land-values, in such a way that a particular tract of land was evaluated in terms of all the views to which it contributed. The land-values could then be expressed in map-form. There were three aspects of this method which are of particular interest. Firstly, the view–surveyors were instructed to disregard their personal preferences and the effects of sentiment, interest, and surprise. Craik cites two studies that give some support to the idea that aesthetic and preferential judgments may be distinguishable. It is important that this point should be clearly established. Preferences which inevitably reflect a variety of individual and socio-cultural factors will be poor criteria for landscape policy on any scale. But the concept of aesthetic standards suggests a more stable and consensual basis which could be useful. Nor is there any reason why it should not be intelligible and acceptable to laymen. It is necessary that surveyors should be trained to distinguish preferences and evaluations; and only the common component of several surveyors' evaluation of a view should be used.

To help his surveyors Fines provided them with illustrative markers at different points along the rating scale. There were twenty landscape photographs whose values had been determined by ten experts. This is a realistic procedure since evaluation must in some sense be comparative. Provided that the marker values are carefully established the surveyors' judgments will be more likely to reflect common aesthetic standards. Finally, the East Sussex surveyors were allowed to use their discretion in selecting the viewpoints from which they made their evaluations in each kilometre square.

Technical considerations

This is significantly different from the method adopted in other studies. In a survey of river valleys, for example, (Leopold and Marchand, 1968) the viewpoint chosen was of an observer standing by the water and looking up and down the valley. Other studies have taken considerable trouble to perform evaluations on a wide range of systematically or randomly selected photographs. These procedures, however, over-emphasize a pictorial approach to landscape appraisal, and do not cater for an interactive and dynamic involvement with the environment. Where it is known that the principal experience of the landscape will be limited to the view from a motorway, or nature trail, for example, it may be realistic to carry out inventories for standard pathways or 'corridors' in the way that Lowenthal and Riel (1972a) and Litton (1969) have done. But, as Craik suggests, studies are needed at present which combine and compare free exploration by the surveyor, the use of randomly selected pathways and viewing stations, and randomly determined sets of photographs. One might add that the factors of season and weather should be incorporated, however difficult that might be.

A common aim of landscape appraisals is not simply to map its quality, but to determine which physical features — such as relative relief, afforestation, the presence of water — contribute to the quality as judged. Of particular interest will be those features which are susceptible to conservation or development policies. It is a comparatively simple numerical operation, using multivariate regression procedures, to relate physical attributes to landscape evaluations. But it does rely for its validity both on the care with which the evaluation has been made, and also on an adequate specification of physical attributes. This latter requirement may be problematic. Specifying only those attributes which have clear policy implications for example could result in an incomplete and misleading picture. Attempts to analyze the landscape in terms of such variables as the 'perimeter of intermediate vegetation' or 'area of distant water' (Shafer *et al*, 1969) may lead one into a wilderness of complex arrays in which one loses contact equally with planning practicalities and psychological plausibility. What is needed is to use both a reliable basis in the psychology of perception and aesthetic judgment, and also a firm statement about areas of manoeuvre in planning decisions. If the specified physical attributes satisfy these two sets of criteria, one is not guaranteed an infallible solution, but at least it is supportable.

Conclusion

In many ways the research into natural — and man-made — hazards is the most satisfactory work discussed in these three chapters. It deals with critical, life-and-death problems, the solutions to which, when achieved, are quite clear. Man's relationship to the natural environment and to extreme geophysical events intrigues both our romantic and dramatic sensibilities. Work on the perception of hazards and of landscape has tended to use instant methodology. But systemic models, such as Kirkby's, of the dynamic networks involved in adjustment to hazard are sophisticated and promising.

Strictly psychological interest appears to be injected more forcibly when responses to wilderness and the landscape are under consideration. We have seen examples of spurious theorizing. The application of adaptation level theory by Sonnenfeld and role theory by Craik is interesting. But it is very evident that a theory is being *applied*. When one reads Kirkby's approach to the study of man-made hazards one has much more of an impression that here is a *peculiarly appropriate* context for probing theoretical questions relating to awareness, attribution or communication.

Whether or not the outcome is successful, there is a strong motivation in nearly all the work on the natural environment to influence policy decisions fairly directly. This tendency is more marked even than in the last chapter. The hazard research is aimed at alleviating appalling losses of life and of economic resource. Wilderness research is carried out by those who are responsible for its management, who have to decide the competing claims of recreational use and symbolic conservation. One's major criticism of the general policy orientation is that it is insufficiently activist and participatory. The position at the end of the last chapter has just been reached (*cf.* Swan, 1970; Buckhout, 1972) in concern for the natural environment. We anticipate that much of the effort of environmental psychology will soon move in that direction.

Chapter Ten

Contributing to Environmental Decision Making

David Canter

The contribution
of environmental psychology

Where are we, then? We have run the gamut from clos to crowding. We have examined the thermal, acoustic and luminous environments. We have attempted to make some sense of the way people use space, and have examined the agglomeration of environmental aspects, how they may be studied together and apportioned weights. In the subsequent chapters we considered studies of the large scale environment. This included a detailed consideration of urban man, his delights, and difficulties and the possibilities for his participation in decisions about his surroundings. But where does all this leave us?

In the opening chapter a stand was taken on a number of points. The key ones may be recapitulated here. First, it was argued that that branch of existing academic psychology which was concerned with perception had surprisingly little *specific* to offer to the field of environmental psychology, although the *general* scientific approach and viewpoints developed therein had much to commend them. Secondly, that models of man in relation to his physical environment were necessarily complex. We did not anticipate, in the near future, a general model that would explain response, for example, to heat and to landscape in the same terms. Thirdly, environmental psychology is nothing if not applied. It is about actual people in real-world physical environments and is of little value if it cannot eventually influence the interaction of people with their surroundings.

For the first two of these points the preceding nine chapters have produced ample supporting evidence. Traditional psychological research or theories *have* been present but the casual reader could be forgiven for believing that we had never read the works of the leading perceptual psychologists, but the same reader would also have difficulty in demonstrating their relevance.

On the second point even the casual reader will now appreciate the complexities of the interactions we have with our physical surroundings. It is the third of our points, possibly the most significant, which may not have appeared to gain support from the preceding text. The reasons for this lack of support for the applied nature of environmental psychology are such central issues that we shall devote this final chapter to examining them.

The question we are concerned with is: why it is so difficult to produce results from the study of the physical environment which will contribute to design decision making? This is not to suggest that the research covered in this book is all irrelevant, contributing only to the development of some abstract, academic theory. Nor is it to dismiss the 'early days' argument, that it is not more than five or ten years since research in environmental psychology started in earnest, and thus any search for applied pay-off is premature. Rather, we wish to examine some of the factors which separate environmental decision making from environmental research, so that we may better understand the types of bridge which may link the two.

In looking for bridges between research and practice we are implicitly assuming that, in the majority of cases at least, there is a gap. Few practitioners would question this. Yet the gap is greater in some areas than in others. In the area of heating, for instance, or airport noise, the results of early psychological research have found their way directly into design guides and government recommendations (as discussed in Chapters Two and Three,

respectively). Yet even in these areas, recent research developments have not influenced practice significantly. When it comes to
the broader, more complex, issues dealt with in later chapters it is
difficult to find any evidence of influence on practise.

Of course, the commonly held belief that 'pure' research will
eventually find its way into technological development has long
been discredited by historical analyses of the links between
academic discoveries and applications of them. For instance, in
1969 it was pointed out (Hafstad, 1966) that, although the time
between technological innovation and its application has steadily
reduced over the past century, no such relationship exists for the
time between academic discovery and its use in some technical
application. The links for this often appear so tenuous that the
innovation may well have emerged without the scientific discovery. However, the gaps between science and technology in
general appear to be considerably less than those between
environmental research and environmental decision making. What
is it which makes these two activities so difficult to link?

Concepts and language

Probably the greatest area of difference between researcher and
practitioner is in the concepts which they use to describe the
problems which they are tackling. The designer works with a set of
concepts uniquely geared to the decisions he has to make.
Researcher's concepts are built upon their theoretical orientations,
or more particularly, upon the aspects of the situation which they
feel they can measure. For example, the lighting engineer is often
concerned with the number and type of light fittings he will need
to place in a building, and how to bring the electrical energy to
them, whereas the environmental researcher, thinks more naturally
in terms of perceived brightness and its influence upon performance. Although this distinction is, of course, being eroded.
Another example may be given from the area of landscape in
which the landscape designer may conceive of his problem in
terms of the amount of soil to be moved, the environmental
conditions available to him and the passage of the seasons. Even if
he starts from the ambience he is trying to create his concepts will

be directly linked to the materials he manipulates. The researcher will be more excited by the roles of natural landscape facilities and the measurements of people's reactions to landscape beauty.

It is important to appreciate that these are not just differences in the vocabulary available to the various specialists. There are frequent references to difficulties in 'communication' between those involved in the design process and those doing related research. Suggestions such as the preparation of glossaries of technical terms, or the appointment of "translators who will convert the language of one specialist into the language of the other", seem to be based upon the idea that the communication difficulty is only a matter of the understanding of another discipline's terminology. This is to miss the point that the vocabulary is derived from a specific set of processes. Although, as has been pointed out in other places (for example Canter, 1974) there are many parallels between the activities of the architect or planner and the activities of the research worker, there can be no simple translation of the language of a book such as the present one, its 'variables' 'experimental designs' and 'correlation coefficients', into the language of the designer. His 'sketch designs', 'cost accounting' and 'weathering of materials' are concepts which are part of a separate system. The distinction between the researcher's and the designer's system which provides context for their different vocabularies derive from the fact that they both have to function within a different set of real-world constraints. Constraints to which we will now turn our attention.

The immediacy of design

An important aspect of the constraints upon the designer are the *immediacy* of the decisions he must make. He has a rigid sequence to which to work. Contractors and client alike are expecting a finished product from the designer at a specific date in the future. Although the research worker may well have deadlines for reports, the scale of time to which he works is at once both longer and shorter than the architect's or other designers. It is shorter in that usually a research project from beginning to completion takes, at most, two or three years, but it is longer in that he may well devote his life to the resolution of one particular set of problems.

324

Of more importance, he will see the value of his contribution in the way in which it fits into the contributions of other scientists, who have worked before and will come after him, as well as those who are working at the same time.

As a consequence, the research worker is concerned with getting the 'true' answer as effectively as he possibly knows how. He will, for example, wish to measure human annoyance with noise by the 'best' means. This will entail him trying out a variety of measures until he finds one that gives him the maximum relationships to his validity criteria. Rightly too, the designer will frequently not find the time to concern himself with the minutiae of the scientist. The designer is certainly not able to wait for the results of research, which may be germane to his own particular design problem. He may also find that the details (which the researcher has felt necessary to examine, in order to be sure that his answer is accurate) are not the details, which are crucial to the designer. Similarly, the broad overview which the research scientist takes as read, and which he needs to refine and specify before it can be converted into particular research projects, is often the most important contribution which the researcher can make to the design process.

There are a range of ways in which research and design are conducted. The cross fertilization of these two human activities may well be in unexpected combinations. General principles from research may find their way into particular environmental decision making. Of possibly even greater significance, although hardly ever mentioned, is the parallel possibility that a general orientation towards a design may find its way into specific research projects.

Stages in design

The differences in concepts and in time scale grow out of different goals, and the processes which develop to achieve these goals. The processes of research are discussed in detail in many introductory texts (see, for instance, Chapter Two of Canter, 1974). Although these accounts are usually somewhat idealized and do not fully capture the details of the actual activity, they are a lot closer to it than parallel accounts of the design process. For instance,

Broadbent and Ward (1969) in their edited summary of the various design methods in architecture, are really more concerned with proposals for methods which designers *may/should* use than with an account of what they actually *do*. Indeed, Broadbent (1973) in his later writings throws considerable scorn upon the design methodologists and argues that design proceeds by a quite different route to that laid out by the theorists. An important distinction between the characteristics of the research and the design process may be drawn out of the literature which exists. It is the difference between critical analysis on the one hand and the synthesizing of information to make a decision on the other. Any designer reading previous chapters in this book will have been aware of the niggling, almost fretful, search for weaknesses which frequently appear in the text next to accounts of research. For instance, in Chapter Five, Newman receives short shrift for the ideas underlying his design proposals. In Chapter Seven the studies of distance estimation are criticized for being concerned with something other than distance. In other words, ask a researcher the relationship between A and B and he will immediately give you three 'ifs' and two 'buts' before a hesitant indication of the possible relationships in terms of the 'information he has available at the present time'. He is trained to take problems apart, examine their various pieces and to specify the conditions under which they may be expected to fit together again.

Contrast this with asking a designer for help with an environmental decision (whether it be for a new wallpaper or a new metropolis), he will soon have at least one possibility for you to choose from. This is demonstrated clearly in schools of architecture where there is an emphasis often in the early years on holding students back from making a decision until they have sufficient information on which to make it. This facility for coming up with an answer is essential if the designer is to survive. Think even of the complexity of deciding whether to get out of bed in the morning, only when all the relevant information had been amassed. If, in addition one also wished to consider all the possible alternatives to actually getting out of bed, the intricacies are multiplied considerably. As Maver (1971) has pointed out the information store necessary to generate the full range of possible design solutions for a simple building is astronomic, let alone having spare capacity to actually evaluate the solutions. There is thus a real sense within which a designer can have too much information. Yet, as we have seen, a researcher can never have enough.

Career structure

There is one further distinction between the professional activities of academics and designers which, although it is scarcely ever mentioned, may well have the greatest influence on the interactions between the two. This difference lies in what we may call the political or career structure of their jobs.

The comment is often heard that academics must 'publish or perish'. While this may be less true in applied areas, such as environmental research, than it is in the 'pure' area of say, elementary particle physics, and is certainly more true on the North American side of the Atlantic than on the European side, nonetheless, it is a force which undoubtedly leaves its mark on all research activities. Its influence is to nudge research in the direction of relatively small scale, self-contained studies, which fit conventionally into the rubric of existing science. The research councils, for instance, will more readily give funds to a project which has its origins deep in psychology, than one which is structured independently of existing psychological research. Furthermore, certain sorts of topics, studied in a particular way, are more likely to produce results which will lend themselves to publication in a scientific journal, than are others. For example, the study of the effect of noise upon performance is far more likely to produce clear cut, publishable results than is a case study of the acoustic environment of a modern office building. When this influence is put against the complexity of the problems which the environmental psychologist is attempting to resolve, it is little wonder that much of the research can be readily criticized as of little applied relevance.

In some ways these professional limitations may be viewed as an essentially financial problem. If one were to calculate the number of variables, and the number of levels of these variables, which it was necessary to control and measure in order to fully study, say, the psychological processes underlying the response of people to a given building, and then to compare this to the complexity of the problems being studied in a typical chemical laboratory, it is likely that the building problem would emerge as notably more complex. The resources made available for the study of people are only a fraction of those made available to study chemicals. This again, forces the environmental psychologist into small scale experiments with relatively few variables. This implies that even where the research psychologist is attempting to deal directly with real-world problems, the whole structure of his profession will militate against him coming up with a truly real-world answer.

When we consider the designer, the professional inhibitions on him using research are of a different order to those on the researcher in producing usable research. Taking architecture as an example it may be seen that the pressures are essentially organizational ones. It is true that the attitudes of architects towards the behavioural sciences are changing, but even where the architect is keen to make use of whatever psychological information he can obtain, he must use this information in a distinctly unsympathetic context. Besides the time scale which we have already discussed the architect also usually has clear, frequently stringent cost limitations. Indeed, in Britain, much of his concern may be concentrated on producing a building which is within the cost limit. But even independently of the limitations of time and finance the architect must respond to a wide range of influences upon him. Not only must he attend to the advice of his various environmental design consultants, he must also be sensitive to the pleadings of his client and the local council, the fire prevention officer and the contractor. These people will make very specific demands on his design. They will have, for example, things to say about corridor width and the depth of the building's foundations. If the building project is at all large there may well be other directly political influences upon him. Not uncommonly, these influences are of such a form that if a building is not produced quickly, there is a real risk that a building will never be produced at all. These pressures give the design process an urgency which is usually missing in exercises in schools of architecture. Yet even in these exercises it is frequently the case that the student finds the extra burden of incorporating psychological information too much to bear.

328

To summarize, it has been argued that the concepts, professional orientation, and urgency of actual design activity creates a process into which it is difficult to feed psychological information. It is necessary to emphasize that this does not imply any deficiency on the part of either existing designers or existing research workers, or that some new hybrid breed of professional will better bridge the gap. As the text of this book demonstrates, when an architect attempts to do research, or even in the rarer instances when a research scientist attempts to contribute directly to design, they both come up against the difficulties we have been discussing. It is the two systems of human activity which undergo an inherent strain when attempting to cohabit.

The design process

The above account of the difficulties should not be taken to mean that contact between research and practice is impossible. Although we do not have the space to examine the parallels between the environmental design and other professional practice, it should be apparent that some professions have managed to build very strong links to their parent academic disciplines. The medical profession is a good example of practitioners drawing very heavily upon a scientifically based technology. It should certainly be possible for similar links to be forged in the future, for environmental design. In order to see how these links may come about, we must now look more closely at the design process itself. This will enable us to identify those points within it at which the psychological contribution may be most significant.

Most designers seem to accept that the design process is made up of at least three distinct phases (Broadbent and Ward, 1969). The first of these phases is the recognition of the need for a design, and an attempt to analyze the requirements which it will meet. The second stage is the creation of some design solution, often referred to as 'synthesis'. This stage draws together the requirements identified in the first stage and attempts to generate one or a number of solutions which will meet them. The third stage consists of some sort of check that the solution produced does in fact meet the requirements identified. This check may take the form of a formal design evaluation, but it is more likely to be 'the test of time'.

Broadbent (1973) has demonstrated the ways in which this sequence may take place in a variety of contexts. In particular, Broadbent has pointed out that designers, especially architects, have generally used four distinct ways of synthesizing their design solutions. He argues that one of the earliest of these was the pragmatic approach. The pragmatic designer draws upon the materials available to him and creates his design solution directly from the properties of those materials. Usually, the most simple and obvious functions for the building, such as keeping the elements at bay, are taken as the requirements to be met for a truly pragmatic design.

It is easy for pragmatic design to become what Broadbent called 'iconic' design. In this case the designer is attempting to reflect or capture the fixed notion of his culture as to what the design should be like. He attempts to build a 'fixed mental image'.

Moving on from the iconic, designers may break new ground by attempting to build analogies for other forms, usually those found in nature. Probably the most famous example of analogic design is Le Corbusier's Chapel at Ronchamp, for which it is maintained that analogies with the shell of a crab were drawn on, particularly for the roof.

Finally, the designer can draw upon a system which will generate his design. Usually these are proportional systems which give the designer "authority for a great many decisions about the shape of the figure, the size and shape of a facade, a window, a doorway and so on which would otherwise depend upon his personal judgement". This 'canonic' design seems to have a very long history and can be traced at least to the first millennium BC. It probably was essential to the distinction between the vernacular builder and the professional architect. For it is only when a person has a system, preferably esotoric, by which to generate his forms, that he can truly argue that he is a professional with his own unique skills.

Incorporating psychology in design

The above discussion of the process and types of design should be enough to illustrate that there could never be one single way for psychological information to be incorporated in design decision making. There certainly are stages for which the psychological contribution would appear more appropriate. Chapter Six, for example, testifies that there is considerable evidence that psychological research may contribute to the final feedback or evaluation stage of the design process. There is much in common between psychological research and the notion of appraisal. Like most psychological research it is essentially historical, attempting to find out what the effects over time have been of an environment on its inhabitants.

The difficulties of incorporating feedback research information into the design process may be gleaned from the discussion at the beginning of this chapter. Certainly, the small scale over which most building appraisals have been carried out is one factor which must go a long way to circumscribing their usefulness. Nonetheless, it is noticeable that those building types in which there is a constant repetition and development of designs by a central authority, such as school building in Britain, are often some of the most successful designs. This is the case because there is a real possibility that the central authority oversees the continuous production of buildings and can thus actually incorporate information gained from one design in the production of the next.

At the other end of the design process, the inception stage, a stage which might be more effectively called the conception stage, there has been relatively little attempt to look for psychological input. However, there is growing support for the notion that it is at this very early stage that some of the crucial design decisions are made. Hillier *et al* (1972) devoted a paper to the argument that "if research is to make an impact on design it must influence designers at the pre-structuring and conjectural stages". To emphasize their points the authors suggested that "design proceeds by conjecture/ analysis rather than by analysis/synthesis".

It is of little importance whether we consider the conjecture as part of the analysis stage or a separate stage but what is important is that in the early stages of analyzing the design problem there are already present the powerful germs of a design solution. Canter's (1972) study of a children's hospital demonstrated that there were formulations in existence dealing with the actual three dimensional shape of the finished building, long before a detailed analysis of the design requirements had been made. Indeed, we have argued earlier that this preconceptualization of the design problem, the preformulation of potential design proposals, are essential if the designer is to earn a living, especially if he is to earn a living and maintain his sanity. As a consequence, for psychological research to have an impact it is necessary for its influences to be felt at these very early stages of conceptualization. Hillier and his colleagues come down heavily on the side of the values of a theory in providing such an influence. We may perhaps go a stage further and suggest that it is the views that the designer holds of the nature of his building's users which is crucial. In other words, the model of man to which the designer subscribes may well be the most significant single influence on his design.

Possible man-environment relationships

We will return to models shortly, but there is a third type of psychological contribution, which possibly appears the most obvious to the psychologist. This is the contribution which may be made during the process of synthesis, at what is referred to as, the stage of 'scheme design'. At this stage it may be thought that the relationship between physical variables and psychological variables may be drawn upon. It may be argued that if the designer is provided with details of the links say, between room size and

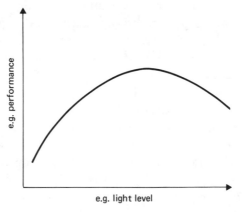

Figure 10.1 Schematic curvilinear relationship

satisfaction then he may simply choose the level of satisfaction he thinks his client can afford and from that read off the room size he should build. This prospect has a number of attractions but it depends upon the form of the relationships which exist.

For example, it became clear in Chapter Three that levels of lighting may be both too high as well as too low. Below a certain level visual accuracy is reduced and above a certain level the problems of glare are introduced. This implies that there is a curvilinear relationship like that shown in Figure 10.1. which may relate performance and probably satisfaction to light intensity. When we have such a curvilinear relationship the possibilities for contributing to scheme design are apparent. The peak of the curve is clearly the ideal situation for which to aim. In a design situation for which it is not possible to get actually the peak of the curve it is still possible to estimate the reduced quality of the environment by establishing how far from the peak the lighting intensity is. Of course, the abstract relationship illustrated begs a number of questions. Certainly, the question of the actual measurement used for the two axes can be raised and the variety of such measurement has been illustrated in Chapter Three. There is also the very real problem of predicting in advance the lighting levels at any particular point. This, however, is a truly technological problem and one which is rapidly being solved by such people as Lynes (1972).

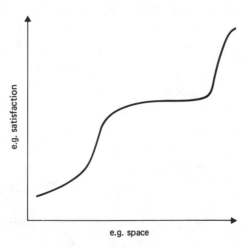

Figure 10.2 Schematic step-function relationship

If we consider now the relationship illustrated in Figure 10.2, we will see that its implications for design are less clear cut. Such a relationship which we may call a step function, might be drawn from the work discussed in Chapter Five. Along the vertical axis we may have some indication of dissatisfaction or a feeling of intrusion and along the horizontal axis we may have the distances which people sit from one another. If the arguments of such writers as Sommer (1969) are correct, and there really is a specific area of personal space in which intrusion is felt, then there will be a relatively small distance over which dramatic changes in response will take place. Such functions are to be expected when dealing with spatial variables, the most obvious being door width. Up to a certain width only one person may get through a door comfortably, but once the width is achieved it then becomes possible for a person to get through with a parcel. Once a further width is achieved, he may get through while continuing a conversation with somebody else. Such notions based upon step functions are built into regulations for buildings such as those relating to means of escape. In this case, for example, unit widths of exits are specified often around 500 mm and designers are often requested to increase their escape. route widths in units of this. Thus, the implication of such functions is that the designer is aware that he must keep close to certain units, above or below those units he is simply wasting his resources.

A third type of relationship, by far the most common between

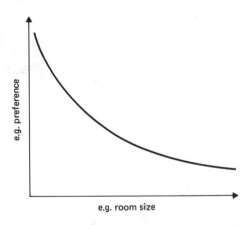

Figure 10.3 Schematic monotonic relationship

physical and psychological variables, is illustrated in Figure 10.3. The relationship between house-to-house distance and privacy, for example, may well be of such a form. Certainly, the relationships between preference and light level described in Chapter Four are of precisely this form, or room size and satisfaction in Chapter Six. Given a relationship like this the designer's job of selection is much more difficult. There are no clear points of change present to guide his decision making. Somehow he has to determine a point of entry on the horizontal or vertical axis and read off the implications of this. If he is able to assign cost values to the physical variables he may be able to decide the range in which he could afford to build certain aspects of the building and then to read off the likely consequences. Alternatively, he could decide on the level of satisfaction, or whatever, which he felt he ought to achieve, and then to work backwards from this to determine the level of physical variable he should select. But in this case, possibly even more so than in the previous two, the exact conditions under which the relationship is established and the details of it may be crucial.

Models of man/environment interaction

It is worth noting that we have found it easier to select examples for these relationships from earlier chapters in the book rather than later. This is because the underlying models to which they all relate are probably more appropriate for the single physical variables of heat, light, sound and space than they are for dealing with complex environmental situations.

The three relationships illustrated all represent mechanical models for human interactions with the environment. They assume that a given level of environmental input will give rise to a given level of psychological response.

This mechanical model may be developed to take into the consideration the properties of systems complete with homeo-static controls. In Chapter Two considerable evidence was presented to demonstrate that the human body does function like a machine in certain respects, especially when it is coping with the thermal environment. However, as we proceeded through Chapters Three, Four and Five the mechanical model was slowly eroded until we were dealing with situations in which interpretations made by the individual played a dominant role, and, as a consequence, it was possible for relationships to develop and evolve in the light of the individual interactions with his situation. This returns us to the discussion that we had earlier when considering the contribution to the architect's preconceptualizations. If he is attempting to use a mechanical model he will look for cut and dried relationships between response and the environment. In some cases this may be appropriate but in others it will not be. He will need a different model.

In Chapter Five we found it necessary to examine a different model of human interactions with his physical surroundings. This was the animal model. From this viewpoint it was thought that existing processes could be established in human beings which had their origins in man's animal ancestry. The importance of the animal origins of these processes was that they would lead to the universal existence of processes and the consequent possibility of designers drawing upon them for their design solutions. Although not quite as unsophisticated as mechanical analogies, because it allows a wide range of interaction with the physical environment, the animal model still has a specific structure to it which would lend itself particularly to the canonical form of design creation. From the point of view of design strategy it certainly puts the architect into the position of a superhuman. He can look down upon his users as animals to be manipulated by his environment.

We saw that there was little evidence for the validity of the animal model of people's interactions with buildings. As a consequence in subsequent chapters, we moved onto a mainly cognitive approach. The range of variations possible within the cognitive model is easily as great as those within the mechanical model. For although we are concerned with people making sense of their environment and actively searching out information in order to facilitate that goal, we may deal with this comprehension either with an emphasis on the social aspects which give rise to it or with the cognitive structures which underlie it. In Chapter Nine, for instance, there was a discussion of the roles which the landscape facilitated. On the other hand, in Chapter Six we laid particular emphasis on the pattern of relationships between the various aspects of building satisfaction. If the landscape architect took up the role model seriously, he would try and create a situation where the 'properties' were provided to facilitate the structuring by the individual, of his own interpretation of the roles which he considers appropriate. This would be quite different from the mechanical approach of setting specific levels of the environment in the confident hope that these will produce responses of satisfactions from it's users.

The problem of criteria

Even when we have identified the most appropriate model, or sub-model, for the particular stage and type of design process, there is still one other important question to be considered. This is the question which found its fullest force in the discussion of distance estimation in Chapter Seven. There the studies of distance estimation were criticized because they had not been demonstrated to relate directly to actual behaviour. The argument put forward there was that the concern with distance estimation was a concern for people's behaviour in cities. People were studying distance estimation as a mediating variable between wishes and actions. It was further argued that until this variable was validated by demonstrating its relationships to the way in which people use cities it was only of tangential academic interest.

This theme also runs through a number of other chapters. In Chapter Four, for instance, the comparison was made between rated satisfaction and its links to the luminous environment and various forms of performance in relation to aspects of the environment. Here again, the distinction is being made between what people say and what people do. In Chapter Six it emerged that two quite different approaches to evaluating total buildings could be discerned. On the one hand, there were the building appraisals, in the main, based on people filling in questionnaires indicating their responses to the environment. On the other hand, there was the observational work, behavioural mapping, which gave an account of what people did within the building.

There are a number of interesting psychological questions about the links between these two sorts of measurements. Clearly, behaviour is much more specific and related to the particular situation in which it occurs, whereas what people say, verbal response, may be much more abstract and more independent of a particular context. Furthermore, there is some debate as to whether behaviour can be taken at its face value or needs interpretation, and as to whether we can deal with the expressed meanings of words or need to explore their underlying dimensions or psychological implications.

The significance of this debate for our present examination of the contribution of research to practice is in the acceptability of a particular form of information. Certainly, the opinion is commonly expressed by designers that designs may not be based upon what people say, because of the confusions and the ambiguities of people's verbal responses. The argument is that behaviour is a criterion in its own right, the goal of a building or a city is to influence what people do and, as a consequence, psychological information of the ways in which people are influenced in their behaviour by their physical surroundings is often taken at its face value. It is accepted as a crucial criterion.

On the other hand, some architectural theorists such as Broadbent (1973) have argued that the central goal of buildings is to influence people's emotional state, particularly their satisfaction. Behaviour is only a means to the achievement of this stage. Therefore, valid and reliable measures of people's emotional responses to physical forms may be taken as acceptable criteria.

The question of criteria as expressed in these two viewpoints can only be resolved by reference to the goals of the organization for which the building is being constructed. There are clearly situations in which one form of criteria or the other is directly applicable. In designing a building which is commercially established so as to attract people to it, such as a discotheque or restaurant, people's comments about how pleasant the building is are not nearly so telling as the frequency with which they actually use the building. Of course, their verbally expressed emotional reactions are very useful indications of the reasons why one building might be successful and another not. They certainly provide useful insight into the process which may be of assistance to the decision maker. Nonetheless, there are other situations in which the organization's goals are not so directly commercial and in which the emotional, or at least the subjective, state of the users are the key consideration. Buildings, such as hospitals for children

338

or housing for the elderly may well fall into this latter category.

In general, we may say that there is considerable advantage in having both forms of criteria available. If we know the links between people's expressed emotional reactions, their actual behaviour and the physical forms of the environment, then we are in a strong position to understand the underlying causal links and, as a consequence, to generate meaningful abstractions or models, of people's interactions. These abstractions may then be of value to the designer.

We need to have as full a picture as possible of people's interactions. This includes what is going on inside of them as well as what we can observe outside of them. This point has been argued elsewhere (Canter, 1970a) demonstrating that there is considerable value in treating building users, both as subjects of research, in that they express their own viewpoints, and as objects of research in which they are studied by observing them. The key point to emerge from this discussion then, is that although as wide a range of information as is possible, is of considerable value in enabling the decision maker to draw upon psychological information, the ways in which he does draw upon that information depends upon the goals of the organization for which he is designing. The application of psychological information cannot be dealt with in the abstract as some simple input. Just as it is meaningless to think of all human action as essentially mechanical response to stimulus, so it is meaningless to think of the design process as a mechanical activity into which new forces can be fed. We may influence the ways in which the environmental designer considers his design problem and we may even contribute, to some degree, towards the particular areas in which he will look for a solution to those problems, but we cannot set up a series of correct answers which will stand for all time and all decision making problems.

Roles for the psychologist in the design process

We have looked at a wide range of man environment interactions. We have further argued that the contribution of the knowledge of these interactions may be very varied and occur in a wide variety of ways. To emphasize and clarify this we must finally turn our attention to one further set of possibilities. This is the question of the *role* of the environmental psychologist within the design process.

One of the key roles which the psychologist may be called on to play may appear as a remarkably simple one. This is related to the fact that the central problem of decision making is in formulating the design requirements. As a consequence, the specialist often finds himself in a position in which his major task is to reformulate the issues with which the design team is concerned and to express them in a more rigorous and coherent language. As will be apparent from earlier chapters the teasing out of the nub of the argument, examination of confusion in concepts, is the central job of the research scientist. He plays with words, he examines theories, formulates hypotheses and, indeed, writes reports. Yet the architect or planner, whose skills lie in manipulating spaces, must nonetheless transmit his ideas, orientations and attitudes to the many others with whom he works, (this includes clarifying these concepts to himself).

Many of these orientations are concerned with the ways in which the environment produced interacts with those who are using it. Thus, there is a value to be gained by drawing upon the language of psychology to reiterate the goals which the building is designed to achieve. For example, the planner concerned with controlling the amount of crowding in a new community may find considerable advantage, especially in talking to others about his problems, in reformulating concepts in terms of the issues which were raised in Chapter Eight. For instance, is it the number of people in a room or the resources available for people to draw on which are crucial factors?

Another role may be called the role of the mediator. Generally speaking the designer is approaching the social scientist or psychologist because of his concern for the actual users of his design. Thus it frequently occurs that the designer is drawing upon the psychologist *in place of* the actual building users. It is thus not surprising that much of the psychological research in relation to the physical environment takes the form of a glorified opinion poll. In Chapter Three, for instance, in dealing with reactions to noise or in Chapter Six when dealing with reactions to the total environment, we were frequently concerned with surveys of user reactions. In this case the psychologist is often only trying to summarize the responses of the potential user, so that he may present them more readily to the decision makers.

An important question here is the degree to which the psychologist should *translate* the user's reactions instead of simply *replaying* them as best he can. The difficulty with only reproducing the responses is that the users may not have a clear idea of what they want. Certainly, if the building is not yet produced there might be great difficulty in determining the validity of the opinions of the potential users.

If the psychologist takes his advocacy role seriously he may become a professional revolutionary, for he is actively attempting to change the decision making process. This does not necessarily remove him from his empirical scientific background. He may well argue, that if the architect is to effectively respond to the feelings and reactions of the potential users, that a totally different design process, which incorporates the users as integrated decision makers, is the only psychologically meaningful solution. It should further be noted that the psychologist's skill will be, in part, in proposing the most appropriate 'revolutionary' solution for each design problem. Not necessarily, in putting forward the same decision making strategy for all environmental matters.

If the environmental psychologist is to function as a revolutionary, or as a specialist or even as a mediator, advocate or verbalizer, a variety of different strategies and skills are necessary. He will need a core of approaches and information to structure his activities, but he will further require some common ground with the designer. The designer will need to understand the basis and framework within which communications from the psychologist are structured. The designer will need to know something of the subject matter and language upon which the psychologist is basing his actions. In other words, both groups need to understand and agree upon the methods, practices and ideas inherent in psychological approaches to the physical environment. It is hoped that this book is a step in that direction.

Bibliography

Abey-Wickrama, I. *et al*, 1969, 'Mental Hospital Admissions and Aircraft Noise', *The Lancet*, (2), 1275, (13 Dec.).

Acking, C.A. and Kuller, R., 1973, 'Presentation and Judgement of Planned Environment and the Hypothesis of Arousal', in Preiser, W.F.E., ed., 1973, 72–83.

Aiello, J. and Aiello, T., 1974, 'The Development of Personal Space: Proxemic Behaviour of Children 6 Through 16', in *Human Ecology*, 2 (3), 117–189.

Akin, O., 1973, 'Contextual Fittingness of Everyday Activity Encounters', in Preiser, W.F.E., ed., 1973, 123–137.

Altman, I., 1971, 'An Ecological Approach to the Functioning of Small Social Groups', in Rassmussen, J.E., *Individual and Group Behaviour in Isolation*, Aldine, Chicago.

Altman, I., 1970, 'Territorial Behaviour in Humans: An Analysis of the Concept', in Pastalan, L. and Carson, D., eds., *Spatial Behaviour of Older People*, University of Michigan, Ann Arbor.

Altman, I. and Haythorn, W., 1967, 'The Ecology of Isolated Groups', *Behavioural Science*, 12, 169–181.

Altman, I. and Taylor, P., 1973, *Social Penetration–The Development of Interpersonal Relationships*, Holt, Rinehart, Winston, New York.

Ammons, C.H., 1955, 'A Task for the Study of Perceptual Learning and performance variables', *Percept. Mot. Skills*, 5, 11–14.

Andersen, J.J. and Olesen, S., 1968, MS thesis, Technical University of Denmark.

Anderson, C.M.B., 1971, *The Measurement of Attitude to Noise and Noises*, National Physical Laboratory Aero Report Ac 52.

Andersson, B., Gale, C. and Sundsten, J., 1964, 'Preoptic Influences on Water

Intake', in Wayner, M.J., ed., *Thirst: 1st International Symposium on Thirst in the Regulation of Body Water*, Pergamon, Oxford.

Anon, 1960, *DIN 1946: Ventilation Plants*, Deutsche Institut für Normalisation.

Appleyard, D., 1969, 'City Designers and the Pluralistic City', in Rodwin, L. *et al*, eds., *Planning for Urban Growth and Regional Development*, MIT Press, Cambridge.

Appleyard, D., 1970, 'Styles and Methods of Structuring a City', *Environment and Behaviour*, 2, 100—117.

Appleyard, D., Craik, K.H., Klapp, M. and Kreimer, A., 1974, 'The Berkeley Environmental Simulator', *Institute of Urban and Regional Development Working Paper No. 206*, University of California, Berkeley.

Archea, J., 1970, *A Beginning Bibliography in socio-physical Technology*, National Bureau of Standards, Washington.

Archea, J. and Eastman, C., 1970, *EDRA Two*, Carnegie-Mellon University, Pennsylvania.

Ardrey, R., 1966, *The Territorial Imperative*, Atheneum, New York.

Argyle, M., ed., 1973, *Social Encounters*, Penguin, Harmondsworth.

Argyle, M., 1969, *Social Interaction*, Methuen, Atherton.

Argyle, M. and Dean, J., 1965, 'Eye Contact, Distance and Affiliation', *Sociometry*, 28, 289—304.

Aston, S.M. and Bellchambers, H.E., 1969, 'Illumination, Colour Rendering and Visual Clarity', *Ltg. Res. and Tech.*, 1, 259—261.

Balder, J.J., 1957, 'Erwunschte Leuchtdichten in Buroraumen', *Lichttechnik*, 9, 455—461.

Ballantyne, E.R., Barned, J.R. and Spencer, J.W., 1967, 'Environment Assessment of Acclimatized Caucasian subjects at Port Moresby, Papua', *Proceedings of the 3rd Australian Building Research Congress*.

Barash, P., 1973, 'Human Ethology: Personal Space Reiterated', in *Environment and Behaviour*, 5.

Barker, M. and Burton, I., 1969, 'Differential Response to Stress in Natural and Social Environments; An Application of a Modified Rosenzweig Picture-Frustration Test', *Natural Hazard Research Working Paper No. 5*, Department of Geography, University of Toronto.

Barker, R. and Wright, H., 1955, *Midwest and its Children*, Harper and Row, New York.

Barker, R.G., 1968, *Ecological Psychology*, Standford, California.

Barker, R.G. and Gump, P.V., eds., 1964, *Big School, Small School: High School Size and Student Behavior*, Stanford University Press.

Bartlett, F.C., 1932, *Remembering*, Cambridge University.

Bechtel, R.B., 1971, 'A Behavioral Comparison of Urban and Small Town Environments, in Archea, J. and Eastman, C., eds., *EDRA Two: Proceedings of the 2nd Annual Environmental Design Research Association Conference*, Carnegie-Mellon University, Pittsburgh.

Bedford, T.A., 1964, *Basic Principles of Ventilation and Heating*, H.K. Lewis, London.

Bednar, M.J., 1970, *User Evaluation of the Spatial Environment: A Study of Methodology*, Rensselaer Polytechnic Institute, New York.

Bellchambers, H.E. and Godby, A.C., 1972, 'Illumination, Colour Rendering and Visual Clarity', *Ltg. Res. Tech.*, 4, 104—106.

Benzinger, T.H., 1959, 'On Physical Heat Regulation and the Sense of

Temperature in Man', *Proceedings of the National Academy of Sciences*, 45, 645–659.

Benzinger, T.H., 1960, 'The Sensory Receptor Organ and Quantitative Mechanism of Human Temperature Control in Warm Environments', *Federation Proceedings*, 19, 32–41.

Benzinger, T.H., Pratt, A.W. and Kitzinger, C., 1961, 'The Thermostatic Control of Human Metabolic Heat Production', *Proceedings of the National Academy of Sciences (USA)*, 47, 730–739.

Benzinger, T.H., 1963, 'Peripheral Cold and Central Warm–Reception, Main Origins of Human Thermal Discomfort', *Proceedings of the National Academy of Sciences*, 49, 832–839.

Beranek, L.L., 1962, *Music, Acoustics and Architecture*, John Wiley, New York.

Berry, P.C., 1961, 'Effect of Colored Illumination upon Perceived Temperature', *Journal of Applied Psychology*, 45, 248–250.

Beutell, A.W., 1934, 'An Analytical Basis for a Lighting Code', *Illum. Engr.*, 27, 5–16.

Biesele, R.L., 1950, 'Effect of Task-to-Surround Lighting ratios on Visual Performance', *Illum. Engng.*, 45, 733–740.

Bitter, C. and Van Ierland, J.F.A.A., 1965, 'Appreciation of Sunlight in the Home', in Hopkinson, R.G., ed., *Sunlight in Buildings*, 27–37.

Blackwell, H.R., 1972, 'A Unified Framework of Methods for Evaluating Visual Performance Aspects of Lighting', *C.I.E. Publication 19*.

Blackwell, H.R. and Smith, S.W., 1970, 'Additional Visual Performance Data for Use in Illumination Specification Systems', *Illum. Engng.*, 65, 389–410.

Blasdel, H.G., 1972, 'Identification of Performance Criteria Using Multi-dimensional Scaling of User Evaluations', *NBS Special Publication 361, Performance Concept in Buildings*, and 'Multi-dimensional Scaling for Architectural Environment', *Environmental Design Association, 3rd Conference*, Los Angeles.

Blaut, J.M., McLeary, G.S. Jr. and Blaut, A.S., 1970, 'Environmental Mapping in Young Children', *Environment and Behaviour*, 2, 335–349.

Bodmann, H.W. and Sollner, G., 1965, 'Glare Evaluation by Luminance Control', *Light and Lighting*, 58, 195–199.

Bodmann, H.W., Sollner, G. and Voit, E., 1963, 'Bewertung von Beleuchtungsniveaus bei Verschiedenen Lichtarten', *Proc. C.I.E. 15th Session (Vienna)*, C. 502.

Boyce, P.R., 1973, 'Age, Illuminance, Visual Performance and Preference', *Ltg. Res. Tech.*, 5, 125–144.

Boyce, P.R. and Lynes, J.A., 1975, 'Illuminance, Colour Rendering Index and Colour Discrimination Index', to be published in the *Proceedings of the CIE*, London.

Boynton, R.M. and Boss, D.E., 1970, *The Effect of Background Luminance upon Visual Search Performance*, University of Rochester, Kent.

Bratfisch, O., 1969, 'A Further Study of the Relation Between Subjective Distance and Emotional Involvement', *Acta Psychologica*, 29, 244–255.

Briggs, R., 1973, 'On the Relationship Between Cognitive and Objective Distance', in Preiser, W.F.E., ed., *Environmental Design Research*, 1, Dowden, Hutchinson and Ross, Stroudsburg.

British Standards Institution, 1967, *BSS4198: Method for Calculating Loudness*, The Institution, London.

Broadbent, D.E., 1958, *Perception and Communication*, Pergamon, Oxford.

Broadbent, G., 1973, *Design in Architecture*, Wiley, New York.

Broadbent, G. and Ward, A., 1969, *Design Methods in Architecture*, Lund Humphries, London.

Brookes, M.J., 1970, *Changes in Employee Attitudes and Work Practices in the Office Landscape*, Human Factors Design and Research Inc., New York.

Brundrett, G.W., 1974, 'Human Sensitivity to Flicker', *Ltg. Res. Tech.*, 6, 127–143.

Brunswick, E., 1956, *Perception and the Representative Design of Psychological Experiments*, University of California, Los Angeles.

Bryan, M.E. and Tempest, W., 1973, 'Are Our Noise Laws Adequate?', *Applied Acoustics*, 6, (3), 219.

Buckhout, R., 1972, 'Pollution and the Psychologist: a call to action', in Wohlwill, J.F. and Carson, D.H., eds., *Environment and the Social Sciences: Perspectives and Applications*, American Psychological Association.

Building Performance Research Unit, 1972, *Building Performance*, Applied Science Publishers, London.

Building Performance Research Unit, 1972a, *Criteria of Sunshine, Daylight, Visual Privacy and View in Housing*, University of Strathclyde, Glasgow.

Burton, I. and Kates, R.W., 1964, 'The Perception of Natural Hazards in Resource Management', *Natural Resources Journal*, 3, 412–441.

Burton, I., Kates, R.W. and White, G.F., 1968, 'The Human Ecology of Extreme Geophysical Events', *Natural Hazard Research Working Paper No. 1*, Department of Geography, University of Toronto.

Buttimer, A., 1972, 'Social Space and the Planning of Residential Areas', *Environment and Behavior*, 4, 279–318.

Bycroft, P. and Wolff, P.M., 1974, 'Effects of Energy Restrictions on Working Attitudes in the Office Environment', *Journal of Architectural Research*, 3, No. 3, 70–73.

CIE International Lighting Vocabulary, 1970, Publication No. 17, (available from Bureau Centrale, 4 Av. du Recteur Poincare, 75-Paris 16^e, France).

Cadwallader, M.T., 1973, 'A Methodological Examination of Cognitive Distance', in Preiser, W.F.E., ed., *Environmental Design Research*, II, Dowden, Hutchinson and Ross, Stroudsberg.

Calhoun, J.B., 1966, 'The Role of Space in Animal Sociology', *Journal of Social Issues*, 22, 46–59.

Calvin, J.S., Dearinger, J.A. and Curtin, M.E., 1972, 'An Attempt at Assessing Preferences for Natural Landscapes', *Environment and Behavior*, 4, 447–470.

Canter, D., 1968a, *The Study of Meaning in Architecture*, University of Strathclyde, Glasgow.

Canter, D., 1970a, *Architectural Psychology*, RIBA, London.

Canter, D., 1970b, 'Need for a Theory of Function in Architecture', *Architect's Journal*, 4 February, 299–302.

Canter, D., 1970, 'Individual Differences in Response to the Physical

346

Environment', *Bulletin of the Bristol Psychological Society*, 23, 123 (abstract).

Canter, D., 1971, *The Development of Scales for the Evaluation of Buildings*, University of Strathclyde, Glasgow.

Canter, D., 1972, 'Royal Hospital for Sick Children: A Psychological Analysis', *Architect's Journal*, 6 September, 525—564.

Canter, D., 1972a, 'Reactions to Open Plan Offices', *Built Environment*, October, 465—467.

Canter, D., 1974, *Psychology for Architects*, Applied Science Publishers, London.

Canter, D., 1968, 'Office Size: An Example of Psychological Research in Architecture', *Architect's Journal*, 24 April, 881—888.

Canter, D., 1969, 'An Intergroup Comparison of Connotative Dimensions in Architecture', *Environment and Behavior*, 1, 37—48.

Canter, D. and Lee, T., 1974, eds., *Psychology and the Built Environment*, Architectural Press, London.

Canter, D. and Wools, R., 1970, 'A Technique for the Subjective Appraisal of Buildings', *Building Science*, 5, 187—198.

Carey, L. and Mapes, R., 1971, *'The Sociology of Planning: A Study of Social Activity on New Housing Estates*, Batsford, London.

Carlson, L.D. and Hsieh, A.C.L., 1965, 'Cold', in Edholm, O.G. and Bacharach, A.L., eds., *The Physiology of Human Survival*, Academic Press, London.

Carpenter, C., 1958, 'Territoriality: A Review of Concepts and Problems', in Roe, A. and Simpson, G., eds., *Behaviour and Envolution*, Yale University Press, New Haven, 224—250.

Chapman, D. and Thomas, G., 1944, 'Lighting in Dwellings', *The Lighting of Buildings, Post War Building Studies*, No. 12 Appendix VI, HMSO, London.

Cheyne, J. and Efran, M., 1972, 'The Effect of Spatial and Interpersonal Variables in the Invasion of Group Controlled Territories', in *Sociometry*, 35, 3, 477—489.

Chrenko, F.A., 1953, 'Heated Ceilings and Comfort', *Journal of the Institute of Heating and Ventilating Engineers*, 20, 375—396, and 21, 145—154.

Christie, A.W. and Fisher, A.J., 1966, The Effect of Glare from Street Lighting Lanterns on the Vision of Drivers of Different Ages, *Trans. Illum. Engng. Soc.*, London, 31, 93—108.

Clamp, P.E., 1973, 'Approach to the Visual Environment', *Arch. Res. Teach.*, 2, 153—160.

Coates, G. and Sanoff, H., 1972, 'Behaviour Maping: The Ecology of Child Behaviour in a Planned Residential Setting', in Mitchell, W.J., ed., *EDRA 3*, 13-2-1 to 13-2-11, University of California, Los Angeles.

Collins, J.B., 1969, *Perceptual Dimensions of Architectural Space Validated against Behavioural Criteria*, University of Utah, Ph.D. Thesis (unpublished).

Collins, J.B. and Hopkinson, R.G., 1954, 'Flicker Discomfort in the Lighting of Buildings', *Trans. Illum. Engng. Soc.*, 19, 135—158.

Colquhoun, W.P. and Goldman, F.R., 1968, 'The Effect of Raised Body Temperature on Vigilance Performance', *Ergonomics*, 11, 48.

Cooper, J.R., Hardy, A.C. and Wiltshire, T.J., 1974, 'Occupier Attitudes to

347

Solar Control Glasses', *J. Arch. Res.*, 3, 29—43.

Cornsweet, T.N., 1970, *Visual Perception*, Academic Press, New York.

Craik, K.H., 1968, 'The Comprehension of the Everyday Physical Environment', *AIP Journal*, January, 34, 29—37.

Craik, K.H., 1970, 'Environmental Psychology', in Newcombe, T.M., ed., *New Directions in Psychology*, Holt, Rinehart and Winston, New York.

Craik, K.H., 1972, 'Psychological Factors in Landscape Appraisal', *Environment and Behavior*, 4, 255—266.

Cunningham, M.C., Carter, J.A., Carter, P.R. and Webb, B.C., 1973, 'Towards a Perceptual Tool in Urban Design: A Street Simulation Study', in Preiser, W.F.E., 1973, *op.cit.* 62—71.

Cuttle, C., 1971, 'Lighting Patterns and the Flow of Light', *Ltg. Res. Tech.*, 3, 171—189.

Cuttle, C., Valentine, W.B., Lynes, J.A. and Burt, W., 1967, 'Beyond the Working Plane', *Proc. CIE 16th Session*, (Washington), B, 471—482.

Davies, D.R., 1968, 'Physiological and Psychological Effects of Exposure to High Intensity Noise', *Applied Acoustics*, 1, (3), 215.

Davis, G. and Roizen, R., 1970, 'Architectural Determinants of Student Satisfaction in College Residence Halls,', in Archea, J. and Eastman, C., 1970, *op.cit.*, 28—44.

Dean, R.D. and McGlothlen, C.L., 1965, 'Effects of Combined Heat and Noise on Human Performance, Physiology and Subjective Estimates of Comfort and Performance', *Proceedings of Institute of Environmental Sciences 1965 Annual Technical Meeting.*

de Jonge, D., 1962, 'Images of Urban Areas', *Journal of the American Institute of Planners*, 28, 266—276.

Delany, M.E., 1972, *A Practical Scheme for Predicting Noise Levels (L_{10}) Arising from Road Traffic*, National Physical Laboratory Acoustics Report Ac 57.

Delong, A., 1970, 'The Micro-Spatial Structure of the Older Person: Some Implications of Planning the Social and Spatial Environment', in Pastalan, L. and Carson, D., eds., 1970, *Spatial Behaviour of Older People*, University of Michigan, Ann Arbor.

Delong, A., 1970a, 'Seating Position and Perceived Characteristics of Members of a Small Group', *Cornell Journal of Social Relations*, 5, 2.

Denton, T., McCollum, J.I., McCollum, C.P. and Stutsman, R., 1973; 'Types of User Building Evaluation', in Preiser, W.F.E., 1973, *op.cit.*

Department of the Environment, 1973, *Planning and Noise*, Circular 10/73, HMSO, London.

Downs, R.M. and Stea, D., 1973, *Image and Environment: Cognitive Mapping and Spatial Behavior*, Aldine, Chicago.

Dubos, R., 1968, 'Environmental Determinants of Human Life', in Glass, D.C., ed., *Environmental Influences*, Rockefeller Press, New York.

Duck, S., 1973, *Personal Relations and Personal Constructs: A Study of Friendship Formation*, Wiley, London.

Duffy, E., 1962, *Activation and Behavior*, Wiley, New York.

Eastmann, A.A., 1968, 'Colour Contrast versus Luminance Contrast', *Illum. Engng.*, 63, 613—620.

Edholm, O.G., 1967, *The Biology of Work*, Weidenfeld and Nicolson, London.

Edwards, M., 1974, 'Comparison of Some Expectations of a Sample of

Housing Architects with Known Data', in Canter, D. and Lee, T., eds., 1974, *op.cit.*, 38—47.

Ekman, G. and Bratsfisch, D., 1965, 'Subjective Distance and Emotional Involvement: A Psychological Mechanism', *Acta Psychologica*, 24, 446—453.

Ellis, F.P., 1953, 'Thermal Comfort in Warm and Humid Atmospheres', Observations on Groups and Individuals in Singapore', *Journal of Hygiene*, 51, 386.

Epaneshnikov, M.M. and Sidorova, T.N., 1965, *The Evaluation of the Saturation with Light of the Rooms of Public Buildings*, 11—14, Svetoteknika.

Eschenbrenner, J., 1971, 'Effects of Intermittent Noise on the Performance of a Complex Psychomotor Task', *Human Factors*, 13, 59—63.

Esser, A., Chamberlain, A., Chappler, E., and Kline, N., 1970, 'Territoriality of Patient on a Research Ward', in Proshansky, H. *et al*, eds., *Environmental Psychology: Man and His Physical Setting*, Holt, Rinehart and Winston, Inc., New York.

Esser, A., 1970, 'Interactional Hierarchy and Power Structure on a Psychiatric Ward: Ethological Studies of Dominance Behaviour in a Total Institution', in Hutt, S. and Hutt, C., eds., *Behaviour Studies in Psychiatry*, Pergamon Press, Oxford.

Eysenck, H.J. and Willett, R.A., 1962, 'Cue-utilisation as a function of drive: an Experimental Study', *Perceptual and Motor Skills*, 15, 229—230.

Fanger, P.O., 1967, 'Calculation of Thermal Comfort: Introduction of a Basic Comfort Equation', *ASHRAE Transactions*, No. 73, Pt. II.

Fanger, P.O., 1972, 'Improvement of Human Comfort and Resulting Effects on Working Capacity, *Biometeorology*, 5, (2), 31—41.

Fanger, P.O., 1970, *Thermal Comfort: Analysis and Applications in Environmental Engineering*, McGraw-Hill, New York.

Fanger, P.O., 1973, 'The Influence of Age, Sex, Adaptation, Season, and Circadian Rhythm on Thermal Comfort Criteria for Man, *Bulletin de l'Institut International du Froid*, Annexe 1973—2, 91—97.

Faris, R.E.L. and Dunham, H.W., 1939, *Mental Disorders in Urban Areas*, University of Chicago.

Feldman, E.E., 1968, *Journal of Personality and Social Psychology*, 10.

Festinger, L., Schacter, S. and Back, K., 1950, *Social Pressures in Informal Groups*, Harper and Row, New York.

Fines, K.D., 1968, 'Landscape Evaluation: A Research Project in East Sussex', *Regional Studies*, 2, 41—55.

Finkleman, J.M. and Glass, D.C., 1970, 'Reappraisal of the Relationship Between Noise and Human Performance by Means of a Subsidiary Task Measure', *Journal of Applied Psychology*, 54, 211—213.

Flynn, J.E., Spencer, T.J., Martyniuk, O. and Hendrick, C., 1973, 'Interim Study of Procedures for Investigating the Effect of Light on Impression and Behaviour', *Journal Illum. Engng. Soc.*, 3, 87—94.

Forster, R.E. and Macpherson. R.K., 1952, 'The Regulation of Body Temperature During Fever', *Journal of Physiology*, 125, 210—220.

Fouilhé, P., 1960, 'Evaluation Subjective des Prix', *Revue Française Sociologique*, 1, 163—172.

Fox, R.H., 1965, 'Heat', in Edholm, O.G. and Bacharach, A.L., eds., *The Physiology of Human Survival*, Academic Press, London.

Freedman, J.L., Klevansky, S. and Ehrlich, P.R., 1971, 'The Effect of Crowding on Human Task Performance', *Journal of Applied Social Psychology*, 1, 7—25.

Fried, M. and Gleicher, P., 1961, 'Some Sources of Residential Satisfaction in an Urban Slum', *Journal of the American Institute of Planners*, 27, 305—315.

Fry, G.A., 1962, 'Assessment of Visual Performance', *Illum. Engng.*, 57, 426—437.

Gagge, A.P., Stolwijk, J.A.J. and Hardy, J.D., 1967, 'Comfort and Thermal Sensations and Associated Physiological Responses at Various Ambient Temperatures', *Environmental Research*, 1, 1—20.

Galloway, W.J. and Bishop, D.E., 1970, *Noise Exposure Forecasts: Evolution, Evaluation, Extensions and Land Use Interpolations*, FAA-NO-70-9.

Garner, W.R., 1962, *Uncertainty and Structure as Psychological Concepts*, Wiley, New York.

Gibson, J.J., 1966, *The Senses Considered as Perceptual Systems*, Houghton Mifflin, Boston.

Goffman, E., 1963, *Behaviour in Public Places*, The Free Press, New York.

Golant, S. and Burton, I., 1969, The Meaning of a Hazard-Application of the Semantic Differential', *Natural Hazard Research Working Paper No. 7*, Department of Geography, University of Toronto.

Golledge, R.G., Briggs, R. and Demko, D., 1969, 'The Configuration of Distances in Intra-urban space', *Proceedings of the Association of American Geographers*, 60—66.

Golledge, R.G., and Zannaras, G., 1973, 'Cognitive Approaches to the Analysis of Human Spatial Behavior', in Ittleson, W.H., ed., *Environment and Cognition*, Seminar Press, New York.

Gould, P. and White, R., 1974, *Mental Maps*, Harmondsworth, Penguin.

Graham, C.H., 1965, *Vision and Visual Perception*, Wiley, New York.

Griffiths, I.D. and Boyce, P.R., 1971, 'Performance and Thermal Comfort', *Ergonomics*, 14, (4), 457—468.

Griffiths, I.D. and Langdon, F.J., 1968, 'Subjective Response to Road Traffice Noise', *Journal Sound. Vib.*, 8, (16).

Griffiths, I.D. and McIntyre, D.A., 1972, 'Radiant Heating and Comfort', *Building Services Engineer*, 40.

Griffiths, I.D. and McIntyre, D.A., 1973a, 'Subjective Responses to Relative Humidity at Two Air Temperatures', *Actes du Colloque International*, 'Prévision Quantitative des Effets Physiologiques et Psychologiques de l'Environnement Thermique Chez l'Homme', *Collection des Colloques Internationaux du CNRS*, Paris.

Griffiths, I.D. and McIntyre, D.A., 1973b, 'The Balance of Radiant and Air Temperature for Warmth in Older Women', *Environmental Research*, 6, (4), 382—388.

Griffiths, I.D. and McIntyre, D.A., 1974, 'Subjective Response to Overhead Thermal Radiation', *Human Factors*, 16, (4), 415—422.

Griffiths, I.D. and McIntyre, D.A., 1974a, 'Sensitivity to Temporal Variations in Thermal Conditions', *Ergonomics*, 17, (4), 499—507.

Haas, J.E., Boggs, K.S. and Bonner, E.J., 1971, 'Weather Modification and the Decision Process', *Environment and Behaviour*, 3, 179—189.

Hafstad, L.R., 1966, 'The Role of Industrial Research', *Science Journal*, September, 2, No. 9, 79—84.

Hall, E.T., 1963, 'A System of Notation of Proxemic Behaviour', *American Anthropologist*, **65**, 1003–26.

Hall, E.T., 1966, *The Hidden Dimension*, Doubleday, New York.

Hansard, 1943, 'House of Commons Rebuilding', *Parliamentary Debates House of Commons*, **393**, No. 114, 403–474, HMSO, London.

Hardy, J.D., 1960, 'The Physiology of Temperature Regulation', *US Navy Bureau of Medicine and Surgery, Task MR 995. 15–2002. 1.*

Harker, S.D.P., 1971, 'Investigations into Subjective Reactions to High Intensity Lighting', *Luterg Report No.40*, Loughborough University, Leicester.

Harman, D.M., 1969, 'The Role of the dB(A)', *Applied Acoustics*, **2**, (2), 101.

Hart, R.A. and Moore, G.T., 1971, 'The Development of Spatial Cognition: a Review', *Place Perception Research Reports, No.7*, Department of Geography, Clark University.

Hawkes, R.J., 1970, 'Multi-dimensional Scaling: A Method for Environmental Studies', *Building*, 19th June, 69–72.

Hawkes, R.J., 1970a, 'A Study of Lighting Quality', *IERI Project*, 96–70.

Hawkes, R.J. and Douglas, H., 1971, 'Subjective Acoustic Experience in Concert Auditoria', *Acustica*, **24**, 5, 235.

Hearn, G., 1957, 'Leadership and the Spatial Factor in Small Groups', *Journal of Abnormal and Social Psychology*, **104**, 269–272.

Hediger, H., 1962, 'The Evolution of Territorial Behaviour', in Washburn, S., ed., *The Social Life of Early Man*, Methuen, London.

Heinemeyer, W.F., 1967, 'The Urban Core as a Centre of Attraction', in *Urban Core and Inner City*, Brill, Leiden.

Helson, H., 1964, *Adaptation Level Theory: An Experimental and Systematic Approach to Behavior*, Harper and Row, New York.

Hershberger, R.G., 1972, 'Towards a Semantic Scale to Measure the Meaning of Architectural Environments' in Mitchell, W.J., ed., *EDRA 3*, University of California, Los Angeles, 6-4-1 to 6-4-10.

Heshka, S. and Nelson, Y., 1972, 'Interpersonal Speaking Distance as a Function of Age, Sex and Relationships', *Sociometry*, **35**, 4, 491–498.

Hillier, B., Musgrove, J. and O'Sullivan, P., 1972, 'Knowlege Design' in Mitchell, W.J., ed., *EDRA 3*, University of California, Los Angeles, 29-3-1 to 29-3-14.

Hinde, R., 1956, 'The Bibliological Significance of the Territories of Birds', *Dissertation Abstracts International: Series B.*, **31**: 7572.

Hochberg, J.E. and Brooks, V., 1962, 'Pictorial Recognition as an Unlearned Ability: A Study of One Child's Performance', *American Journal of Psychology*, **75**, 624–628.

Hoinville, G., 1971, 'Evaluating Community Preferences', *Environment and Planning*, **3**, 33–50.

Hole, W.V. and Attenburrow, J.J., 1966, *Houses and People*, HMSO, London.

Holladay, L.L., 1926, 'The Fundamentals of Glare and Visibility', *J. Opt. Soc. Amer.*, **12**, 271–319.

Holmberg, I. and Wyon, D.P., 1969, 'The Dependence of Performance in School on Classroom Temperature', *Educational and Psychological Interactors*, No.31, School of Education, Malmo.

Hopkinson, R.G., 1963, *Architectural Physics–Lighting*, HMSO, London.

Hopkinson, R.G., 1970, 'Glare from Windows', *Construction Research and*

Development Journal, 2, 98—105.

Hopkinson, R.G. and Collins, J.B., 1970, *The Ergonomics of Lighting,* McDonald.

Horowitz, M., Duffy, D. and Stratton, L., 1964, 'Body-Buffer Zone', *Archives of General Psychiatry,* 11, 651—656.

Houghten, F.C., Teague, W.W., Miller, W.E. and Yant, W.P., 1929, 'Thermal Exchanges Between the Human Body and its Atmospheric Environment', *American Journal of Physiology,* 88, 386—406.

Howard, E., 1920, *Territory in Bird Life,* Murray, London.

Howard, R.B., Mlynorski, F.G. and Saner, G.C., 1972, 'A Comparative Analysis of Affective Responses to Real and Represented Environments' in Mitchell, W.T., ed., *EDRA 3,* University of California, Los Angeles.

Hudson, P., McGraw, W. and McGraw, P., 1971, 'Attention Structure in a Group of Pre-School Infants' in Honikman, B., ed., *Proceedings of the Architectural Psychology Conference at Kingston Polytechnic,* Kingston Polytechnic and RIBA Publications.

Hudson, R., 1974, 'Images of the Retailing Environment: An Example of the Use of the Repertory Grid Methodology', *Environment and Behavior,* (in press).

Humphreys, M.A., 1973, *Personal Communication,*

Huntington, E. and Cushing, S.W., 1921, *Principles of Human Geography,* John Wiley, New York.

Hutt, C. and McGrew, W.C., 1967, 'Effects of Group Density upon Social Behaviour in Humans' in *Changes in Behaviour with Population Density,* Association for the Study of Animal Behaviour Symposium, Oxford.

Hutt, C. and Vaizey, M.J., 1966, 'Differential Effects of Group Density on Social Behaviour', *Nature,* 209, 1371—1372.

Hutte and Cohen, 1964, study cited in Tom Burns' 'Nonverbal Communication', in *Discovery,* 31—35.

Iltis, H.H., Loucks, D.L. and Andrews, P., 1970, 'Criteria for an Optimum Human Environment', *Ekistics,* 29, 449—452.

Ittelson, H., 1959, 'Adaptation Level Theory' in Koch, S., ed., *Psychology: A Study of a Science,* 1, McGraw-Hill, New York.

Ittelson, W.H., 1952, *The Ames Demonstrations in Perception,* Princeton University, Princeton.

Ittelson, W.H., Proshansky, H.M. and Rivlin, L.G., 1970, 'The Environmental Psychology of the Psychiatric Ward', in Proshansky *et al,* eds., 419—439.

Ittelson, W.H., Proshansky, H.M., Rivlin, L.G. and Winkel, H., 1974, *An Introduction to Environmental Psychology,* Holt, Rinehart and Winston, New York.

Johansson, C.R. and Lofstedt, B., 1969, 'The Effects of Classroom Temperatures on School Performance: A Climate Chamber Experiment', *Nordisk Hygien. Tid.,* XLX, 9—19 (in Swedish).

Jones, E.E., Kanouse, D.E., Kelley, H.H., Nisbett, R.E., Valins, S. and Weiner, B., 1971, 1972, *Attribution: Perceiving the Causes of Behavior,* General Learning Press, Morristown.

Jourdain, F., 1921 in Howard, E., *Territory in Bird Life,* Fontana.

Kahneman, D. and Tversky, A., 1973, 'On the Psychology of Prediction',

Psychological Review, **80**, 237—251.

Kamino, K., 1968, *Studies of Pedestrian Movement,* Osako University, Osako.

Kaplan, S., 1973, 'Cognitive Maps, Human Needs and the Designed Environment' in Preiser, W.F.E., ed., *Environmental Design Research,* I, Hutchinson and Ross, Dowden, Stroudsburg.

Kates, R., 1970, 'Natural Hazard in Human Ecological Perspective: Hypotheses and Models', *Natural Hazard Research Working Paper No.14,* Dept. of Geography, University of Toronto.

Keighley, E.C., 1973a, 'Visual Requirements and Reduced Fenestration in Office Buildings in a Study of Window Shape', *Build. Sci.,* 8, 311—320.

Keighley, E.C., 1973b, 'Visual Requirements and Reduced Fenestration in Offices in a Study of Multiple Aperture and Window Area', *Build. Sci.,* 8, 321—331.

Kelly, D.H., 1961, 'Flicker Fusion and Harmonic Analysis', *J. Opt. Soc. Amer.,* 51, 917—918.

Kelly, D.H., 1961a, 'Visual Responses to Time-Dependent Stimuli', 'Amplitude Sensitivity Measurement', *J. Opt. Soc. Amer.,* 51, 422—429.

Kelly, G.A., 1955, *The Psychology of Personal Constructs,* Norton, New York.

Kenshalo, D.R. and Nafe, J.P., 1962, 'A Quantitative Theory of Feeling', *Psychological Review,* 69, 17—33.

Kepes, G., 1956, *The New Landscape,* Theobald, Chicago.

Khck, J. and Krivohlavy, J., 1967, 'Evaluation of the Criterion to Measure the Suitability of Visual Conditions', *Proc. C.I.E., 16th Session,* (Washington), B., 306—317.

Kirkby, A., 1973, *Some Perspectives on Environmental Hazard Research,* Department of Psychology, University of Bristol.

Klopfer, P., 1969, *Habitats, and Territories: A Study of the Use of Space by Animals,* Basic Books, London.

Kosten, C.W. and Van Os, G.J., 1962, 'Community Reaction Criteria for External Noises: Paper F-5 in NPL Symposium No.13, *The Control of Noise,* HMSO, London.

Kruithof, A.A., 1941, 'Tubular Luminescence Lamps for General Illumination', *Philips Tech. Rev.,* 6, 65—73.

Kryter, K.D., 1959, *J. Acoust. Soc. Amer.,* 31, No.1415.

Küller, R., ed., 1973, *Architectural Psychology: Proceedings of the Lund Conference,* Student Litteratur, Lund.

Kuper, L., 1953, 'Blue Print for Living Together' in Kuper, L. *et al, Living in Towns,* Cressent Press, London.

Landsberger, H.A., 1961, *Hawthorn Revisited,* Cornell University, Cornell.

Langdon, F.J., 1966, *Modern Offices: A User Survey,* HMSO, London.

Langdon, F.J. and Scholes, W.E., 1968, 'The Traffic Noise Index: A Method of Assessing Noise Nuisance', *A.J.,* 147, 17 April.

Lansing, J.B. and Marans, R.W., 1969, 'Evaluation of Neighborhood Quality', *Journal of the American Institute of Planners,* 35, 195—199.

Latané, B. and Darley, J., 1970, *The Unresponsive Bystander,* Appleton-Century-Croft, New York.

Lau, J.J.H., 1970a, 'Differences Between Full-Size and Scale Model Rooms in the Assessment of Lighting Quality', in Canter, D.V., ed.

Lawson, B.R. and Walters, D., 1974, *The Effects of a New Motorway on an Established Residential Area.*

Lawton, M.P., 1972, 'Some Beginnings of an Ecological Psychology of Old Age' in Wohlwill, J.F. and Carson, D.H., *Environment and the Social Sciences*, American Psychological Association, Washington.

Leavitt, H., 1951, 'Some Effects of Certain Communication Patterns on Group Performance', *Journal of Abnormal and Social Psychology*, 46, 38—50.

Lee, T.R., 1962, ' "Brennan's Law" of Shopping Behaviour', *Psychological Reports*, 11, 662.

Lee, T.R., 1970, 'Perceived Distance as a Function of Direction in the City', *Environment and Behavior*, 2, 40—51.

Lee, T.R., 1971, 'Psychology and Architectural Determinism (part 3)', *Architects Journal*, 154, 651—659.

Lee, T.R., 1968, 'Urban Neighborhood as a Socio-Spatial Schema', *Human Relations*, 21, 241—267.

Lee, T.R., 1971, 'Psychology and Architectural Determinism (part 2)', *Architects Journal*, 154, 475—483.

Lee, T.R., 1971, 'Psychology and Architectural Determinism', *Architects Journal*, 4 August, 253—262.

Lee, T.R., 1957, 'On the Relation Between the School Journey and Social and Emotional Adjustment in Rural Infant Children', *British Journal of Educational Psychology*, 27, 101—114.

Leibman, M., 1970, 'The Effects of Sex and Race Norms on Personal Space', *Environment and Behaviour*, 2, (2), 208—246.

Leithead, C.S. and Lind, A.R., 1964, *Heat Stress and Heat Disorders*, Cassell, London.

Leopold, L.B. and Marchand, M.O., 1968, 'On the Quantative Inventory of the Riverscape', *Water Resources Research*, 4, 709—717.

Leyhausen, P., 1970, 'The Communal Organisation of Solitary Mammals', in Proshansky, H., Ittelson, W. and Rivlin, L., eds., *Environmental Psychology*, Holt, Rinehart and Winston, Inc., New York.

Lindzey, G. and Thorpe, J.H., 1968, 'Projective Techniques' in *International Encyclopedia of the Social Sciences*, 12, Sills, D.L. ed., Free Press, New York.

Lipman, A., 1968, 'Building Design and Social Interaction', *Architects Journal*, 147, 23—30.

Little, K., 1965, 'Personal Space' in *Journal of Experimental Social Psychology*, 1, 237—247.

Litton, R.B. (Jr.), 1969, 'Forest Landscape Description and Inventories: A Basis for Land Planning and Design', *USDA Forest Service Research Paper PSW-49*, Pacific Southwest Forest and Range Experiment Station, Berkeley.

Longmore, J. and Ne'eman, E., 1973, 'The Availability of Sunshine and Human Requirements for Sunlight in Buildings', Conference on 'Environmental Research in Real Buildings', N.I.C./Committee TC 3.3, September, Cardiff.

Lowenthal, D. and Riel, M., 1972a, 'The Nature of Perceived and Imagined Environments', *Environment and Behavior*, 4, 189—207.

Lowenthal, D. and Riel, M., 1972b, 'Environmental Assessment: A Case Study of New York City', *Publications in Environmental Perception No.1*, American Geographical Association, New York.

Lowenthal, D. and Riel, M., 1972c, 'Environmental Structures: Semantic and

354

Experiential Components, *Publications in Environmental Perception No.8'*, American Geographical Association, New York.

Lowrey, R.A., 1971, 'Distance Concepts of Urban Residents', in Archea, J. and Eastman, C., eds., *EDRA Two: Proceedings of the 2nd Annual Environmental Design Research Association Conference*, Carnegie-Mellon University, Pittsburgh.

Lynch, K., 1960, *The Image of the City*, MIT Press, Cambridge.

Lynes, J., 1972, *Principles of Natural Lighting*, Applied Science Publishers, London.

Lynes, J., 1971, 'Lightness, Colour and Constancy in Lighting Design', *Ltg. Res. and Tech.*, 3, 24—42.

Lynes, J.A., Burt, W., Jackson, G.K. and Cuttle, C., 1966, 'The Flow of Light into Buildings', *Trans. Illum. Eng. Soc.*, 31, 65—91, London.

Lythgoe, R.J., 1932, *The Measurement of Visual Acuity*, Medical Research Council Special Report No.173.

McCormick, E.J., 1970, *Human Factors Engineering*, McGraw-Hill, New York.

McGrath, J.J., 1963, 'Irrelevant Stimulation and Vigilance Performance', in Buckner, D.N. and McGrath, J.J., *Vigilance, A Symposium*, McGraw-Hill.

McIntyre, D.A., 1973, 'A Guide to Thermal Comfort', *Applied Ergonomics*, 4, 2, 66—72.

McIntyre, D.A. and Griffiths, I.D., 1972, 'Subjective Response to Radiant and Convective Environments', *Environmental Research*, 5, 4, 471—482.

McKennell, A.C., 1963, *Aircraft Noise Annoyance Around London (Heathrow) Airport*, Central Office of Information, SS.331.

McKennell, A.C. and Hunt, E.A., 1966, *Noise Annoyance in Central London*, The Government Social Survey, SS.332.

McKenry, K., 1971, *Value Analysis of Wilderness Areas*, unpublished MSc thesis, University of Strathclyde.

McKenzie, R.D., 1933, *The Metropolitan Community*, McGraw-Hill, New York.

Mackey, C.O., 1944, 'Radiant Heating and Cooling Part II', *Cornell University Engineering Experimental Station Bulletin No.33*.

Macmillan, M.G., Reid, C.M., Shirley, D. and Passmore, R., 1965, 'Body Composition, Resting Oxygen Consumption and Urinary Creatinine in Edinburgh Students', *Lancet*, 1, 728—729.

McNall, P.E., Jaax, J., Rohles, F.H., Nevins, R.G. and Springer, W., 1967, 'Thermal Comfort (Thermally Neutral) Conditions for Three Levels of Activity', *ASHRAE Transactions* No.73.

McNall, P.E. and Biddison, R.E., 1970, 'Thermal and Comfort Sensations of Sedentary Persons Exposed to Asymmetric Radiation Fields', *ASHRAE Transactions* No.76.

Mackworth, N.H., 1950, *Researches on the Measurement of Human Performance*, Medical Research Council Special Report Series No.268, HMSO, London.

Manning, P., 1965, ed., *Office Design: A Study of Environment*, University of Liverpool, Liverpool.

Markus, T., 1969, 'Design and Research—Co-operation Not Conflict', *Conrad*, July, 1, No.2, 35—38.

Markus, T.A., 1965, 'The Significance of Sunshine and View for Office

Workers', in Hopkinson, R.G., ed., *Sunlight in Buildings*, 59—93.

Marsden, H., 1971, 'Intergroup Relations in Rhesus Monkeys (Macacca Mulatta)', in Esser, A., ed., *Behaviour and Environment, The Use of Space by Animals and Men*, Pleum Press, New York, London.

Marshall, A.H., 1967, 'A Note on the Importance of Room Cross-section in Concert Halls', *J. Sound Vib.*, 5, 100.

Maurer, R. and Baxter, J.C., 1972, 'Image of the Neighborhood and City Among Black-, Anglo- and Mexican-American Children', *Environment and Behavior*, 4, 351—388.

Maver, T., 1971, *Building Services Design: A Systemic Approach*, RIBA, London.

Mehrabian, A. and Diamond, S., 1971, 'Seating Arrangements and Conversation', in *Sociometry*, 34, 281—289.

Milgram, S., 1970, 'The Experience of Living in Cities', *Science*, 167, 1461—1468.

Milova, A., 1971, *The Influence of Light of Different Spectral Composition on Visual Performance*, C.I.E., Barcelona, 7107.

Ministry of Housing, 1967, 'Housing at Coventry', *Official Architecture and Planning*, 30, No.12.

Morgan, M.H., 1960, *Vitruvius' Ten Books on Architecture*, Dover Publications, New York.

Morris, D., 1967, *The Naked Ape*, McGraw-Hill, New York.

Moos, R.H. and Insel, P.M., eds., 1974, *Issues in Social Ecology: Human Milieus*, National Press Books, Palo Alto.

Muck, E. and Bodmann, H.W., 1961, 'Die Bedeutung des Beleuchtungsniveaus bei Praktischer Sehtatigkeit', *Lichttechnik*, 13, 502—507.

Munro, A.F. and Chrenko, F.A., 1949, 'The Effect of Radiation from the Surroundings on Subjective Impressions of Freshness', *Journal of Hygiene*, Cambridge, 47, 288.

Munroe, R.H. and Munroe, R.L., 1971, 'Household Density and Infant Care in an East African Society', *Journal of Social Psychology*, 83, 3—13.

Murray, A., 1943, *Thematic Apperception Test: Pictures and Manual*, Harvard University Press, Cambridge.

Murray, R., 1974, 'Influence of Crowding in Children's Behaviour' in Canter, D. and Lee, T., eds., *Psychology and the Built Environment*, Architectural Press, London.

Ne'eman, E. and Hopkinson, R.G., 1970, 'Critical Minimum Acceptable Window Size: A Study of Window Design and Provision of View', *Ltg. Res. Tech.*, 2, 17—27.

Ne'eman, E., 1974, 'Visual Aspects of Sunlight in Buildings', *Ltg. Res. Tech.*, 6, 159—164.

Nevins, R.G., Rohles, F.H., Springer, W. and Feyerherm, A.M., 1966, 'A Temperature-humidity Chart for Thermal Comfort of Seated Persons', *ASHRAE Transactions*, No.27.

Newburgh, L.H., 1968, *Physiology of Human Heat Regulation and the Science of Clothing*, Hafner, New York.

Newcomb, T., 1956, 'The Prediction of Interpersonal Attraction', *American Psychologist*, 11, 575—586.

Newman, O., 1972, *Defensible Space*, MacMillan, New York.

Nielsen, M. and Pedersen, L., 1952, 'Studies on the Heat Loss by Radiation and Convection from the Clothed Human Body', *Acta Physiol. Scand.*, 27, 272—294.

Niesser, U., 1971, *Cognitive Psychology*, Appleton-Century-Crofts, New York.

Norum, G., Russo, N. and Sommer, R., 1967, 'Seating Patterns and Group Task', *Psychology in the Schools (4)*, 276—280.

Osbourne, R.M., 1971, 'An Office Landscape Experiment in the Post Office', *Commonwealth Government Management Services Journal*, 14—22.

Osgood, C.E., 1970, 'Interpersonal Verbs and Interpersonal Behaviour', in Cowan, J.L., ed., *Studies in Thought and Language*, University of Arizona, Tucson.

Osgood, C.E., Suci, G.J. and Tarrenbaum, P.H., 1956, 'The Measurement of Meaning', *Urbana*, University of Illinois Press.

Osgood, C.E., Suci, G.J. and Tannenbaum, P.H., 1957, *The Measurement of Meaning*, University of Chicago Press, Chicago.

Orne, M.T., 1962, 'On the Social Psychology of the Psychological Experiment: with particular reference to demand characteristics and their implications', *American Psychologist*, 17, 776—783.

Pastalan, L., 1970, 'Privacy as an Expression of Human Territoriality', in Pastalan, L. and Carson, D., eds., *Spatial Behaviour of Older People*, The University of Michigan, Ann Arbor.

Patterson, M. and Holes, P., 1966, 'Social Interaction Correlates of the MPI Extraversion-Introversion Scale', *American Psychologist*, 21, 724—725.

Patterson, M., 1971, 'Compensatory Reactions to Spatial Intrusion', *Sociometry*, 34, 114—121.

Patterson, M. and Sechrest, L., 1970, 'Interpersonal Distance and Impression Formation', *Journal of Personality*, 38, 161—166.

Pederson, P.M. and Shears, L.M., 1973, 'A Review of Personal Space Research in the Framework of General System Theory', *Psychological Bulletin*, 80, No.5, 367—388.

Pepler, R.D., 1958, 'Warmth and Performance: An Investigation in the Tropics', *Ergonomics*, 2, (1), 63—88.

Pepler, R.D., 1963, 'Performance and Well-being in Heat', in *Temperature: its Measurement and Control in Science and Industry*, 3, Part 3 Reinhold Publishing Corporation, New York.

Peterson, J.M., Woodman, D. and Eaton, R., 1969, *Slides versus Buildings*, University of Cincinnati, Mimeo.

Poulton, E.C. and Kerslake, D. McK., 1965, 'Effect of Warmth on Perceptual Efficiency', *Aerospace Medicine*, 36, 29—34.

Porter, M. Argyle, M. and Salter, V., 1970, 'What is Signalled by Proxemity', *Perceptual and Motor Skills*, 30, 39—42.

Preiser, W.F.E., 1972, 'The Use of Ethological Methods in Environmental Analysis: A Case Study', in Mitchell, W.J., ed., *EDRA Three*, University of California, Los Angeles.

Preiser, W.F.E., 1973, *Environmental Design Research*, Dowden, Hutchinson and Ross, Pennsylvania.

Proplan Ltd., 1966, *Housing, Tenant Survey prepared for Wates*, Proplan Ltd., Croydon.

Proshansky, H.M., Ittelson, W.H. and Rivlin, L.G., 1970, eds., *Environmental*

357

Psychology: Man and his Physical Setting, Holt, Rinehart and Winston, New York.

Provins, K.A., 1966, 'Environmental Heat, Body Temperature and Behaviour: An Hypothesis', *Australian Journal of Psychology*, 18, 118—129.

Pyron, B., 1972, 'Form Diversity in Human Habitats', *Environment and Behaviour*, 4, No.1, March, 87—120.

Rainwater, L., 1966, 'Fear and the House-as-Haven in the Lower Class', *Journal of the American Institute of Planners*, 32, 23—31.

Rapoport, A. and Watson, N., 1972, 'Cultural Variability in Physical Standards', in Guttman, R., ed., *People and Buildings*, Basic Books, New York.

Rasmussen, O.B., 1971, 'Man's Subjective Perception of Air Humidity', *Proceedings of 5th International Congress for Heating, Ventilating and Air-Conditioning*, Copenhagen, 1, 79—86.

Reed, S.K., 1973, *Psychological Processes in Pattern Recognition*, Academic Press, London.

Rivlin, L.G. and Wolfe, M., 1972, 'The Early History of a Psychiatric Hospital for Children: Expectations and Reality', *Environment and Behaviour*, 4, No.1, 33—72.

Robinson, D.W., 1969, *National Physical Laboratory Aero Report*, Ac. 38, March.

Roethlisberger, F.J. and Dickson, W.J., 1939, *Management and the Worker*, Harvard University, Cambridge, Massachusetts.

Rosenberg, G., 1967, 'City Planning Theory and the Quality of Life', *Ekistics*, 24, 411—414.

Rosenzweig, S., 1945, 'The Picture-Association Method and its Application in a Study of Reactions to Frustration', *Journal of Personality*, 14, 3—23.

Ross, H., 1974, *Behaviour and Perception in Strange Environments*, George Allen and Unwin, London.

Rotter, J.B., 1966, 'Generalised Expectancies for Internal Versus External Control of Reinforcement', *Psychological Monographs*, 80, 1—28.

Rowlands, E., Waters, I., Loe, D.L. and Hopkinson, R.G., 1973, 'Visual Performance in Illumination of Differing Spectral Quality', *UCERG Report*, University College, London.

Russo, N., 1969, Study cited in Sommer, R., *Personal Space: The Behavioural Basis of Design*, Prentice-Hall, Englewood Cliffs, New Jersey.

Ryd, H. and Wyon, D.P., 1970, *Methods of Evaluating Human Stress due to Climate*, National Swedish Institute for Building Research No.D6/70.

Saarinen, T.F., 1966, 'Perception of the Drought Hazard on the Great Plains', Department of Geography Research Paper No.106, University of Chicago, Chicago.

Saarinen, T.F., 1973, 'The Use of Projective Techniques in Geographic Research' in Ittleson, W.H., ed., *Environment and Cognition*, Seminar, New York.

Saegert, S., 1970, 'Crowding: Cognitive Overload and Behavioral Constraint,' Graduate School and University Centre of the City University, New York.

Sanoff, H., 1969, 'Visual Attributes of the Physical Environment' in *Response to Environment*, Student Publication of the School of

Design, No.18, Raleigh, North Carolina State University.

Sarbin, T.R. and Allen, V.L., 1968, 'Role Theory' in Lindzey, G. and Aronson, E., eds., *Handbook of Social Psychology*, I, Addison-Wesley, Reading, Mass.

Sarbin, T. and Vernon, A., 1968, 'Role Theory' in Lindzey, G. and Aronson, E., eds., *The Handbook of Social Psychology*, *2nd Edition*, 488–567, Addison-Wesley, Reading, Mass.

Sargent, S., 1974, 'Crowding: Cognitive Overload and Behavioural Constraint', Paper received from the Environmental Psychology Program, City University of New York.

Saunders, J.E., 1969, 'The Role of the Level and Diversity of Horizontal Illumination in an Appraisal of a Simple Office Task', *Ltg. Res. Tech.*, 1, 37–46.

Schlegel, J.C. and McNall, P.E., 1968, 'The Effect of Asymmetric Radiation on the Thermal and Comfort Sensations of Sedentary Subjects', *ASHRAE Transactions No.74.*

Scholes, W.E. and Sargent, J.W., 1971, 'Designing Against Noise from Road Traffic', *Applied Acoustics*, 4, (3), 203.

Scott, D.E. and Blackwell, H.R., 1970, *Visual Performance in a Landolt Ring Task*, Ohio State University Report.

Seashore, S.E., 1963, 'Field Experiments with Formal Organisations', *Human Organisation*, 164–170.

SEF, 1972, *Academic Evaluation: An Interim Report*, Metropolitan Toronto School Board, Toronto.

Shafer, E.L. (Jr.), and Burke, H.D., 1965, 'Preferences for Outdoor Recreation Facilities in Four State Parks', *Journal of Forestry*, 63, 512–518.

Shafer, E.L. Jr., Hamilton, J.F. (Jr.), and Schmidt, E.A., 1969, 'Natural Landscape Preferences: A Predictive Model', *Journal of Leisure Research*, 1, 1–19.

Shafer, E.L. Jr. and Mietz, J., 1969, 'Aesthetic and Emotional Experiences Rate High With Northeast Wilderness Hikers', *Environment and Behavior*, 1, 187–197.

Shafer, E.L. and Richards, T.A., 1974, 'A Comparison of Viewer Reactions to Outdoor Scenes and Photographs of Those Scenes', in Canter, D. and Lee, T. *op cit.*

Sheehan, L. and Hewitt, K., 1969, 'A Pilot Survey of Global Natural Disasters of the Past Twenty Years', *Natural Hazard Research Working Paper No.11*, Department of Geography, University of Toronto.

Simonson, E. and Brozek, J., 1948, 'Effect of Illumination Level on Visual Performance and Fatigue', *J. Opt. Soc. Amer.*, 38, 384–397.

Sims, J. and Saarinen, T.F., 1969, 'Coping With Environmental Threat: Great Plains Farmers and the Sudden Storm', *Annals of the Association of American Geographers*, 59, 677–686.

Sommer, R., 1970, 'Small Group Ecology in Institutions for the Elderly' in Pastalan, L. and Carson, D., eds., *Spatial Behaviour of Older People*, University of Michigan, Ann Arbor.

Sommer, R., 1966 and 1970, 'The Ecology of Privacy', originally in *The Library Quarterly*, 1966, 36, 234–248. Taken from Proshansky, H., Ittelson, W. and Rivlin, L., 1970, *Environmental Psychology*, Holt, Rinehart and Winston, New York.

Sommer, R., 1969, 'Studies in Personal Space', *Sociometry*, 22, 247–260.

359

Sommer, R., 1967, *Personal Space, the Behaviour Basis of Design*, Prentice-Hall Inc., Englewood Cliffs, New Jersey.

Sommer, R. and Gifford, R., 1968, 'The Desk or the Bed?", *Personnel and Guidance Journal*, May, 876—878.

Sonnenfeld, J., 1966, 'Variable Values in Space and Landscape: An Inquiry into the Nature of Environmental Necessity', *Journal of Social Issues*, 22, 71—82.

Sprague, C.H. and McNall, P.E., 1970, 'The Effects of Fluctuating Temperature and Relative Humidity on the Thermal Sensation (Thermal Comfort) of Sedentary Subjects', *ASHRAE Transactions No.76*, Part I.

Stea, D., 1969, 'The Measurement of Mental Maps: An Experimental Model for Studying Conceptual Spaces', *Studies in Geography*, No.17, Northwestern University, Evanston.

Stevens, S.S., 1961, 'To Honor Fechner and Repeal His Law', *Science*, 133, 80—86.

Stevens, W.R. and Foxell, C.A.P., 1955, 'Visual Acuity', *Lt. and Ltg.*, 48, 419—424.

Stevens, K.N. and Pietrasanta, A.C., 1957, *Procedures for Estimating Noise Exposure and Resulting Community Reactions from Airbase Operations*, WADC TN-57-10, Wright—Patterson Airforce Base, Ohio.

Stiles, W.S., 1928, 'The Effect of Glare on the Brightness Difference Threshold', *Proc. Roy. Soc.*, B., 104, 322—351.

Stilitz, I., 1970, 'Pedestrian Congestion', in Canter, D., ed., *Architectural Psychology*, RIBA Publications Ltd., London.

Stokols, D., 1972, 'On the Distinction Between Density and Crowding: Some Implications for Future Research', *Psychological Review*, 79, 275—277.

Stone, P.T. and Harker, S.D.P., 1973, 'Individual and Group Differences in Discomfort Glare Responses', *Ltg. Res. Tech.*, 5, 41—49.

Stone, P.T. and Groves, S.D.P., 1968, 'Discomfort Glare and Visual Performance', *Trans. Illum. Eng. Soc. (London)*, 33, 9—15.

Stratton, L., Tekippe, D. and Flick, G., 1973, 'Personal Space and Self-Concept', in *Sociometry*, 36, 424—429.

Stringer, P., 1972, 'Some Remarks on People's Evaluation of Environments' in Wilson, A.G., ed., *Patterns and Processes in Urban and Regional Systems*, 316—324, Pion, London.

Swan, J.A., 1970, 'Response to Air Pollution—A Study of Attitudes and Coping Strategies of High School Youths', *Environment and Behavior*, 2, 127—152.

Tagg, S.K., 1974, 'The Subjective Meaning of Rooms: Some Analyses and Investigations' in Canter, D. and Lee, T., eds. *op. cit.*

Tars, S.E. and Appleby, L., 1973, 'The Same Child in Home and Institution: An Observational Study', *Environment and Behaviour*, 5, No.1, 3—28.

Teichner, W.H. and Wehrkamp, P.F., 1954, 'Visual Motor Performance as a Function of Short-Duration Ambient Temperature', *Journal of Experimental Psychology*, 47, 447—450.

Thornton, W.A., 1973, 'Fluorescent Lamps With High Colour-Discrimination Capability', *J. Illum. Eng. Soc.*, 3, 61—64.

Tinbergen, N., 1957, 'The Functions of Territory', *Bird Study*, 4, 14—27.

Uitterhoeve, W.L. and Kebschull, W., 1973, 'Visual Performance and Visual

Comfort in Offices', Second European Light Congress, Brussels.

Van der Ryn, S. and Boie, W.E., 1963, *Value Measurement and Visual Factors in the Urban Environment*, College of Environmental Design, University of California.

Van Ierland, J., 1967, 'Two Thousand Dutch Office Workers Evaluate Lighting', *Working Report E. 39*, T.N.O., Delft.

Vielhauer, J.A., 1966, 'The Development of a Semantic Scale for the Description of the Physical Environment', *Dissertation Abstracts*, 26, 4821.

Vielhauer-Kasmar, J., 1970, 'The Development of A Usable Lexicon of Environmental Descriptors', *Environment and Behaviour*, 2, No.2, 153—169.

Vine, I., 1974, 'Social Spacing in Animals and Man', *Social Science Information*, 12, No.5, 7—50.

Von Frey, M., 1904, *Vorlesungen Über Physiologie*, Berlin.

Walsh, J.W.T., 1958, *Photometry*, Dover Publications, New York.

Walters, D., 1970, 'Annoyance due to Railway Noise in Residential Areas', in Canter, D., ed., *Architectural Psychology*, RIBA Publications, London.

Watson, O. and Graves, T., 1966, 'Quantative Research in Proxemic Behaviour', *American Anthropologist*, 68, 971—985.

Westin, A., 1967, *Privacy and Freedom*, Atheneum, New York.

Weston, H.C., 1945, 'The Relation Between Illumination and Visual Performance', *Industrial Health Research Board Report No.87*, HMSO, London.

Wheeler, L., 1967, *Behavioural Research for Architectural Planning and Design*, Ewing Miller Associates, Indiana.

Wheeler, L., 1969, *The Office Environment*, Interior Space Designers, Chicago.

Whitbeck, R.H., 1918, 'The Influence of Geographical Environments on Religious Beliefs', *The Geographical Review*, 5, 316—324.

White, G.F., 1952, 'Human Adjustment to Floods: A Geographical Approach to the Flood Problem in the United States', *Research Paper 29*, Department of Geography, University of Chicago.

White, G.F., 1966, 'Formation and Role of Public Attitudes', in *Environmental Quality in a Growing Economy*, Essays from the Sixth RFF Forum, John Hopkins Press, Baltimore.

Wicker, A.W., 1969, 'Size of Church Membership and Members' Support of Church Behavior Settings', *Journal of Personality and Social Psychology*, 13, 278—288.

Wicker, A.W., 1972, 'Behaviour-Environment Congruence: A Model of Behavioural Ecology', in Mitchell, W.J., ed., *Environmental Design: Research and Practice*, University of California, Los Angeles.

Willems, E.P., 1973, 'Behavioural Ecology as a Perspective for Man-Environment Research' in Preiser, W.F.E., ed., 152—165.

Williams, J., 1963, 'Personal Space and its Relation to Extraversion-Introversion', Master's Thesis, University of Alberta.

Wilner, D.M., Walkley, R.P., Pinkerton, T.C. and Tayback, M., 1962, *The Housing Environment and Family Life: A Longitudinal Study of the Effects of Housing on Morbidity and Mental Health*, John Hopkins Press, Baltimore.

361

Wilson Committee, The, 1963, *Noise: Final Report of the Committee on the Problem of Noise*, Cmnd. 2056, HMSO, London.

Winkel, G.H. and Bonsteel, D., 1968, *Response to Roadside Environments*, Arthur D. Little, San Francisco.

Winkel, G. and Hayward, D., 1974, 'Some Major Causes of Congestion in Subway Stations', in Ittelson, W., Proshansky, H., Rivlin, L. and Winkel, G., *An Introduction to Environmental Psychology*, Holt, Rinehart and Winston, Inc., New York.

Wohlwill, J.F., 1973, 'The Environment Is Not in the Head!', in Preiser, W.F.E., ed., *Environmental Design Research*, **II**, Dowden, Hutchinson and Ross, Stroudsburg.

Wood, D., 1971, *Fleeting Glimpses: Adolescent and Other Images of the Entity Called San Christobal las Casas, Chiapas, Mexico*, Unpublished M.A. Thesis, Clark University.

Wools, R., 1970, 'The Assessment of Room Friendliness' in Canter, D., ed., *Architectural Psychology*, RIBA Publications Ltd., London.

Wools, R. and Canter, D.V., 1970, 'The Effects of the Meaning of Buildings on Behaviour', *Applied Ergonomics*, 1, 144—150.

Wyon, D.P., Bruun, N.O., Olesen, S., Kjeruff-Jensen, P. and Fanger, P.O., 1971, 'Factors Affecting the Subjective Tolerance of Ambient Temperature Swings', *Proceedings of 5th International Congress for Heating, Ventilating and Air-Conditioning, Copenhagen*, 1, 87—108.

Wyon, D.P., 1970, 'Studies of Children Under Imposed Noise and Heat Stress', *Ergonomics*, 13, (5), 598—612.

Yancey, W.L., 1972, 'Architecture, Interaction and Social Control: The Case of a Large Scale Housing Project', in Wohlwill, J.F. and Carson, D.H., eds., *Environment and the Social Sciences: Perspectives and Applications*, American Psychological Association, Washington D.C.

Young, M. and Willmott, P., 1957, *Family and Kinship in East London*, Penguin, Harmondsworth.

Zannaras, G., 1973, 'The Cognitive Structures of Urban Areas', in Preiser, W.F.E., ed., *Environmental Design Research*, **II**, Dowden, Hutchinson and Ross, Stroudsburg.

Zlutnick, S. and Altman, I., 1972, 'Crowding and Human Behavior', in Wohlwill, J.F. and Carson, D.H., eds., *Environment and the Social Sciences: Perspectives and Applications*, American Psychological Association, Washington D.C.

Subject Index

363

Author Index

370